Public Enterprises

Economics and Management

Public Enterprises
Economics and Management

Volume–II

K.R. Gupta

ATLANTIC
PUBLISHERS & DISTRIBUTORS (P) LTD

Published by

ATLANTIC

PUBLISHERS & DISTRIBUTORS (P) LTD

7/22, Ansari Road, Darya Ganj,
New Delhi-110002
Phones : +91-11-40775252, 23273880, 23275880, 23280451
Fax : +91-11-23285873
Web : www.atlanticbooks.com
E-mail : orders@atlanticbooks.com

Branch Office
5, Nallathambi Street, Wallajah Road,
Chennai-600002
Phones : +91-44-64611085, 32413319
E-mail : chennai@atlanticbooks.com

Printed in India at Nice Printing Press, A-33/3A, Site-IV, Industrial Area, Sahibabad, Ghaziabad, U.P.

Preface

Public enterprises assume great importance, especially in developing countries like India. These enterprises are considered to be a powerful engine of economic development and an important instrument of attaining the widely cherished goal of a socialist society. These were set up to meet the immense task of facilitating the industrial development in the country in a manner that no region was left behind in the process.

During the period since Independence, public enterprises have been reliable partners in advancing growth in the country. They remain relevant as they have demonstrated the ability to adjust to the changing environment. Many public enterprises have been able to withstand the intense competition that ensued from domestic and global firms since the early 1990s when India began the process of liberalizing its economy. In recent times, some of the public enterprises have emerged as effective players in international markets. The 2010 Forbes Global List of 2,000 companies includes 56 Indian companies; among these 28 were Indian public sector companies.

Public enterprises will continue to be important if they take steps to keep their performance under constant review and strive for efficiency and competitiveness. In order to maintain sustained profitability and consistently give good performance, public enterprises need to adopt best practices of management and keep themselves abreast of market orientation.

India's sustained economic growth requires that all stakeholders, both in the public and the private sector, contribute their very best, so that there is overall development in the country. Public enterprises have a huge responsibility on them to excel in their fields and through their work to serve the national goal of socio-economic development. It should be their endeavour to maintain high level of standards so that these become best practices in the industry, setting benchmarks for other companies to emulate.

The reputation of an organization depends upon the strength and values of its personnel. There should be continuous efforts to upgrade human resources through skill development, attitudinal change and team building, including through more women in the higher echelons of public sector management.

Starting with a modest investment of ₹ 29 crore in 5 enterprises on the eve of the first Five Year Plan in 1956, enterprises in the public sector have steadily progressed to 246 in number with an investment of ₹ 5,29,950 crore till 2009. This rapid growth of public enterprises has given rise to a number of debatable issues like the forms of organization, financing, price policy, governing boards, public accountability, goals and measurement of management, personnel management, financial management, industrial relations, efficiency and disinvestment. *Public Enterprises: Economics and Management* analyses these issues with a detached and scientific outlook and provides suitable suggestions. Although benefit has been taken of, and illustrations cited about the experience of working of public enterprises abroad, the book is written primarily in the setting of working of public enterprises in India. Report of Ad hoc Group of Experts on Empowerment of Central Public Sector Enterprises (CPSEs), Guidelines on Corporate Governance for CPSEs, and White Paper on Disinvestment of CPSEs are given in Annexures.

I had the privilege of working in a large public enterprise (State Trading Corporation of India) for four years which provided me an opportunity to study the problems of public enterprises from a very close angle. This has enabled me to be more realistic, as compared with pure academicians who often have a tendency to be idealistic, in analyzing problems and making suggestions.

I am highly indebted to many top executives of several public enterprises for providing me an opportunity for free and frank discussions and supplying me useful information.

The book will be useful not only to the students of Economics, Commerce and Business Management but also the executives of public enterprises, government officials and parliamentarians deeply concerned with the setting up and working of public enterprises.

K.R. Gupta

Contents

Annexures

Industrial Relations

10

In regard to industrial relations, public enterprises differ from private enterprise in an important respect. To cite from the First Five-Year Plan, "the profit-motive and the exploitation of workers for private gain have no significance in the State-owned enterprises. The undertakings have no doubt to show the same, if not greater, efficiency of working as private-owned undertakings. They have also to show profits. But the nature of these profits is different. The profits which these undertakings make are not profits intended for any individuals or group of individual but are extra wealth for the whole country".[1] The worker in a public enterprise stands on a different footing from a worker in a private enterprise. "He has a dual role of master and servant; master as a citizen of the country and servant as a worker of the undertaking. It is therefore necessary that he should be made conscious that in serving the undertaking he is serving himself and that the better he works and the greater his efficiency the better he will serve and help himself. He must be made to feel that the responsibility for the success or failure is as much his as that of the management and that the undertaking belongs to the country as a whole including himself. He should take pride in his contribution to the success of the undertaking".[2] But the absence of profit-motive in public enterprises should not be used to justify exemption of public undertakings from labour laws applicable to the private sector. To cite from the Second Five Year Plan, "In view of the fact that public sector will grow in future, the manner of administration of industrial relations in public enterprises is of great importance for the success of the undertakings and for the fulfilment of the aspirations of labour. Any attempt, therefore, on the part of public employer to avoid the responsibility of an employer on the ground that he is not working for profit has to be discouraged. Managements of public undertakings should not normally seek exemptions from labour laws or ask for other concessions not available to the private sector."[3]

From the ordinary workers' point of view, however, the working conditions and industrial relations in public enterprises have not been much different from those prevailing in the private enterprises. The attitude of management towards workers, causes of disagreement and clashes of personality, working conditions and wages, stresses and strains borne by workers resulting from the working procedures and methods, effects of changes in demand, experience of competition and fear of unemployment are still more or less the same as in the private sector. In fact, the fear of unemployment has increased with the government deciding to disinvest in several undertakings.

Model Employers

The labour policy and programmes of the Government of India do not distinguish between the private and public enterprises. But public enterprises can legitimately be expected to act as model employers and set an example of enlightened management and employer-employee relationships. The Guide on 'Labour Laws and Practices' brought out by the Ministry of Labour and Employment tries to provide an indication about the special obligations of public sector managements. It suggests that managements should discharge their responsibilities with exceptional care and should adopt a really enlightened policy in labour matters treating workers as real partners ensuring that their just grievances are promptly redressed and taking timely remedial measures after ascertaining the causes of labour unrest. It is, however, desirable that the Government should clearly spell out the special responsibilities of the management in public sector undertakings.

It is very important for the management of public enterprises to show a lively interest in the welfare of the employees. The promotion and training policies of public enterprises should be so framed as to convince the workers of the interest that management has in developing their skills and qualifications and in improving their prospects and standard of living. The public enterprises should set the pace and serve as a model in regard to wage rates, working conditions, and welfare activities. The Board of Directors of public enterprises should include persons having a sympathetic appreciation of labour problems. The workers should be progressively associated with the working of the enterprises so that they feel that in practice, as well as in theory, they are partners in the enterprise. Healthy unionism should be encouraged and no restrictions should be placed on industrial and commercial employees exercising their trade union rights like the employees of private enterprises. Agreements should be concluded for increasing output and reducing costs, combating absenteeism and checking offences against discipline. Collective bargaining between workers and management should be encouraged and the management should be given on the spot full discretion and power to enter into commitments within certain prescribed limits. Similarly, government conciliation and arbitration machinery should be made available to the workers of state undertakings. It may, however, be made clear that the 'model employer' concept should not be interpreted to mean that management is bound to accept any demand that any organisation of workers may put forth. Nor should this concept be construed to mean that supervising officers would be expected to condone or be lenient to laziness, indifferent work and acts of indiscipline.

Statutory Obligations

The management must be efficient in detecting causes of dissatisfaction among employees and prompt in initiating speedy measures to redress the grievances or moving the conciliation machinery to deal with disputes. One of the basic requirements for proper labour-management relations is that the employers discharge their statutory obligations promptly and effectively. But in this regard, the record of several enterprises has been far from satisfactory. Even now there some public undertakings which have not yet framed a regular procedure for the redress of employees' grievances. It is unfortunate that these deficiencies continue in spite of the fact that the government have circulated model standing orders and grievance procedure for the guidance of the managements. This state of affairs is partly because of lack of efficient and effective personnel departments in some enterprises.

Labour Management

The personnel departments in many enterprises are manned by officers who are not professionally qualified or adequately experienced in labour matters. The public enterprises should take measures to have their personnel managers trained in industrial relations and labour management and to strengthen their personnel departments in this regard. Further, the organisation of the personnel and labour department is not appropriate in many public enterprises. The same set of officers have been entrusted with functions relating to industrial relations and labour welfare on the one hand, and other aspects of personnel management like recruitment, promotions and conduct and discipline, on the other. If labour officers are to be effective in dealing with workers, it is essential that they do not have to share responsibility for decisions which might become the subject matter of disputes. The officers entrusted with labour relations should not bear any direct responsibility in matters like recruitment, promotions and disciplinary action against workers. Further, it would be very useful if the chief executive can obtain impartial and objective advice on labour matters from a senior officer who does not bear responsibility for any matters other than industrial relations and labour welfare. In smaller public undertakings, a separate section should be set up exclusively for labour relations within the personnel department. In larger undertakings, a separate labour department should be created exclusively for labour relations. In such undertakings, it would be essential to ensure the closest co-ordination between the personnel department and the department for labour relations. The heads of these two departments must work in co-operation with each other and take important decisions after joint consultation.

Labour-Management Relations

In many public enterprises, the relations between management and the workers have not been cordial. In many cases, the trouble arose from inter-union or intra-union rivalries and the problem faced by the management in determining which union or group within a union actually represented the majority point of view. It has been found that the communication between workers and management was, by and large, not satisfactory and that the machinery for joint consultation and joint councils of management had either not been organized adequately or were not functioning effectively. The agitations were launched by workers' unions for a variety of reasons, e.g. non-acceptance of awards, disputes regarding bonus, project allowance and other allowances, disciplinary action against workers, alleged assignment of extra work, retrenchment of staff, and sometimes individual grievances.

In many cases, disputes between management and labour have resulted into unfortunate incidents involving acts of violence and disturbance of law and order at the site of the factory. The problem has become serious, especially in backward regions, with labour resorting to potentially militant measures in their attempt to secure acceptance of their demands by the managements. These incidents, commonly known as gheraos, have introduced a new and dangerous element in the field of labour-management relations. It is highly desirable that the agreements between labour and management are arrived at through collective bargaining and voluntary agreement and not through collective coërcion and exaction of concessions by the use of terror, veiled threats of force and violence. If unchecked, these tendencies are bound to damage the normal machinery of labour-management consultations and of conciliation. The property of the public enterprises belongs to the society and the managements act as agents of the state charged with the management of this social property in the collective interest. In such a situation, violence and gheraos in public enterprises are particularly incongruous and harmful. While public enterprises should take appropriate measures to ensure that the just grievances of labour are satisfactorily redressed and the awards of labour tribunals, wage boards, etc. are promptly implemented by the management, the Central and State Governments should take immediate and effective measures to check the spread of violence and gheraos in all enterprises, whether in the public or the private sector.

In essence, a strike or agitation reflects a breakdown of the normal processes of negotiations between labour and management and a failure of conciliation. This may be the consequence of wrong handling by the management, unjustified demands and irresponsible action on the part of the workers' union, or the ineffectiveness of the settlement machinery of the government concerned.

In a democratic society, although strikes, except under certain circumstances, have been recognised as a legitimate weapon in the armoury of labour, they should be used only as a last resort when all other avenues of settling the dispute with the management have been exhausted. It should be appreciated that the rule of law of a very extensive and fundamental nature prevails in the country. If judicial interpretation is final as between the government and the citizens, there is no reason why it should not be so as between the managements and workers of public enterprises. The strikes adversely affect not only the workers and the employers but also the community at large. Since public undertakings operate mostly in the field of public utility services and basic industries, strike in them a cause a lot of inconvenience to society and result in a rise in the price which consumers have to pay for their products. It is, therefore, very essential that the strikes in public enterprises are avoided, whatever may be their cause. The Industrial Disputes Act lays down certain conditions under which a strike becomes illegal and punitive action can be taken against the workers and other persons participating in it. But there have been cases where strikes have taken place in public undertakings in contravention of the provisions of the Industrial Disputes Act and yet no effective action has been taken subsequently. In order to discourage such strikes, any union resorting to an illegal strike should be immediately de-recognised and the workers participating in it rendered liable to removal from service after a summary inquiry. At the same time, it may be pointed out that an illegal lock-out should be dealt with as firmly as an illegal strike.

Settlement of Industrial Disputes

The Industrial Disputes Act, 1947, which is a Central Act regulating the settlement of industrial disputes, applies to various public enterprises also. The machinery prescribed by this Act consists of (i) the Works Committee, at the unit level, (ii) the Conciliation Officers, appointed by the governments concerned for mediating in and promoting the settlement of disputes, and (iii) the adjudication authorities like Labour Courts, Tribunals and National Tribunals. Provision also exists for Boards of Conciliation and Courts of Enquiry.

Most of the public enterprises owned by the Central Government fall in the 'State sphere' for the purpose of this Act. In other words, when an industrial dispute arises, the State Conciliation Officers intervene and make efforts for the settlement of the dispute. In case the conciliation fails, the State Government orders adjudication, wherever necessary. However, before an adjudication is ordered, as a matter of convention, the State Government consults the Central Government in view of the repercussions that are likely to follow an award. In the Central sphere, the Chief Labour Commissioner's Organisation is the agency which undertakes conciliation and looks after the maintenance of cordial relations in the enterprises falling in his jurisdiction.

In addition to the statutory authorities, a Standing Committee of representatives of the Ministries of the Government of India has also been functioning since August 1957 to consider measures for the speedy settlement of disputes which take place in the public enterprises of the Central Government.

The Industrial Disputes (Amendment) Act, 2010 states that in case of a dispute between a contractor and the contract labour employed through the contractor in any industrial establishment, the appropriate government shall be the Central Government or the State Government, as the case may be, which has control over such industrial establishment.

For the resolution of disputes arising out of individual grievances, the Industrial Disputes (Amendment) Act, 2010, envisages setting up of Grievance Redressal Machinery by every industrial establishment employing twenty or more workmen. The Committee so constituted should consist of equal number of member from the employer and the workmen. The total number of member of the Committee shall not exceed more than six, provided, as far as practicable, half of them are women. The chairperson of the Grievance Redressal Committee shall be selected from the employer and from among the workmen alternatively on rotation basis every year.[4]

Recognition of Trade Unions

Trouble has arisen in many cases in public enterprises because of the inter-union or intra-union rivalries and the problem faced by the management in determining which union or group within a union actually represented the majority point of view. There is no Central Act providing for statutory recognition of unions. The Indian Trade Union Act, 1926 contains provisions for registration under certain conditions but does not make it obligatory for the unions to seek registration under the Act, nor does it impose any obligations on the management. However, the Rajasthan and Madhya Pradesh Industrial Relations Acts contain provisions for statutory recognition of unions under specified conditions, and confer certain rights on the unions which are granted recognition. In other states, managements are expected to grant recognition to unions in accordance with the procedure and criteria laid down in a voluntary code, viz. the Code of Discipline. But the Code does not lay down the rights of a recognised union as against a non-recognised union. Moreover, even an unrecognised union can raise a dispute, get conciliation proceedings started, or take the dispute to adjudication.

The present position leads to an unnecessary proliferation of unions and an unhealthy rivalry between them. This not only leads to an escalation of demands by competing unions but also weakens the trade unions on the whole and makes the process of labour-management negotiations more complicated.

Sometimes the unions call for a strike or launch some kind of agitation simply to attract greater membership and raise more funds.

A simple way of overcoming the difficulties created by the proliferation of unions and inter-union rivalries would be to provide for all the workers electing their representatives who would bargain on their behalf. Each worker should be entitled to vote in electing these representatives by secret ballot once every two years. A Labour Council elected in this way would truly represent workers and would be competent to negotiate with the management on labour matters. The elections might be held by the management organisations with the help of the Government machinery. Implementation of this scheme, however, would require necessary changes in the labour laws in their application to public undertakings. Labour-management relations in the public sector should not be treated as in the private sector.

Communication and Joint Consultation

Inadequate communication between workers and management and the lack of joint consultative machinery are important reasons for the unsatisfactory state of industrial relations. Many times disputes occur in public undertakings because of misinformation and lack of understanding on the part of workers about the changes initiated by the management. The representatives of workers and employees often make a grievance of the fact that information on several matters which they consider vital is withheld from them. They contend that in arriving at a satisfactory settlement all the relevant information should be disclosed to them just in the same way as in all judicial proceedings, all relevant information on which the decision of the dispute is likely to depend is disclosed to both the parties. Many disputes remain unresolved and, in fact, embitter the relations with mutual suspicion and distrust between the management and its employees, simply because the information which the employees consider to be of vital importance in finding out a satisfactory settlement was inadequate or not disclosed to them. Keeping information secret creates suspicion which, according to Somervell, "will invariably set people guessing the wrong way where they feel their interests are at stake".[5] Keeping in view the delicate nature of the confidence factor which governs the modern industrial world, a state enterprise should supply all the material information to its employees, of course, keeping always in view the public interest. An effective way of obtaining good communication between labour and management is by developing the joint consultative machinery in the undertakings. Under the Industrial Disputes Act, 1947, the government concerned can require an undertaking to set up Works Committees consisting of an equal number of representatives of management and workers. The functions envisaged for the Works Committee are to promote measures for securing and maintaining amity and good relations between the employer and the workers, and towards that end to comment upon matters of common interest or concern and to try to compose differences of opinion regarding such matters. Unfortunately, the Works Committees are not functioning effectively in public enterprises mainly because of lack of positive response from workers, absence of strong unions and inter-union rivalries.

The importance of communication has also to be viewed from the angle of the size of the enterprise. The public enterprises are generally characterised by a large size and complexity of organization. This increases the problem of securing good human relations among the employees. Inadequate communication in these enterprises is likely to lead to misunderstandings among the employees and diminish their cooperation with the management.

The attainment of higher morale, discipline and improved incentives largely depends on facilitating and promoting communication within the enterprise. The communication does not simply consist of making available more and better factual information about the enterprise but includes certain positive aspects which are more important and probably more difficult to attain. The most important is the need to instill in the workers a sense of partnership, a sense of pride in the public enterprise and a sense of responsibility for its efficiency and well-being. It is very essential to infuse among employees a sense of purpose and an awareness of the fact that they are working in an enterprise which is engaged in serving the collective interest of the community. The workers of the public enterprises must also be made aware of the important problems which the country and industry are facing, e.g. shortage of basic goods and materials and dependence on imports, shortage of capital resources, the overriding need for improving productivity and ensuring the maximum possible utilisation of the huge amount of capital invested in the public enterprises.

A very important reason for the failure of Works Committees is the fact that they are convened in a routine manner without adequate preparation of agenda papers. The result is that members do not find discussions very worthwhile. The managements should take Works Committee meetings as opportunities to inform the workers of their plans and difficulties and to explain the reasons for the changes being initiated. The proceedings of the Works Committees should be given due publicity so that the workers' representatives may feel more interested and responsible for what emerges from the discussions.

In addition to Works Committees, another joint body of the management and workers is the Joint Management Council, which exercises supervisory, advisory and administrative functions in matters regarding safety, welfare, etc. It has been possible to introduce the scheme of Joint Management Councils sponsored by the government as a purely voluntary scheme only in a few undertakings. An important condition for the formation and success of Joint Management Councils is that there should be a well-established and strong trade union functioning in the undertaking. In most cases, this condition is not satisfied. In order to overcome this difficulty the Management Council should take a form in which the members on the workers' side are elected by all the workers themselves and not nominated by unions. This would improve the chances of successful working of the Joint Management Councils.

Bonus

A bonus, which started off originally as a distribution of part of the profit as a reward, has come to take the form, through a series of judicial decisions, of a part of the emoluments earned by employees. Some people consider profit bonus to be entirely wrong in principle. In order to provide a true incentive and reward for good work, the system of bonuses should be so devised as to provide incentives for the most productive use of installed capacity. The volume profits as shown in the profit and loss accounts for a particular period is not necessarily the only, or even the best, test of productivity or good work. It is further contended that all earnings from public enterprises should go to the general fund because it would, to that extent, obviate the necessity of further taxation. It is also pointed out that the public enterprises provide amenities which are far better than those provided by the private sector and, therefore, payment of bonus is not justified.

The Ministry of Labour, however, did not approve of this stand because the application of labour legislation would become difficult if the public sector were to be accorded a privileged treatment. But it suggested that the public enterprises could be usefully classified into two categories for the payment of bonus. The first category includes public utility undertakings like Posts and Telegraphs, Railways, Defence establishments, etc., where the primary objective is to provide a service rather than to make profits. The second category includes the bulk of remaining public enterprises and it is in this category that a bonus is likely to be paid on a parallel with private industry.

Welfare Activities

The public enterprises have been quite liberal in their expenditure on townships and ancillary facilities like medical and educational facilities, shopping and community centres, play grounds, etc. The Committee on Public Undertakings, in its eighth Report, has commented upon the different standards followed in the scales of accommodation and the scales at which services and other facilities were being provided. The Committee also recommended that steps should be taken to lay down "suitable guiding principles, norms and standards without any delay...to ensure that public undertakings follow a balanced approach in incurring expenditure on productive and non-productive activities". Glaring disparities in the scales of amenities provided to workers in different enterprises are bound to lead to a cycle of escalating demands in the public sector, which would result in avoidable additional expenditure. In this regard, it is fully recognised that laying down of rigid financial limits may not be possible. Expenditure is bound to vary from enterprise to enterprise depending upon its location and the availability of housing, medical and educational facilities in the vicinity of the enterprise. But still broad guidelines and norms can be worked out in order to ensure a certain degree of uniformity among different public enterprises.

Workers' Participation in Management

One of the measures suggested for obtaining co-operation between the workers and the managements is the association of workers in the management of enterprises. Probably the most significant success attained in this regard has been in the erstwhile Yugoslavia where the workers' council elects the chief executive and holds him accountable for the working of the enterprise. But there also the chief executive and the managerial staff were responsible for the administrative control of the enterprise, and the workers are not responsible for the day-to-day administration. These limiting factors must be kept in mind while examining the extent to which workers' association in management can be obtained in the conditions prevailing in our country.

In regard to association of labour in management, it has often been suggested that a labour representative should be included in the Board of Directors of the enterprise. This suggestion does not appear to be very appropriate because it is difficult for the labour representative to simultaneously discharge the different responsibilities of a board member and a labour representative. Such an approach is likely to detract from the constructivenss of discussions in the Board without bringing about any significant improvement in the transaction of business relating to industrial relations. What the workers actually want is association with matters which affect them more intimately, matters which are of immediate and vital interest to them like security of service, information about the enterprise, future prospects, wages, etc. and not high policy decisions. The best way would be that a person having experience of trade union work should be appointed to the board, not as a representative of the labour but as an expert on labour matters.

NOTES

1. Planning Commission, Government of India, *First Five-Year Plan*, p. 580.
2. *Ibid.*
3. Planning Commission, Government of India, *Second Five-Year Plan* (New Delhi, 1956), p. 577.
4. Industrial Disputes (Amendment) Act, 2010 (No. 24 of 2010), dated 18-8-2010.
5. Hubert Somervell, *The Industrial Peace in Our Time* (London, 1950), p. 127.

Efficiency

11

Measurement of Efficiency

Measurement of efficiency in public enterprises is a very complicated problem. "...like so many terms having a very large and indeterminable connotation, the term 'efficiency' is so wide and porous that there is little interpretation that it can successfully resist."[1] It involves a large number of interdependent variables. Even if all of them were amenable to precise measurement, which is not true in actual practice, there still remains the problem of attaching suitable weights to different variables. Consideration has to be given, for instance, to the cost of production of service per unit of resource, the satisfaction of the consumers in respect to quantities, qualities, and prices, the state of labour relations and the degree to which a spirit of willing co-operation has been created among members of staff, and the ability of the whole organisation to adjust itself to changing circumstances, its readiness to make experiments and to quickly adopt the latest technical improvements.[2]

The problem is made more complicated by the entrance of value considerations through the term 'public interest'. The public enterprises are expected to serve public interest. The term 'public interest' is amenable to different interpretations. "...it is not always possible to provide a list of what is contained in the bag of this term."[3] "The performance record of the nationalised industries had been the subject of lively controversy, with government official, parliamentarian, layman or economist attacking or defending it on the basis of concepts, often not clearly defined, of how enterprises should be run in the public interest. In practice the record is a highly complex one and defies simple description or evaluation."[4]

The most difficult problem is that of the selection of suitable standards. "The suitability of any unit of measurement will depend much upon the significance we attach to the word 'efficiency'".[5] If industrial efficiency consists, as E.A.G. Robinson maintains, "in trying to do with eight men what we have hitherto been doing with ten men", labour productivity per man-hour would be a satisfactory criterion of measuring industrial efficiency. If, however, the term "efficiency" is used in a wider sense, that is, obtaining the greatest results at least cost, cost of production per unit would be an appropriate criterion of efficiency. A private industrialist would, however, view efficiency from a different angle. His objective is to maximise profits and, therefore, his criterion would be the rate of profit that he can earn. We briefly examine below the important criteria of measuring efficiency in public enterprises.

Criterion of Profits

This criterion has the great advantage that it is simple to calculate and understand. It provides a common standard of measuring efficiency of different enterprises. It is a general criterion which indicates the overall efficiency combining all the different operations together.

In private enterprise, guided by the objective of profit maximisation, profits provide the most important criterion of efficiency. In contrast, the public sector is normally not guided entirely by the profit motive and therefore the profits earned by a public enterprise are not a very appropriate criterion of its efficiency. "Private investment is only held justifiable on business principles if in the foreseeable future there are reasonable prospects of a fair rate of return on the capital invested therein. Public investment, on the other hand, while not shunning profits, would move in whatever the social benefit/social cost ratio justified it".[6]

While applying profits as a criterion of efficiency in a public enterprise, an important thing that has to be kept in mind is whether the enterprise is operating under monopolistic or competitive conditions. A public enterprise operating under monopolistic conditions can inflate profits by restricting output and thereby artificially raising prices, which is not possible under competitive conditions. Such profits are the result not of the efficient conduct of the enterprise but of the monopolistic position enjoyed by it. The profits, to be a test of efficiency, must not be the result of exploitation.

Though the profits are an important yardstick of efficiency, it would be a mistake to adopt them as the sole criterion of efficiency. In addition to efficiency, profits are affected by a number of other factors, viz., intensity of capital structure, size or scale of operation, location, degree of integration, efficiency of various inputs, imperfections of markets, changes in demand, fiscal and taxation policies, inflationary conditions, cyclical fluctuations, etc. All such factors should be taken into consideration while evaluating the efficiency of a public enterprise.

A public enterprise may come into existence as a result of nationalisation of a private-owned industry or from state venturing into a new field of economic activity. The public enterprise may operate along with its counterparts in the private sector or may be the sole producer in that field. The objective as well as the method of operation would differ from enterprise to enterprise and this would have to be kept in view in evaluating the efficiency of an enterprise.

In case of nationalised industries, comparison is possible between two periods before and after the nationalisation. A transport undertaking under private management, for instance, may be exploiting only the most profitable areas. After nationalisation, in the larger interest of the country, it may decide to extend services to the unexploited, sparsely populated and apparently unprofitable regions. In such cases efficiency before and after nationalisation cannot be compared on the basis of profits. Similarly, comparison on the basis of profits may be vitiated if the enterprise functions in the two periods under different market structures. Before nationalisation the enterprise, for instance, may be operating under competitive conditions and after nationalisation it may have monopoly and as a result enjoy certain direct and indirect benefits in hiring labour and capital, purchasing raw materials and marketing the products. Even when the public enterprises operate in a competitive market along with private enterprises, the objectives and the principles being followed in the two sectors would have to be kept in view while making a comparison of efficiency on the basis of profits. Keeping in view the national objective of attainment of a socialist society, the public enterprises, for instance, may be offering more favourable conditions of service to labour than those offered by the private enterprises. For purposes of comparison, the profits of enterprises in the two sectors would have to be suitably adjusted to take account of such factors.

Some enterprises may not yield profits during the initial stages of their operation. They may take some time for their construction before they can gear to full operation. In such circumstances, the enterprises would take time to fructify. Here profits cannot be used as a yardstick of efficiency. In such cases, efficiency would have to be judged with reference to the judicious application of men and resources in keeping with the time-schedule and cost-estimates.

Lord Latham, a former chairman of London Transport Executive, points out that if circumstances are favourable, satisfactory profits can conceal inefficiency while in unfavourable circumstances a proper degree of efficiency may be achieved in spite of an absence of profits.[7] He emphasizes that in a public enterprise consideration must be paid to other criteria also. According to him, the test of efficiency should be whether the service provides facilities which are reasonably adequate to meet the public needs at prices which are also reasonable and which will enable the undertaking to pay its way. The pursuit of maximum efficiency in this sense becomes the most economical use of resources for a given return in goods and services.

Professor Sargant Florence and Gilvert Walker contend that breaking even or making a surplus is the best primary test of efficiency in the public sector provided that certain conditions are fulfilled.[8] In the first place, the surplus should not be the result of exploitation. Secondly, money costs should reflect real costs and must not leave social costs out of account. Thirdly, the surplus should result from a small margin on a large output rather than a large margin on a small output. In short, the prime measure of efficiency is the ability to break even, or slightly more than even, at the greatest level of production. Ancillary tests of vigorous management are lower prices, higher quality, or an extended range of goods and services.

Adherence to Time-Schedule and Cost Estimates

Though adherence to time-schedule and cost estimates is one of the important criteria of efficiency, it may be foiled by inaccurate budget estimates. If the estimates are revised frequently, the efficiency of the enterprise cannot be evaluated with the help of this criterion. The cost of DVC, for instance, was originally estimated at ₹ 55 crores and was subsequently revised from time to time. According to the 1960 estimates, it stood at ₹ 107 crores.[9] Such frequent and large revisions indicate lack of farsightedness in regard to possible variation in cost of factors to be utilized in constructing the undertaking including wage structure and cost of capital goods and other accessories. In such cases, the efficiency of the enterprise can hardly be judged with the help of this criterion. Similar has been the case of the estimates for three steel plants at Rourkela, Durgapur and Bhilai. The original estimate for these three plants was ₹ 353 crores and subsequently it was revised to ₹ 439 crores raising the investment within a short period by about 25 per cent. The foreign exchange component increased from ₹ 228.5 crores to ₹ 292 crores rising by about 28 per cent.[10]

The time schedule is another measure of efficiency. A public enterprise would be expected to adhere to the time schedule laid down in the project plan. But often there are difficulties in keeping the time schedule. Shortage of competent technicians is one of the important difficulties. It took more than two years, for instance, for the DVC to find a chief engineer and it was confessed that the person appointed was not the best under the circumstances because other foreigners either did not respond or demanded much higher remuneration which the DVC could not afford to pay. Secondly, there is the difficulty of obtaining capital goods in time. The target dates for the construction of various dams in the DVC have been frequently extended because of the non-availability of capital goods in time.[11]

Labour Productivity

Labour productivity per man-hour is a fairly satisfactory indication of efficiency. There are, however, a number of difficulties in its actual application. It is difficult to precisely measure the labour productivity per man-hour. Even if such computations are possible, they cannot be used for inter-comparisons because the statistical data of different units are not homogeneous. The goods produced by different units differ widely in regard to dimension, texture, design, finish and quality. Further, the equipment employed by different mills differs so widely in respect of machinery employed, capacity and actual output that it is difficult to find any satisfactory basis for comparing the relative efficiency of different units.

Cost of Production

Cost of production per unit of output is an important criterion of efficiency. The lower the cost per unit of output, the higher would be the efficiency of the enterprise.

There are, however, difficulties in inter-comparison of cost data of different units working under widely different conditions. The units are located at different places and, therefore, enjoy economies of location to different degrees. "The distance of mills from the centres of raw materials, and from the source of power, the varying rates of wages and conditions of labour in different parts of the country, the marked divergences as regards the character and accessibility of the principal markets and other differences arising from the local environment of the industry are so great that the costing data available for comparison will not be truly homogeneous."[12] Even if we confine the comparison to units located in the same area and enjoying the same benefits in regard to location, there will still remain considerable differences in respect of technical equipment and type of goods manufactured. When the different units operate under widely different conditions, there does not appear much basis for inter-comparison of the cost data.

In comparing the cost-structure of different units, there arises the question whether the costs should be expressed as "per unit of output" or as "percentage of the value of goods produced". In industries producing more or less homogeneous type of goods like sugar or cement, the efficiency of different units can be compared on the basis of cost of production per unit. But in industries whose products differ considerably in regard to quality, cost of production per unit of output cannot form a satisfactory basis for comparing the efficiency of different units. The efficiency of a unit producing coarse cloth, for instance, cannot be compared with that of another unit producing finer varieties of cloth on the basis of their cost of production per unit of output. The cost of production per unit of output would vary according to the quality of output. In such cases, for making comparisons of efficiency, the cost would have to be expressed as "percentage of the value of goods produced" or as "percentage of total turnover".

In addition to difficulties of inter-comparison, the criterion suffers from several shortcomings and its actual application involves many problems. The unit cost of production depends on a number of factors, e.g. technique of production, organisation, labour relations, productive enthusiasm, skill and training, etc., which are all partially independent variables. As a result, a decline in unit cost, which may at first sight be taken to indicate a general improvement in efficiency, may conceal the fact that a deterioration in, say, the administrative organisation has been more than counterbalanced by the introduction of a new machine.[13] Similarly cordial labour relations may lead to decreased unit costs in spite of technical stagnation and organisational obsolescence. Thus, there is the need for techniques of measuring the movement and the mutual interaction of the various factors which influence the efficiency of public enterprises in contrast to criteria which measure efficiency in terms of a few arbitrarily selected factors.

Cost reduction criterion presupposes some basic concept of cost already in vogue which would supply the yardstick of cost of production per unit of service. If standard norms regarding the cost of production are laid down, the efficiency of the enterprise can be judged by its success in keeping the actual costs within these limits. The usefulness of this measure will obviously depend on the care with which the norms are set up. If they are based on purely historical costs, they may provide only a rough measure of efficiency. In spite of this the norms based on historical costs may have to be used in the earlier stages of an enterprise as the building of norms on the basis of detailed study takes time. Some experience of the actual working of the enterprise would be necessary before they are built up. If prices of most of the inputs remain more or less unchanged, such norms will provide a rough basis for measuring efficiency. Even if the prices are fluctuating, costs at fixed prices of inputs can be specially calculated to provide a basis for comparison.

There are always some reserves in any production process which provide an opportunity for the efficient management to reduce costs below the norms set up on the basis of previous history. This, however, involves the difficulty that as these reserves are utilised and wastes eliminated, such efforts will yield progressively diminishing returns. This will be more so because year after year the norms themselves will be lowered according to the cost level actually obtained. If cost reduction in relation to norms historically established is the sole measurement of efficiency and every attainment in cost reduction leads to a lowering down of cost norms, the management may have a tendency to be cautious not to attain a very large cost reduction in any particular year. "The experience of Polish industrial management where such methods were used for some time indicates that such difficulties are likely to arise".[14]

Though cost norms based purely on historical data may be used in the early stages, efforts should be made to calculate standard costs for various inputs on the basis of proper study of the processes of production. The general cost norms will be an addition of these with a certain allowance for overheads.

An important disadvantage of an overall measure of efficiency like profitability or cost reduction is that in a complex undertaking producing a number of products, the overall measure of efficiency may not satisfactorily reveal the level of efficiency in particular sections of the enterprise. Efficiency in some parts may be quite high and conceal low efficiency in other parts of the enterprise. This shows the need for maintaining separate accounts for different parts of the undertakings so as to provide a measure of efficiency in different parts.

The operating costs may sometimes rise because of factors which are beyond the control of the public enterprise; this should be kept in view while evaluating the efficiency of a public enterprise.

Care should be taken that the reduced cost is not at the cost of quality. "Efficiency, in terms of reduced cost without quality production, amounts to nothing except inefficiency".[15].

Comparative Data

Appraisal of performance is basically an exercise in comparisons. These comparisons can be made in three possible ways. In the first place, management's performance in different periods can be compared to assess the changes recorded over time. Secondly, comparisons can be made between the performance of different enterprises over the same period. Thirdly, actual performance can be measured against certain hypothetical standards. In regard to the first two methods, it is essential that the same set of indicators is used whether for measuring performance in different periods of time or in different enterprises. For the third method, standards have to be laid down based on the performance data of similar enterprises in the past and on a detailed analysis of the various elements of production. This is a very difficult task.

The criteria for evaluating performance mentioned above only indicate the strategy for undertaking the task. To give them an operational shape, it is necessary to select certain ratios to serve as indicators of performance. The ratios relevant to the first criterion would depend upon the non-commercial objectives prescribed for the public enterprises. The objective may be to develop a particular industry or provide a service to the community at reasonable cost or develop the economic conditions of a particular area or section of the community. The success in these matters may be judged by the volume of output, the distribution of the products or services and the less tangible social value of the capital investment. In regard to the second criterion, namely, that of maximising profits, the return on capital employed, which is itself ratio, is the most important indicator. The variable indicating the quality of output would differ from one enterprise to another depending upon the nature of the product or service provided by the enterprise. In case of public utilities like electricity and transport undertakings, for instance, important indicators would be the punctuality and regularity with which services are provided. In case of engineering and manufacturing concerns, useful indicators are the extent of consumers' demand for the products and their acceptability in the market. These indicators, however, involve difficulties in case of enterprises operating under monopoly conditions. As regards the last criterion, namely, economy and efficiency in the use of resources, it is not very difficult to select ratios indicating the utilisation, in physical and financial terms, of each category of input per unit of output.

Some people suggest a comparison of public enterprises with their counterparts in the private sector. Such an evaluation will be reasonable if done scientifically and with reference to comparables. This suggestion has not been well received because of a number of reasons.[16] In the first place, common denominators for making such a comparison exist only for a limited field of activity. One of the important reasons for this is the different motives of operation. Secondly, there are difficulties in making comparisons over a period of time. There may take place substantial differences over two periods in regard to important matters like technique of production, size of demand, etc. Thirdly, the comparison may be difficult because of differences in age, methods of raising capital, facilities available, etc.

Some enterprises have a number of units. For example, "in France the tobacco monopoly consists of twenty-two factories, the National Stud Farms have twenty-one stables of stallions, the national aircraft construction corporations...consists of several factories".[17] Since different units of the enterprise perform more or less the same operation, it would be useful to compare costs in each unit. Thus inter-unit comparisons in public enterprises would be more meaningful and useful than comparisons of public enterprises with their counterparts in the private sector.

Overall Index of Efficiency

The foregoing analysis shows that none of the criteria by itself is adequate to evaluate the efficiency of a unit. If all these criteria are used, there is every possibility that the distortions attributable to any one criterion taken singly may be offset. Further, if the application of all these criteria reveals the dominance of the same tendencies, the general conclusions are verified and confirmed.

In fact, there is the need to explore the possibilities of constructing an overall Index of Efficiency not only to compare the relative efficiency of different units but also to keep a continuous watch over the progress made by an individual unit over a period of time in the reduction of costs, maximization of output and most economic utilisation of the human and material resources available to the community. Such an index should also take into account the direct and indirect social costs and benefits accruing to the community as a result of the setting up of the enterprise.

There are, of course, conceptual, technical and statistical difficulties in measuring the social benefits and costs. Many social costs and benefits are not amendable to measurement with any degree of precision or scientific exactitude. There is also the problem of assigning appropriate weights to different items of economic and social costs in an overall index of industrial efficiency because this involves value judgments and ideological preferences for end-objectives.

Comparison with Private Sector

The public sector undertakings in India have been criticised for showing poor returns. This criticism is true in case of many public undertakings which have shown a very low rate of returns or even losses. But at the same time, some public undertakings have shown quite good returns. In fact, even in the private sector, there are profit-earning enterprises as well as sick enterprises. No doubt, the average rate of return in the public sector is lower than that in the private sector; but this does not mean that the performance in the public sector is correspondingly poor. While fully recognising the need and scope for improvement in the performance of public sector undertakings, it may be pointed out that it would be wrong to compare the profitability of public enterprises with that of private enterprises without keeping in view certain important distinctive features of the public undertakings. To cite the Study Team on Public Undertakings, "The distinctive features of the public sector in our country should be borne in mind while comparing the profitability of public enterprises with that of private concerns".[18] The fact that the prices of commodities like steel, oil, coal and fertilizers which substantially account for the total turnover of the industrial enterprises of the Central Government are regulated or fixed by the government cannot be ignored. Since most of these goods are what can be described as essential commodities, the government tries to give full protection to the interests of consumers. The result is that the prices fixed are often on the low side and do not make sufficient allowance for the increased capital costs of setting up new plants in these sectors. These factors which bring down the average figures of performance are often overlooked while evaluating the performance of the public sector in terms of profitability.

Professor K.N. Raj has contended that the loss in public sector basic industries essentially flows from their financial structure. An important portion of the capital employed in these industries, for instance, is in the form of loan capital. This tends to get reflected in the rates of return when they are calculated as percentages of paid up capital and after deducting interest payments as a cost item. The practices in regard to depreciation provisions also differ and the public sector plants have a tendency to provide for significantly higher rates.

Rate of return in public sector is also low because of the long gestation period involved in capital-intensive industries like steel, engineering, chemicals, fertilizers, petroleum and heavy machinery. Another cause of low returns is heavy expenditure on townships, hospitals, schools, etc. which is rather on the high side. Social responsibilities in terms of labour welfare also find greater reflections in the public sector investment than in the private sector.

There exists considerable tax evasion in the private sector while the public sector pays full taxes. This is one of the reasons for low returns in the public sector. The loss to the government on account of low returns is partly compensated by the higher tax collections resulting from absence of tax evasion.

Factors Contributing Towards Poor Performance

Low returns in the public undertakings are also partly because of poor performance of the public undertakings. We briefly describe below some of the important factors which have contributed towards poor performance of the public undertakings.

Over capitalisation. The Study Team on Public Undertakings found that many public undertakings were overcapitalised. This leads to surplus machine capacity and avoidable expenditure. Over-capitalisation is because of bad planning.

Large Overhead Expenditure. In many undertakings cost of production is high and return low because of excessive overhead expenditure. There is extravagance in overhead expenditure particularly on township and other welfare activities which needs to be curtailed.

Overemployment. Owing to defective planning and forethought and delay in construction, many public undertakings have got burdened with man-power far in excess of their needs. This has led to heavy recurring expenditure.

Delay in Construction of Projects. Delay in the completion of projects has often led to a large increase in the cost of construction. For example, Trombay Unit of Fertilizer Corporation took 6-7 years to complete against the original estimate of three years. As a result, estimated cost of constructionrose from ₹ 27 crores in 1959 to ₹ 40 crores in 1965.

Absence of Trained Man-power. Many public undertakings were set up in India at a time when technological competence was inadequate to conceive, plan and implement such large projects. Some of these projects were set up in India for the first time and, therefore, the required trained man-power or technical know-how was not readily available.

Poor Management-Labour Relations. In many public undertakings, production, sales and revenue have been affected adversely by indiscipline among workers and poor management-labour relations. Production and sales have been hit by lockouts, sitdown strikes, work to rule agitation and violent disturbances.

Plants Operating Below Rated Capacity. Unutilised plant capacity involves heavy losses or eating away a considerable portion of profits. Some enterprises have not laid down precise targets of production to be attained within a given period based on proper assessment of capacities.

Absence of Sound Pricing Policy. No doubt, it would not be desirable to raise prices in basic and essential industries like fertilizers, coal, oil, electricity, transport, etc., which are directly connected with the development of the economy and the welfare of the masses, but certainly due weightage can be given to adequate returns in pricing the products of other industries. 'Public sector for public good' sentiment has to be judged with reality. Further, external influences on optimum pricing policy, optimum price structures and price regulation, however, desirable, often interfere with the single-minded devotion of the management to commercial efficiency and profitability.

Recruitment and Promotion Policy. The public enterprises in India have not followed a scientific recruitment policy. There have been frequent transfers of staff. More importance has been given to seniority than to merit in staff promotions.

Measures to Improve Efficiency

Objectives and Priorities. The objectives of public enterprise and the priorities in its operations should be clearly laid down.

External Influences. It is not possible to remove external influences on the operations of the public enterprises. The limits of such influences and conventions of their exercise must, however, be appropriately conceived. Clear demarcation, as far as possible, should be made between the autonomy of the management and the influence from the government or parliament. Management should be safeguarded from destructive criticism which deters it from exercising initiative.

Public Relations. Every public enterprise should have a good public relations organisation which regularly receives complaints from the public or consumers and follows them up to action by the top executives.

Presidential Awards. The Government of India has introduced presidential awards for the best public sector undertakings in the form of a Shield, a Certificate of Merit and a Certificate of Honour for outstanding performance, having regard to: (a) financial working; (b) cordial labour relations; and (c) special contribution made to the economy of the country through research, discovery of new processes, design of machinery and equipment, etc. These are to be judged by a Committee of Secretaries of the Ministries of the Government of India assisted by experts, who will evaluate the performance of individual companies. The introduction of presidential awards has provided an incentive to public enterprises for improving their efficiency.

Public Sector Day. The first ever Public Sector day was commemorated on April 10, 2010. This day (10 April) is also significant because in 1973 Standing Conference of Public Enterprises (SCOPE) was formed. The events organized at the Public Sector Day provide a forum for an appraisal of the functioning of public sector enterprises by taking stock of their contribution to the grants of the country.

SCOPE Meritorious Awards. These awards recognize the excellent performance of public sector undertakings. These awards motivate the Chief Executives and employees of public enterprises to work harder and fulfil the expectations of the people.

Cost Accounting. Proper cost accounting is an important method of achieving efficiency. "Information from such accounting, if available promptly, will, besides giving the management an excellent idea of the state of affairs as regards each important operation, enable the application of efficient control at every stage".[19] It is very essential to know, as accurately as possible, the cost incurred on each separate activity of the organisation and the return accruing from it. This enables an assessment of the comparative efficiency of operations.

The costing system of every public enterprise should be thoroughly examined by a body of experts and, as far as possible, a uniform pattern should be recommended for all manufacturing units. Every enterprise should have a well-trained and well-staffed cost accounting unit to serve as an efficient tool of financial and management control.

Statistical Quality Control. As regards the maintenance of highest standards of quality, statistical quality control has shown good results in many manufacturing enterprises abroad and has been introduced in some enterprises in India. "It furnishes a very good check at small cost and should certainly find its way into all suitable state enterprises".[20] All public enterprises should have Quality Control Sections to Facilitate analyse and testing of the products of the factory before they are released for sale. The rigorous standards must conform to those laid down in the advanced countries/internationally accepted standards.

Fixing of Norms of Production. This is very essential for the efficient conduct of a public enterprise. Unless productivity per worker is fixed, it is difficult to evaluate the efficiency. This, however, is likely to change upwards with gaining of experience and expansion of training facilities. A repeated variation from the norm would indicate the necessity for a change in the norm.

The question arises how to fix a norm of workers' productivity in public enterprises, particularly in new fields. The norm can be fixed by two methods, viz., (1) by a comparative data and method of working of the foreign counterparts of the enterprise or (2) in reference to private enterprises in similar fields. The first method is not very appropriate because of the varying conditions prevailing in the two countries and also because of varying policies and methods of operations. The second method is more practicable and can be adopted by public enterprises in India with advantage.

The public enterprises in India utterly lack in norms and scientific management by time and motion study has not been introduced. The Industrial Relations Committee should be consulted in fixing norms so that there is no misunderstanding over it. The workers employed in the undertaking should be made to feel their unity of interests in achieving norms and demonstrating their efficiency.

Supervisory Staff. Adequate incentives should be provided for supervisory staff because supervision is essential not only for larger output but also for perfect jobbing. In the erstwhile U.S.S.R., the manager at the helm of affairs was rewarded for good results and penalised for adverse results. Such practice was followed at every level of production. It is highly desirable that some such practice is introduced in public enterprises in India.

Absence of Industrial Strife. Good industrial moral is very essential for the success of a public enterprise. To secure complete co-operation of the staff and workers, the management should inculcate a sense of public service in employees so that the notion that "we won't work for another's profit" does not find a place in their mind.

Because of the growing consciousness of workers in asserting their rights and the management's reluctance to yield to the demands of labour, industrial disputes have become a common feature of the modern industry and it would be too much to expect complete absence of industrial strife in public enterprises. But all efforts should be made to resolve disputes, as far as possible, by persuasion, conciliation and voluntary methods which will lead to better relations and efficiency in the long run, if not immediately.

Incentive Bonus Scheme. Excepting a few public enterprises like Chittaranjan Locomotive Works, etc., the incentive bonus scheme does not figure in its proper perspective in public enterprises. The introduction of the system of piece-work rating and bonus as an incentive to increased production, efficiency, and earning have shown good results all over the world. The following measures can be taken to introduce the incentive scheme:

(i) The management should introduce time studies of the different operations in workshops, factories and offices and consider suitable methods of recording the reasonable output of individuals or small groups.

(ii) The norms of work to be fixed in consultation with the unions of workers should be based on the standard of reasonable efficiency of an average worker and not on the existing low efficiency.

(iii) Incentive bonus should be paid to individuals or groups of workers for the extra work done and additional production attained over the standards so fixed.

(iv) In a similar manner, reward should be given for outstanding performance over and above the fixed targets to people engaged in marketing and sales at different levels. This will create an incentive among employees to put in their best efforts and promote healthy competition among employees and officers at different levels.

Recognition of Meritorious Works. Special recognition should be given to workers who do some exceptional and outstanding work by grant of honoraria, letter of appreciation or prize medals. Similarly, successful efforts of officers to raise the standard of operational efficiency and to root out corruption and their good work and sense of public duty should be considered as one of the important qualifications for accelerated promotion. Further, if somebody does any meritorious work, his name may be mentioned in the Annual Report and he may also be given a suitable reward.

Cash Awards for Valuable Suggestions and Inventions. Some of the public enterprises have introduced the scheme of offering cash awards for valuable suggestions or inventions in order to provide opportunities to employees to show their inventive ideas which can lead to important economies in the production process, sales or efficient functioning of the enterprises. 'Cash Your Suggestion' scheme has been introduced in some of the public undertakings, e.g. Hindustan Shipyard, Indian Telephone Industries, the Railways, etc. The scheme should be introduced in all other public enterprises also. The management should set up Suggestions Committees consisting of senior and experienced technical officers which should meet periodically to review the suggestions received from employees at different levels. The Suggestions Committee should also co-opt some non-official members and representatives of the labour so as to ensure impartiality. Wide publicity should be given to the scheme in order to make it popular among the employees.

Psychological Approach Towards Staff. A psychological approach is very essential in order to get the best out of workers. For efficient and economic working of an organisation what is required is a humanistic approach to management as against a mechanistic approach so that even the humblest worker is made to feel that his work is important and he develops interest in it. A worker's relation with the enterprise should not be restricted to his obtaining wages for the work done by him. He should be made fully conscious of the place of respect he deserves and he should be made to realise that he is the kingpin on which the success of the enterprise depends and that efficient performance of his day-to-day work is not only in the interest of the enterprise but also in his own interest. The enterprise should not fail to appreciate the work of the employee and look to his personal problems with sympathy and helpful attitude. If his self-respect is boosted up and he is made to develop interest in the work he is doing, his efficiency would be stepped up substantially.

Participation of Employees in Decision-making. For obtaining administrative efficiency, economy and discipline and resultant higher productivity, it is very essential that employees are associated in decision-making on all important issues of the enterprise. This will give a sense of belonging to the employees and the decisions taken by the high-power-committees in which employees are also represented, will be respected and implemented whole-heartedly by the employees. The small matters which often lead to big labour and staff problems later on can be fruitfully sorted out through staff councils. Staff meetings should take place regularly and frequently. The members of the staff should be encouraged to express their views and feelings freely and frankly. The supervisor should try to lead his unit to a group discussion on any matter which affects general work policy rather than reserving this prerogative to himself. Serious group problems of discipline should be discussed frequently and openly with the groups of employees affected in an attempt to obtain their solution of the difficulty.

Deputationists. The Government of India has taken steps to free the public undertakings of officers on deputation from the civil service whose loyalty and inspiration lie not in the undertakings concerned but in their parent office. It has often been found that the deputationists do not possess the technical qualifications and experience required by the enterprise. Further, they are costlier than the regular employees because they have to be paid deputation allowance in addition to their salary. Since the deputationists return to their parent office after a certain period of time, this practice stands in the way of accumulation of experience and building of business contacts. In view of these considerations, the deputationists have been given an option by the government either to return to their parent office or to get permanently absorbed in the public undertakings by resigning from the government. They must merge their identity and future with the undertaking in which they are employed. This will give them a sense of belonging and dedication and make them accountable to the undertaking for their performance and future prospects.

Scientific Recruitment Policy. The public enterprises have often failed to appoint the right type of personnel needed by them, which has resulted in a low level of efficiency. They must formulate a scientific recruitment policy at all levels whether for the top managerial officers or people at middle and low management level.

Recruitment in public enterprises is outside the purview of the Union Public Service Commission. The public enterprises have their own Departmental Recruitment Committees, which have often failed to choose the right type of personnel. In order to recruit right type of personnel for public enterprises, the government should set up an Industrial Public Service Commission which should consist of competent professional and technical experts and public men. The Commission will be able to follow an integrated, co-ordinated and uniform recruitment policy and eliminate all chances of corruption, favouritism and nepotism now prevalent in public enterprises.

Promotion Policy. A satisfactory promotion policy is very essential to improve efficiency and to boost morale of the employees. It should provide reasonable opportunities of promotion to employees at reasonable intervals and enable the management to choose competent employees and promote them to reasonable positions. The promotion should be determined on the basis of merit, qualification, experience and performance alone. The cases of promotion should be considered with complete impartiality. Much weightage should not be given to confidential reports which have lost their earlier sanctity and respect. They no longer reveal the true performance of the employee reported upon. The report is influenced by the fancies, likes and dislikes of the writer of the report. In the absence of reasonable opportunities for promotion, trained hands may move from one enterprise to another, which is not congenial to efficiency.

Training in Management. The days of managing industries in the old traditional way are gone. Today, we are living in the modern age of technological advancement and have to function amidst age of competition. Only the fittest will survive. Today, organising ability and administrative skill alone are not enough in manning technical jobs. Modern industrial management requires a thorough knowledge of economics, finance, accountancy, information technology psychology, marketing and sales. Similarly, for manning technical jobs, we require fully qualified and trained technicians. This calls for an efficient system of training the personnel in different fields of technology and management. In India many specialised institutes have been set up for imparting training in management and technology. The public enterprises should recruit officers trained in modern techniques of management in different fields. They should also depute their existing officers for training in these institutes.

Arrangements should also be made for training staff within the public enterprises also.

Marketing Arrangements. The public sector undertakings are producing machinery and equipments of various types and other goods worth thousands of crores. But most of the undertakings do not have proper marketing arrangements. Each enterprise should have an appropriate marketing and sales organisation equipped with properly trained personnel. This will enable the enterprise to establish a direct contact with the consumer and eliminate the middleman. Bigger enterprises should have a full-fledged market research department which should conduct extensive market surveys for exploring new markets and developing existing markets, both at home and abroad.

Staff Welfare. In a welfare state, an employee should not be treated simply as a cog in the administrative machine. He must be treated as a human being and given full scope for his development and for the performance of his duty towards his family and society. Proper attention should be paid to welfare activities for the employees, e.g. provision of staff quarters, medical facilities, educational facilities, recreation facilities etc., setting up of co-operative stores, providing holiday homes, rest houses, etc. In this respect, it is encouraging to note that public enterprises have a good record and provide liberal welfare amenities to the employees.

Optimum Utilisation of Plant Capacity. The public enterprises must ensure an optimum utilisation of the plant capacity. This would reduce their cost of production and raise profits. In case, the enterprise fails, in spite of best efforts, to create enough market for its product, it should go in for diversification of its production.

NOTES

1. Parmanand Prasad, "Efficiency and its Evaluation in Public Enterprises", *The Indian Journal of Public Administration* (January-March 1961), p. 42.
2. Tirath Raj Sharma, *The Working of State Enterpreses* (Bombay, 1961), p. 167.

3. Prasad, n. 1, pp. 42-43.
4. W.C. Baum, *The French Economy and the State* (New Jersey, 1958), p. 223.
5. M.M. Mehta, "Measurement of the Efficiency of Public Enterprises" in V.V. Ramanadham (ed.), *Pricing, Labour and Efficiency in the Public Sector* (Hyderabad, 1962), p. 81.
6. D.T. Lakdawala, "Contribution of Public Enterprise", *Indian Economic Journal* (April 1960), p. 395.
7. Lord Latham, "London Transport" in Sir W. Houldsworth and others (ed.), *Efficiency in Nationalized Industry* (London, 1952), p. 29.
8. P. Sargant Florence and Gilbert Walker, "Efficiency under Nationalization and its Measurement" in W.A. Robson (ed.), *Problems of Nationalized Industry* (London, 1952), pp. 195-97.
9. D.V.C. *Monthly Statistical Handbook* (August 1960), p. 33.
10. Estimates Committee, *Report on Hindustan Steel (P) Ltd.—Rourkela, Bhilai and Durgapur Steel Projects* (New Delhi, 1958), paras 50-56.
11. D.V.C. *Annual Report 1956-57,* p. 3.
12. Mehta, n. 5, p. 83.
13. Sharma, n. 2, p. 171.
14. H.K. Paranjape, "Measurement of Management in the Public Sector", *The Indian Journal of Public Administration* (January-March 1964), p. 163.
15. Bheemsain Sharma, "Efficiency in Public Enterprises" in *Indian Journal of Commerce* (March 1965), p. 59.
16. Prasad, n. 1, p. 45.
17. Gabriel Ardant, "The Measurement of Productivity in State Undertakings and Public Services", *Annals of Collectivist Economy* (1953) reprinted in A.H. Hanson (ed.), *Nationalisation* (London, 1963), p. 423.
18. Government of India, *Report of the Study Team on Public Undertakings*, p. 199.
19. R.D. Gorwala, *Report on the Efficient Conduct of State Enterprises* (New Delhi, 1951), p. 25.
20. *Ibid.*

Public Enterprises in India

12

In India, the public sector has played a very important role in the economic development by taking up projects which involve highly sophisticated technology and difficult construction. The rapid industrial development in the country is the result of public sector enterprises as they have helped in producing enough infrastructural facilities (production of electricity, coal, steel, petroleum, etc.) which in turn helped the private sector grow. Even the Green Revolution achieved in agriculture can be attributed to Public Sector Enterprises (PSEs) as these provided power and fertilizers. The PSEs have by and large developed substantial capacities for production of coal, iron-ore, steel, petroleum products, fertilizers, heavy machines, basic drugs, electricity, power equipments and ships. In addition to being a source of employment to a large number of people, the PSEs have also contributed to India's export earnings as well as successful efforts towards import substitution.

The reasons that led the public sector to undertake industrial and commercial activities are many. Firstly, the public utility services like electricity, water, transport, etc. could not be left in the hands of private sector, which normally exploit masses. Secondly, industries like steel, heavy industries, oil exploration and refining, fertilizers, etc. which are basic to industrial development require huge investments and they have a long gestation period. The private sector shows reluctance to invest in such projects as it is always interested in earning quick profits. Thirdly, private sector is normally not very keen in production of goods which have mass consumption like milk, bread, etc. due to low profitability. Fourthly, defence and allied industries which are vital to the security of the country require public sector to enter in the interest of the country. Fifthly, development of backward areas may require entry of public sector to ensure balanced regional development in the country. All these factors have led the public sector in India to enter various fields that cover all the economic activities like production, marketing, distribution, exchange, etc.

The main objectives of PSEs, set up and expanded in pursuance of the Industrial Policy Resolutions of 1948 and 1956, are: to build a strong and sound base for heavy industries; to create infrastructural facilities for self-reliance and self-sufficiency in modern technological development; to prevent the concentration of wealth and economic power in few hands; greater welfare of the common man and rise in his standard of living through public ownership of means of production and development. In other words, the PSEs have been set up to serve the broad macro-economic objectives of higher economic growth, self-sufficiency in production of goods and services (wherever so desired), long-term equilibrium in balance of payments and low and stable prices.

The establishment of PSEs in the country has resulted in sustained employment, particularly through nationalization of sick mills. It has also resulted in industrial development in backward areas like Nagaland, Sikkim and tribal areas of Bihar and M.P. Thus, the public sector is responsible for equitable economic development of various regions of the country. Simultaneously, it has also helped in making India a self-reliant country.

The PSEs in India cover all those undertakings which are wholly or partly owned to the extent of at least 51 per cent of the share capital by the state. They are normally of three kinds: (i) Limited Companies formed under Companies Act in which at least 51 per cent shares are held by the state (ii) Statutory Corporations set up through an Act of Parliament, for example, Food Corporation of India, Life Insurance Corporation, Industrial Finance Corporation, Unit Trust of India, etc. and (iii) Holding

Companies formed under Companies Act which have a hold on the already set up Companies Act as an institutional buffer between the companies and the government, for example, Steel Authority of India, National Textiles Corporation, etc. In addition to these three kinds, there are several Departments of Public Undertakings like Ordnance Factories, Railways, Posts and Telegraph, Telephones, etc. Since these Undertakings are directly run by the government, they do not normally come under the purview of public sector enterprises.

The PSEs have made a notable contribution to the economic growth of the country, particularly by creating a diversified industrial base. After the introduction of economic reforms in 1991-92, a policy of disinvestments and privatization was adopted and up to 2001-02 equity had been sold in 123 enterprises and receipt of ₹ 26,012 crore realized. During the first two years of the Tenth Five Year Plan, the process intensified and a sum of ₹ 18,895 crore was realized from disinvestments. In 2004-05, there was a policy shift and the United Progressive Alliance (UPA) government, while expressing a commitment toward a strong and effective public sector, decided that 'generally profit making companies will not be privatized'. Residual disinvestments made in the last three years of the Plan brought in receipts of ₹ 4,335 crore.

Central Public Sector Enterprises

The Central Public Sector Enterprises (CPSEs), besides statutory corporations, comprise those Government companies (defined under Section 617 of the Companies Act, 1956) wherein more than 50 per cent equity is held by the Central Government. The subsidiaries of these companies are also categorized as CPSEs. However, departmentally run public enterprises like banking institutions and enterprises wherein Central Government equity is less than or equal to 50 per cent are generally not categorized as CPSEs. As on 31.3.2009, there were 246 CPSEs (excluding seven Insurance Companies) with a total investment of ₹ 5,28,951 crore. The increase in both the number of enterprises and the total investment in CPSEs can be gauged by the fact that on the eve of the First Five Year Plan, there were only 5 CPSEs with a total investment of ₹ 29 crore.

A large number of CPSEs have been set up as Greenfield projects consequent to the initiatives taken during the Five Year Plans. CPSEs, such as National Textile Corporation Ltd., Coal India Ltd. (and its subsidiaries) have, however, been taken over from the private sector consequent to their 'nationalization'. Industrial units, such as, Indian Petrochemicals Corporation Ltd., Modern Food Industries Ltd., Hindustan Zinc Ltd., Bharat Aluminum Company Ltd., Maruti Udyog Nigam Ltd. etc. on the other hand, which were CPSEs earlier ceased, to be CPSEs after their 'privatization'.

Along with other public sector majors, such as, State Bank of India in the banking sector, Life Insurance Corporation in the insurance sector, Indian Railways in transportation, the CPSEs are the leading companies of India with significant market-shares in sectors such as petroleum products, (ONGC, GAIL and Indian Oil), mining (Coal India Ltd. and NMDC Ltd.), power generation (NTPC Ltd. and NHPC), power transmission (POWERGRID), nuclear energy (Nuclear Power Corporation of India Ltd.), heavy engineering (BHEL), aviation industry (Hindustan Aeronautics Ltd. and NACIL), storage and public distribution system (Food Corporation of India and Central Warehousing Corporation), shipping and trading (Shipping Corporation of India Ltd. and State Trading Corporation Ltd.) and telecommunication group (BSNL and MTNL).

With economic liberalization, post-1991, sectors that were exclusive preserve of the public sector enterprises were opened to the private sector. The CPSEs, as such, are faced with competition from both the domestic private sector companies (some of which have grown very fast) and the large multi-national corporations (MNCs). These large corporations enjoy the advantage of 'economies of scale' as well as have superior technology. Competition in the markets has, therefore, made the CPSEs also spend on Research & Development (R&D), go for technological collaboration and look for growth opportunities within India and abroad. In the case of some CPSEs, however, turnover has been declining over the years and their market share has got much reduced. CPSEs like National Textile Corporation Ltd., Cement Corporation of India Ltd., HMT Ltd.

have currently a market share of less than five percent in the domestic market.

The two main elements of the government's policy have been devolution of full managerial and commercial autonomy to successful, profit-making companies and modernization and restructuring of sick PSUs as well as sell-off or closure of chronically sick CPSEs. The government has introduced a series of measures for enhancement of financial delegation to Navratnas, Miniratnas, and profit-making CPSEs. These include measures for creation of and disinvestment in subsidiaries, transfer of assets to such subsidiaries, and floating of fresh equity.

Performance of CPSEs

Some parameters of CPSEs as on 31.3.2009 are: Total paid up capital in 246 CPSEs—₹ 1,38,843 crore; Total Share application money pending allotment—₹ 3,867 crore in 41 CPSEs; Total investment (equity plus long term loans) in all CPSEs—₹ 5,28,951 crore; Capital Employed (net block plus working capital) in all CPSEs—₹ 7,94,105 Crore; Total turnover of all CPSEs during 2008-09—₹ 12,63,405 crore; Total income of all CPSEs during 2008-09—₹ 13,07,366 crore; Profit of profit making CPSEs during 2008-09—₹ 98,652 crore; Loss of loss incurring CPSEs during 2008-09—₹ 14,424 crore; Reserves & Surplus of all CPSEs—₹ 5,35,840; Net worth of all CPSEs—₹ 5,88,217 crore; Contribution of CPSEs to Central Exchequer by way of excise duty, customs duty, corporate tax, interest on Central Government loans, dividend and other duties and taxes in 2008-09—₹ 1,51,728 crore; Foreign exchange earnings through exports of goods and services in 2008-09—₹ 74,184 crore; Foreign exchange outgo on imports and royalty, know-how, consultancy, interest and other expenditure during 2008-09—₹ 4,28,821 crore; Number of people employed by CPSEs—15.35 lakh (excluding casual workers and contract labours); Salary and wages in all CPSEs in 2008-09—₹ 82,735 crore; Total Market Capitalisation (M_Cap) of 41 listed CPSEs, based on the stock price in Bombay Stock Exchange—₹ 8,13,530 crores.

In terms of Gross Block, the top ten enterprises as on 31.3.2009 were Oil & Natural Gas Corporation Ltd., Bharat Sanchar Nigam Ltd., NTPC Ltd., Indian Oil Corporation Ltd., Power Grid Corporation of India Ltd., Steel Authority of India Ltd., Nuclear Power Corporation of India Ltd., NHPC Ltd., National Aviation Company of India Ltd., and Hindustan Petroleum Corporation Ltd. The gross block of these enterprises inclusive of Capital-work-in progress amounted to ₹ 6,73,864 crore. This was equal to 68.92 per cent of the total gross block in all CPSEs.

In terms of sector-wise and cognate group-wise cumulative investment in CPSEs, the service sector has highest share of 46.12 per cent in financial investment, followed by the electricity sector (26.19 per cent) and manufacturing (18.07 per cent). Mining, under construction, and agriculture had a combined share of less than 10 per cent. While the CPSEs have monopoly in nuclear power generation, they have a major share in domestic/national output in coal, petroleum, power generation, telecommunication, and fertilizers.

The net profit of all CPSEs (aggregate net profit minus aggregate net loss) stood at ₹ 84,228 crore in 2008-09. Cognate group-wise, the best results were achieved by the 'manufacturing' sector followed by the 'electricity' sector. The other sectors of 'mining' and services recorded significant decline in profits. In the manufacturing sector as well, CPSEs belonging to industries such as steel, petroleum refinery, medium and light engineering, and consumer goods recorded significant decline in their profits. CPSEs contribute to the Central Exchequer by way of dividend payment, interest on government loans and payment of taxes and duties.

Performance of State-level Public Enterprises (SLPEs)

No regular survey is carried out for SLPEs. According to a study by Institute of Public Enterprises (IPE), Hyderabad, as on 31 March 2005, 1129 SLPEs were in operation. The majority of SLPEs are in manufacturing followed by utilities, promotional, and welfare enterprises. In the post-economic reform period, the total investment in SLPEs increased every year reaching a peak of ₹ 2,85,564 crore in 2002-03 before going into a declining trend ending up with ₹ 2,59,124 crore in 2004-05. The accumulated losses of SLPEs have been on the increase reaching a figure of ₹ 60,517 crore in 2004-05, with consequential adverse fiscal impact on the States.

579 out of total 1129 SLPEs are in manufacturing sector and constitute a major share of the SLPEs portfolio in States such as Assam, Gujarat, Kerala, Maharashtra, Rajasthan, Tamil Nadu, Uttar Pradesh, and West Bengal. It has to be noted that a considerable number of these enterprises are taken over sick units. The investment in manufacturing enterprises increased from ₹ 17,099 crore in 1997-98 to ₹ 23,912 crore in 2004-05. The CAGR of investment was 4.2 per cent. These enterprises incurred losses during all the years excluding 2003-04 and 2004-05. As a result, their net worth in 2004-05 was ₹ 12,951 crore.

Restructuring of SLPEs: Some states have been active in restructuring sick PSEs. According to IPE, Hyderabad upto 2004-05, 30 units including cooperatives had been privatized in Andhra Pradesh, 3 in Gujarat, and 1 each in Haryana, Orissa, Punjab, and Rajasthan.

Board Structure of CPSEs

The Department of Public Enterprises (DPE) formulates policy guidelines on the Board structure of Public Enterprises and advises on the shape and size of organizational structure of CPSEs. The public enterprises are categorized in four Schedules namely 'A', 'B', 'C' and 'D'. The initial categorization of CPSEs in the mid-Sixties was made on the basis of their importance to the economy and complexities of their problems. Over the years the DPE has evolved norms for the purpose of categorization/re-categorization of CPSEs. Categorization is based on criteria such as quantitative factors (like investment, capital employed, net sales, profit, number of employees) and qualitative factors (like national importance, complexity of problems, level of technology, prospects for expansion and diversification of activities and competition from other sectors, etc.) In addition, other factors such as strategic importance of the CPSE, etc. is also taken into account. The present procedure involves consideration of the proposals in the administrative Ministry concerned and the Department of Public Enterprises which consults the Public Enterprises Selection Board.

The pay scales of Chief Executives and full time Functional Directors in CPSEs are determined as per the Schedule of the concerned enterprise. Proposals received from various administrative Ministries/Departments for initial categorization/ upgradation of CPSEs in appropriate schedule, personal upgradation, creation of posts in CPSEs, etc. are considered in DPE in consultation with the Public Enterprises Selection Board (PESB). As on 31.1.2010, out of the 246 CPSEs, there are 59 in Schedule 'A', 70 CPSEs in Schedule 'B', 45 CPSEs in Schedule 'C' and 6 CPSEs in Schedule 'D'. The rest 67 are covered under the uncategorized category (See Appendix II). The details of the Board level posts (whole time) in the categorized CPSEs are given in Table 1.

Table: 1 Position of Board Level Executives

Schedule	*Chief Executive*	*Whole-time Director*
Schedule A	59	*
Schedule B	70	213
Schedule C	45	183
Schedule D	06	67
Total	**180**	**463**

Note: *Whole-time Directors are one level below that of the Chief Executive

Corporate Governance

In recent times, the concept of corporate governance has generated a great deal of interest and public debate. Corporate governance is intended primarily to ensure transparency in management of the enterprise and encompasses the entire functioning of the company. The 'Guidelines on Corporate Governance for CPSEs' was brought out by the Department of Public Enterprises (DPE) in June 2007, keeping in view relevant laws, instructions and procedures.

For the purpose of Corporate Governance, the CPSEs have been, furthermore, categorized into two groups, namely

(a) those listed on the Stock Exchanges and (b) those not listed in the Stock Exchanges. The listed CPSEs have to follow the SEBI guidelines on Corporate Governance. In addition, they may also follow those provisions of the Guidelines brought out by DPE which do not exist in the SEBI guidelines and also do not contradict provisions in the SEBI guidelines. The non-listed CPSEs are to follow the DPE guidelines on Corporate Governance, although these are voluntary in nature. These guidelines are under implementation by the CPSEs.

Professionalization of Boards

The Department of Public Enterprises has taken several measures to professionalize the Boards of public enterprises in pursuance to the policy on public sector enterprises being followed since 1991. The guidelines issued by the DPE in 1992 provide for induction of outside professionals on the Boards of CPSEs as part-time non-official Directors. The number of such Directors has to be at least 1/3rd of the actual strength of the Board. In the case of listed CPSEs headed by an executive Chairman, the number of non-official Directors (Independent Directors) should be at least half the strength of the Board. The guidelines also provide that the number of Government Directors on the Boards should be not more than one-sixth of the actual strength of the Board subject to a maximum of two.

Apart from the above, there should be some functional Directors on each Board whose number should not exceed 50 per cent of the actual strength of the Board. The proposals for appointment of non-official Directors are initiated by the concerned Administrative Ministries/Departments. In case of Navratna and Miniratna CPSEs, selection of non-official Directors is made by the Search Committee consisting of Chairman (PESB), Secretary (DPE), Secretary of the administrative Ministry/Department of the CPSE, Chief Executive of the concerned CPSE and non-official Members. For remaining CPSEs (other than Navratna/Miniratna CPSEs), Public Enterprises Selection Board (PESB) makes the selection of non-official Directors. The concerned Administrative Ministry/Department appoints the non-official Directors on the basis of recommendations of Search Committee/PESB after obtaining the approval of competent authority, i.e. Appointments Committee of Cabinet (ACC).

Wages/Salaries and Employees Welfare

The Department of Public Enterprises (DPE) functions as the nodal Department in the Government of India, *inter alia*, in respect of policy relating to wage settlements of unionized employees, pay revision of non-unionized supervisors and the executives holding posts below the Board level as well as at the Board level in CPSEs. While the CPSEs largely follow the Industrial Dearness Allowance (IDA) pattern scales of pay, the Central Dearness Allowance (CDA) pattern scales of pay is being followed by some CPSEs.

The government policy relating to pay scales and pay pattern is broadly that all employees of the CPSEs should be on IDA pattern and related scales of pay. The DPE had, in July 1981 and July 1984, issued instructions to all the administrative Ministries that as and when a new CPSE is created or established, IDA pattern and related scales of pay should be adopted *ab initio*. Vide DPE O.M. dated 10.08.2009, it was reiterated and emphasized that 'appointments' including 'promotion' on or after 01.01.1989 in CDA scales of pay has to be in IDA scales of pay. Out of the approximately 15.35 lakh workmen, clerical staff and executives in 246 CPSEs (excluding Banks, Insurance Companies under the administrative control of the Central Government), around 96 per cent of the workmen and executives are on IDA pattern and related scales of pay.

A pay revision for the IDA executives and non-unionized supervisors was done w.e.f. 1.1.97 for a period of ten years based on the recommendations of Justice Mohan Committee (1st Pay Revision Committee). The duration of this pay revision was for 10 years i.e. upto 31.12.2006. The government, after due consideration of the recommendations of the Second Pay Revision Committee (2nd PRC), headed by Justice M. Jagannadha Rao, issued orders on 26.11.2008 and 09.02.2009.

For the employees of the CPSEs following CDA pattern, the DPE vide its OM dated 14.10.2008, revised the pay scales w.e.f. 01.01.2006, based on government decision in respect of Central

Government employees. The benefit of pay revision was allowed only to the employees of those CPSEs which are not loss making and are in a position to absorb the additional expenditure on account of pay revision from their own resources without any budgetary support from the government. It was also indicated that the Board of Directors would consider the proposal of pay revision of all the employees in the CPSE, keeping in mind the affordability and capacity of the CPSE to pay and submit a proposal to its Administrative Ministry/Department, which will approve the proposal with the concurrence of its Financial Adviser.

Employment

One-fourth of the manpower in CPSEs is in managerial and supervisory cadres. Thus, the CPSEs have a highly skilled workforce, which is one of their basic strengths. The CPSEs, in turn, provide lifetime employment to their employees. Since the CPSEs operate under dynamic market conditions, while some of them may face shortage of people, others may have excess manpower.

To help these enterprises to shed excess manpower, the government initiated a Voluntary Retirement Scheme (VRS). The basic parameters of the model VRS which were notified by the Government vide DPE's O.Ms. dated 5.10.1988 and 6.1.1989 were in force since 1988 till April, 2000. The said scheme was improved upon by the government and new VRS schemes were introduced on 5.5.2000 and again on 6.11.2001. Till 31.3.2009, about 3.03 lakh employees opted for VRS. However, many CPSEs, are facing a high rate of 'attrition', as employees are leaving to join other organizations on account of higher salaries being offered elsewhere.

Counseling, Retraining and Redeployment

In the context of more liberalized economies, restructuring of enterprises has become a global phenomenon. This has necessitated rationalization of manpower in many instances. However, the policy of the government has been to implement these reforms with a humane face as they adversely affect the interest of the workers. Accordingly in February 1992, the government established the National Renewal Fund (NRF) to cover broadly the expenses of VRS and to provide retraining to workers in the organized sector. Priority was given on the needs of CPSEs in the wake of the ongoing restructuring exercises in the central enterprises. Subsequently in February 2000, the NRF was abolished.

Since 2001-02, the scheme for Counselling, Retraining and Redeployment (CRR) is under implementation through DPE. Prior to that, the retraining activity for employees opting for VRS was administered by the Department of Industrial Policy and Promotion. The scheme for Counselling, Retraining and Redeployment (CRR) *inter alia* aims: (a) to provide opportunity for self-employment, (b) to reorient rationalized employees through short duration programmes, (c) to equip them for new vocations, (d) to engage them in income generating self-employment, and (e) to help them rejoin the productive process.

For the implementation of CRR, a Plan Fund of ₹ 8 crore was allocated initially during 2001-02, which was enhanced to ₹ 10 crore during 2002-03 and 2003-04. The plan fund was substantially increased to ₹ 30 crore during 2004-05 and 2005-06, and further enhanced to ₹ 31.50 crore during 2006-07. During 2007-08, however, only ₹ 10.00 crore was allocated and during 2008-09, the plan allocation made was ₹ 8.70 crores for the implementation of CRR scheme. The list of 19 nodal agencies with 46 Employees Assistance Centres (EACs) which are operational and help in implementation of CRR is given below:

1. Academy Suburbia, Kolkata
2. Associated Chamber of Commerce & Industry, New Delhi
3. Association of Lady Entrepreneurs of Andhra Pradesh, Hyderabad
4. Central Institute of Plastics Engineering & Technology, Amritsar
5. Central Institute of Plastics Engineering & Technology, Bhubaneswar

6. Central Institute of Plastics Engineering & Technology, Chennai.
7. Central Institute of Plastics Engineering & Technology, Guwahati
8. Central Institute of Plastics Engineering & Technology, Panipat
9. Electronics Service & Training Centre, Ramnagar
10. Indian Council of Small Industries (ICSI), Kolkata
11. Institute of Entrepreneurship Development, Patna
12. Institute of Labour Development, Jaipur
13. Kalinga Centre for Social Development, Bhubaneswar
14. Madhya Pradesh Consultancy Organisation (MPCON), Bhopal
15. MITCON Consultancy Services Ltd., Pune
16. National Institute for Micro, Small & Medium Enterprises (NIMSEM), Hyderabad
17. National School of Computer Education, Kolkata
18. North India Technical Consultancy Services Ltd., Chandigarh
19. U.P. Industrial Consultants Ltd. (UPICO), Kanpur

MoU System

To ensure a level playing field to the public sector enterprises vis-à-vis the private corporate sector, the Memorandum of Understanding (MoU) system has been introduced. The MoU, as applicable to central public sector enterprises, is a negotiated document between the government and the management of the enterprise specifying clearly the objectives of the agreement and the obligations of both the parties. The MoU system is aimed at providing greater autonomy to public sector enterprises vis-à-vis the control of the government. The 'management' of the enterprise is, nevertheless, made accountable to the government through promise for performance or 'performance contract'. The government, on the other hand, continues to have control over these enterprises through setting targets in the beginning of the year and by 'performance evaluation' at the end of the year.

Performance evaluation is done based on the comparison between the actual achievements and the annual targets agreed upon between the government and the CPSE. The targets constitute of both financial and non-financial parameters with different weights assigned to the different parameters. Performance during the year is measured on a 5-point scale in order to distinguish 'excellent' from 'poor'.

Mega and Major Projects Under Implementation

There were altogether 925 projects in the central sector as on 31.3.2009, of which 102 projects (costing ₹ 500 crores and above) belonged to Central Public Sector Enterprises (CPSEs). Of these 102 projects, 75 were mega projects (costing ₹ 1000 crore and above) and 27 were major projects (costing between ₹ 100 crore and ₹ 1000 crore). The total original cost in respect of these 102 projects of CPSE stood at ₹ 3,02,585 crore, while the revised/anticipated cost is equal to ₹ 3,14,798 crore.

CPSEs Under Construction

There were altogether 33 CPSEs 'under construction' as on 31.3.2009, which were yet to go on regular production on a commercial scale. While the total authorized capital of these 33 CPSEs stood at approximately ₹ 14,318 crores as on 31.03.2009, the paid up capital amounted to ₹ 654.92 crores. A large majority of these CPSEs are subsidiary companies with small authorized and paid-up capital. Some of these subsidiary companies are 'shell companies' which have been set up to facilitate the establishment of Ultra Mega Power Projects (UMPP) in the different parts of the country. The objective of 'shell companies' is to develop large capacities of power generation in India and to bring in the potential investors in UMPP after developing such projects to a stage having major clearances. Power Finance Corporation Limited is the Nodal Agency for the development of these projects under the technical guidance of CEA.

Market Capitalisation of CPSEs Stocks

Stocks of the following 40 CPSEs were being traded on the stock exchanges of India with market capitalization of ₹ 8,13,530 (based on BSE prices) as on 31.03.2009:

1. Andrew Yule and Company Ltd.
2. Balmer Lawri and Co. Ltd.
3. Balmer Lawri Investments Ltd.
4. BEML Ltd.
5. Bharat Electronics Ltd.
6. Bharat Heavy Electrical Corpn. Ltd.
7. Bharat Immunologicals & Biologicals Corpn. Ltd.
8. Bharat Petroleum Corpn. Ltd.
9. Bongaigaon Refinery
10. Chennai Petroleum Corporation Ltd.
11. Container Corporation of India Ltd.
12. Dredging Corporation of India Ltd.
13. Engineers (I) Ltd.
14. Fertilizer & Chemicals (Travancore) Ltd.
15. GAIL (India) Ltd.
16. Hind Copper Ltd.
17. Hind Organic Chemicals Ltd.
18. Hindustan Petroleum Corpn Ltd.
19. HMT Ltd.
20. Indian Oil Corporation Ltd.
21. ITI Ltd.
22. Madras Fertilizers Ltd.
23. Mahanagar Telephone Nigam Ltd.
24. Maharashtra Elecktrosmelt Ltd.
25. Mangalore Refinery and Petrochemicals Ltd.
26. MMTC Ltd.

27. National Aluminium Company Ltd.
28. National Fertilisers Ltd.
29. National Mineral Development Corporation Ltd.
30. Neyvelli Lignite Corpn. Ltd.
31. NTPC Ltd.
32. Oil & Natural Gas Corporation Ltd.
33. Power Finance Corpn. Ltd.
34. Power Grid Corpn. Ltd.
35. Rashtriya Chemicals and Fertilizers Ltd.
36. Rural Electrification Corpn. Ltd.
37. Scooters India Ltd.
38. Shipping Corporation of India
39. State Trading Corpn of India Ltd.
40. Steel Authority of India Ltd.

Investment in Central Public Sector Enterprises

The aggregate real investment in Central Public Sector Enterprises (CPSEs) measured in terms of 'gross block' was ₹ 9,77,803 crore in 2008-09. However, in terms of share in 'gross fixed capital formation' (GFCF) of the country, the share of gross block in CPSEs shows a decline over the years. It came down from 10.39 per cent in 2003-04 to 4.96 per cent in 2007-08. But in 2008-09, their share in gross fixed capital formation went up to 6.24 per cent due to investment of ₹ 1,15,572 crore by CPSEs.

Growth in Financial Investment

The aggregate financial investment in CPSEs comprising paid-up share capital, share application money pending allotment and long term loans has increased from ₹ 29 crore in five enterprises in 1951-52 to ₹ 5,28,951 crore in 246 enterprises in 2008-09. The rise in aggregate financial investment and the number of CPSEs over various Plan periods is given in Table 2.

Table: 2 Growth in (Financial) Investment*

Particulars	*Total Investment (₹ in crore)*	*Enterprises (Nos.)*
At the commencement of the Ist Five Year Plan (1.4.1951)	29	5
At the commencement of the 2nd Five Year Plan (1.4.1956)	81	21
At the commencement of the 3rd Five Year Plan (1.4.1961)	948	47
At the end of 3rd Five Year Plan (31.3.1966)	2410	73
At the commencement of the 4th Five Year Plan (1.4.1969)	3897	84
At the commencement of the 5th Five Year Plan (1.4.1974)	6237	122
At the end of 5th Five Year Plan (31.3.1979)	15534	169
At the commencement of the 6th Five Year Plan (1.4.1980)	18150	179
At the commencement of the 7th Five Year Plan (1.4.1985)	42673	215
At the end of 7th Five Year Plan (31.3.1990)	99329	244
At the commencement of the 8th Five Year Plan (1.4.1992)	135445	246
At the end of 8th Five Year Plan (31.3.1997)	213610	242
At the end of 9th Five Year Plan (31.3.2002)	324614	240
At the end of 10th Five Year Plan (31.3.2007)	420771	245
At the end of first year of Eleventh Five Year Plan (31.3.2008)	455367	242
At the end of second year of Eleventh Five Year Plan (31.3.2009)	528951	246

Note: * As in the Balance Sheet.

Components of Financial Investment

The structure of financial investment in CPSEs has undergone some change over the years. While the share of paid-up capital in total financial investment stood at 32.57 per cent during 2002-03, it declined to 26.25 per cent in 2008-09. The share of long-term loans, on the other hand, went up from 66.56 per cent in 2002-03 to 73.02 per cent in 2008-09.

Sources of Financial Investment

The Central Government has the majority equity holding in CPSEs which is about 84.49 per cent. Other parties such as the financial institutions, banks, private parties (both Indian and foreign), State governments and holding companies have also been forthcoming with investment in terms of both equity and long term loans. However, a significant change has been observed in the investment pattern of CPSEs over the period 2004-05 to 2008-09. Whereas the share of Central Government in total (financial) investment stood at 37.78 per cent in 2004-05, it declined to 29.83 per cent in 2008-09. The share of financial institutions/banks (and 'others'), on the other hand, that was 39.89 per cent in 2004-05 has gone up to 54.09

per cent in 2008-09. This development, in a way, shows the greater confidence of Foreign Investors and banks in the CPSEs. The share of 'foreign parties' in total financial investment has also shown increase from 8.37 per cent in 2004-05 to 8.52 per cent in 2008-09.

Plan Investment in CPSEs

In recent years, a major share of investment in CPSEs has been made from internal resources (IR). In absolute terms, Plan outlay in CPSEs, constituting internal resources (IR), extra-budgetary resources (EBR) and Budgetary Support (BS) have showed a continuous increase. Accordingly, Plan outlay in CPSEs went up from ₹ 59,189.79 crore in 2002-03 to ₹ 1,32,253.31 crore in 2008-09. While the share of IR went up from 55.51 per cent of plan outlay in 2002-03 to 55.06 per cent in 2008-09, the share of Budgetary Support came down from 8.98 per cent in 2002-03 to 1.23 per cent in 2008-09. Moreover, a perusal of different components of IR shows that the share of 'retained profit' has been increasing and it went up from ₹ 27,176.50 crores in 2002-03 to ₹ 69,027.46 crores in 2008-09. Whereas the share of 'depreciation' in IR declined from 48.79 per cent in 2002-03 to 31.03 per cent in 2008-09, the share of 'retained profit' in IR went up from 50.07 per cent in 2002-03 to 62.27 per cent in 2008-09.

Pattern of Investment

Cognate group-wise aggregate real investment in CPSEs during 2008-09, as mentioned in terms of gross block showed that the share of 'manufacturing' CPSEs in gross block, was the highest at 26.86 per cent followed by 'mining' (25.15%), 'electricity' (24.58%) and 'services' (23.04%). In terms of national income classification, the share of 'the industrial CPSEs', comprising manufacturing, mining and electricity, was the largest at 76.59 per cent followed by 'the service sector CPSEs' at 23.41 per cent during the same period.

An analysis of state-wise distribution of 'gross block' shows a significant change over the years. While the states of Bihar (21.91 per cent), M.P. (13.04 per cent), West Bengal (6.71 per cent) and Orissa (5.65 per cent) claimed the largest share in investment until 1977, the states of Maharashtra (17.50 per cent), A.P. (6.78 per cent), U.P. (6.77 per cent), Tamil Nadu (6.66 per cent) and Gujarat (5.60 per cent) had the largest share had in terms of investment during the year 2008-09. These changes, in good measure, have occurred mainly on account of higher investments in oil exploration (e.g. Mumbai High), power projects and telecommunications vis-a-vis investments in steel, heavy engineering and coal mining made in the earlier years.

Some changes in investment pattern have also occurred due to bifurcation of states like Bihar into Bihar and Jharkhand, Madhya Pradesh into Madhya Pradesh and Chhattisgarh and Uttar Pradesh into Uttar Pradesh and Uttrakhand as well as closing down of some CPSEs and conversion of other CPSE into joint ventures with private companies. In absolute terms, however, there has generally been increase in investments in most states.

Price Policy in CPSEs

Prices of goods and services produced by public sector enterprises in India, for long, have been determined by the government under the policy regime of 'controlled prices', or following the administered price mechanism (APM). The APM, in most cases, has been governed by the true cost of production plus a reasonable return on investment.

To obtain the cost estimates, the government has relied upon the Bureau of Industrial Costs and Prices (which was merged in 1999 with the Tariff Commission, Ministry of Commerce and Industry) in the case of CPSEs in the core sectors. The Bureau also made recommendations on prices of goods and services of these enterprises.

Generally, the prices of 'primary commodities' such as agricultural products and minerals is determined by the market forces of demand and supply. The prices of 'manufactured products' and 'services', on the other hand, is determined/administered by firms based on the average/marginal cost of production and the mark-up over and above the cost to accommodate profits. In general, the governments fix/administer the price of goods and services produced by public sector entities based on the following principles:

(a) True costs of goods and services plus a reasonable return on investment,
(b) Cross-subsidization between one group and another or between one sector and another,
(c) Differential price norm for peak and off-peak demand,
(d) Below cost to stimulate demand under conditions of excess/unutilized capacity,
(e) Lower price for providing an incentive to encourage consumption (e.g. fertilizer consumption) and higher price as a disincentive to discourage consumption (e.g. petroleum products) and
(f) Different prices/multi-tariffs to include discounts for purchases on larger volumes.

In the post-1991 period due to economic liberalization, industries in the 'core sector' are no more the exclusive preserve of the public sector. Consequently, many CPSEs have ceased to be monopolies and are facing intense competition in the market. The government has gradually dismantled APM in most sectors/ products and the CPSEs have been given the independence to fix the (competitive) prices on their own. The government, however, continues to be sensitive to the needs of the poor and the impact of rise in output prices (in the core sector) on the Wholesale Price Index (WPI).

Whenever there is any rise in price levels of these products that is not acceptable to the government, the prices are moderated through a combination of measures, such as, lowering of customs duties, excise and sales tax, administrative control on prices, grant of subsidies, etc. Since the late 1990s, the government is increasingly relying on various price regulatory commissions/authorities for regulating prices in the best interests of both the consumers and the producers. The writ of these regulatory commissions extends to both the public sector and the private sector enterprises.

Pricing System of Coal

The Central Government was empowered to fix the grade-wise and colliery-wise prices of coal under the Colliery Control Order, 1945 read with the Essential Commodities Act, 1955. However, the Colliery Control Order, 2000 fully deregulated that pricing of all grades of coal. Accordingly, the coal companies are free to fix grade-wise prices for coal produced by them on their own based on cost of production, landed cost of imported coal as well as demand and supply scenario.

Although the Ministry of Coal no longer sets the prices of various grades of domestic coal, the prices have been fixed by the coal companies from time to time under the guidance of the Ministry, as coal is a primary produce. In view of perpetual demand, both in the domestic and the international markets, there is very little price elasticity of coal. The power sector consumes nearly 75 per cent of the domestic coal produce for the generation of electricity.

In view of the substantial impact of salary revision which hit the bottom line of the coal major Coal India Ltd. that accounts for more than 80 per cent of the country's coal reserves, the Government of India allowed an average price hike of 11 per cent w.e.f. 16 October 2009. The price hike was allowed to enable Coal India Ltd. to earn additional revenue of ₹ 4600 crore annually.

Currently, the Tariff Commission is examining the extant pricing policy for coal for the power sector, while the Planning Commission is exploring the possibility of market-determined pricing. In short, the prices of coal are largely in sync with the cost of production and the transportation and handling charges; the latter forming a significant proportion of the total cost.

Pricing of Petroleum and Gas

After the changeover from administered price mechanism (APM) regime to market-determined pricing w.e.f. 1.4.2002, the oil marketing companies (OMC) are fixing the prices of petroleum products after taking into account the prevalent international oil prices. About 80 per cent of crude oil processed by the domestic refineries is imported to service domestic demand. As the cost of crude, besides taxes, constitutes a substantive part of cost of the final products, international oil prices become the determining factors for pricing of domestic petroleum products.

OMCs procure petrol and diesel from refineries as per their agreements. The basic ex-storage selling prices of petrol and diesel are uniform at all refinery locations throughout the country. The Government allowed OMCs to revise retail prices within a band of +/-10 per cent of the mean of rolling average of last 12 months and of last 3 months international C&F (cost and freight) prices. Prices based on this system, were revised for the first time effective 1 August 2004, leading to price increase of ₹ 1.10/ltr and ₹ 1.42/ltr for petrol and diesel respectively. However, the price band mechanism could not be implemented on fortnightly basis due to steep increase in international prices and the Government took back control of price setting for petrol and diesel as per the band mechanism, and restrained the 'pass through' of the international prices to domestic consumers.

Subsequently in June 2006, on recommendations of the Rangarajan Committee, the Government changed the pricing of petrol and diesel to trade parity basis. The principle of trade parity pricing was to be applied to the refinery gate price. Accordingly, the OMCs pay trade parity price (weighted average of import parity price and export parity price in the ratio of 80 : 20) to refineries when they buy petrol and diesel, and import parity price to refineries for PDS Kerosene and domestic LPG.

The retail selling price of petrol/diesel for the consumers is calculated by taking into account the price paid to refinery on trade parity basis, inland freight from refinery to depot and depot to market, marketing cost, returns on capital, dealer's commission, excise duty, Value Added Tax (State VAT) and local levies. The difference between the required price based on trade parity/import parity and actual selling price realized (excluding taxes, dealer commission) represents the under-recoveries of oil companies.

Due to the incessant increase in the international oil prices, the gap between the input price and the retail prices of the sensitive petroleum products has been widening. In order to provide some relief to the OMCs, the Government announced some measures w.e.f. 5.6.2008. These included increase in the price of petrol, diesel and domestic LPG; reduction in Customs duty on crude from 5 per cent to nil and on MS and HSD from 7.5 per cent to 2.5 per cent and on other products like ATF from 10 per cent to 5 per cent; and reduction in Excise duty by ₹ 1/litre on unbranded MS and HSD.

Subsidies on PDS Kerosene and Domestic LPG, in the Post-APM era starting from 1.4.2002, is on a specified flat rate basis for each depot/bottling Plant and is met from the Union budget. After providing for the aforesaid subsidy, the retail prices were to vary as per changes in the international oil prices. It was decided that the subsidy per selling unit for any depot/bottling plant effective 01/04/2002 shall be frozen and remain unchanged for the financial year 2002-03. The subsidy admissible under this scheme for 2003-04 was at 2/3rd level of the rates allowed during 2002-03. The subsidy admissible for 2004-05, 2005-06 and 2006-07 was at one-third level of the rates of subsidy for 2002-03. The government had decided that this subsidy at 1/3rd level of 2002-03, (average rate of subsidy on domestic LPG cylinder was ₹ 22.58/cylinder and on PDS Kerosene was 82 paise per litre) had been allowed till 31/03/2010.

The gap between the retail prices based on trade parity/ import parity pricing principles and the actual retail prices have resulted in huge under-recoveries to the OMCs. Passing on the entire impact of the steep increase in the oil prices to the consumers would have resulted in sharp increase in the domestic prices to unaffordable levels. Hence, it was decided that the burden be shared by all the stakeholders, namely the government, the upstream oil companies, the oil marketing companies (OMC's) and the consumers.

Besides the fiscal subsidy being provided on PDS Kerosene and Domestic LPG, the government decided to provide relief through issue of oil bonds to OMCs which amounted to ₹ 11,500 crore for 2005-06, ₹ 24,121 crore for 2006-07,

₹ 35,290 crore for 2007-08, and ₹ 71,292 crore for 2008-09. Even after the sharing of the financial burden by upstream companies—viz. ONGC, OIL and GAIL—and issue of oil bonds, there still remained a gap which has had to be absorbed by the public sector OMCs.

In order to control impact of high international prices and to keep the consumer prices of these sensitive petroleum products within reasonable limits, the government has taken a number of measures to rationalize taxes and duties on petrol and diesel. The rationalization in duties on sensitive petroleum products since June 2004 include reduction in customs duties, reduction in excise duties, introduction of LPG as "Declared Goods" under CST Act, and reduction in VAT by state governments since 5 June 2008.

Pricing Policy of Power

For creation of Regulatory Commissions at the Centre and in the States with powers, *inter alia*, to regulate/determine power tariffs, the Electricity Regulatory Commission Act was enacted in 1998. Accordingly, the Central Electricity Regulatory Commission (CERC) was created to regulate/determine power tariffs of CPSEs engaged in generation and inter-state transmission of power. The CERC also issues order on Availability Based Tariff (ABT) for ensuring grid discipline.

Though the Electricity Act, 2003 repealed the ERC Act, 1998, the regulatory powers of CERC constituted under the ERC Act, 1998 have been retained in respect of regulation/ determination of tariff for CPSEs involved in generation and inter transmission of power. The provisions of the Electricity Act, 2003 serve to consolidate the different laws relating to generation, transmission, distribution, trading and use of electricity.

In compliance with Section 3 of the Electricity Act, 2003, the Central Government notified the National Electricity Policy (NEP) in February 2005 and the Tariff Policy on 6.1.2006. The tariff for electricity supplied from the CPSEs is determined by the CERC based on the CERC (Terms and Conditions of Tariff) Regulations, 2004. The tariff for electricity consists of Capacity charges comprising Return on Equity, Interest on loans, Depreciation, Advance against depreciation, and Interest on working capital.

In furtherance of the objectives of the Electricity Act, 2003, the Rural Electricity Policy was also announced by the Government of India in August, 2006.

The pricing policy of nuclear power in the country and the associated tariffs are regulated by the Government of India in accordance with the provisions of the Atomic Energy Act, 1962.

Pricing of Steel

The Indian steel industry was one of the first few major sectors to be comprehensively deregulated as part of the general economic reforms. The erstwhile regime of controls was wholly dismantled in 1992 through the following policy changes: (a) prices and distribution (with the exception of a few strategic areas like SSIC) were freed, (b) trade barriers came down with reduction in tariff rates and removal of physical restrictions (canalizing and licensing) on imports and exports, (c) freight ceilings replaced freight equalization, (d) FDI in Iron and Steel was granted automatic entry, and (e) technology imports were made easier, and (f) capacity controls and reservation on the BFBOF sectors were withdrawn.

Post-deregulation, steel prices came to be determined through competition in the market. The Ministry of Steel has, nonetheless, constituted a 'Steel Price Monitoring Committee' (SPMC) to keep a watch on the price movement. The SPMC seeks to provide an interface between the producers and consumers of steel. It functions as a watchdog and ensures that a free and fair environment prevails in the market. The selling prices of steel and steel products are, *inter alia*, based on factors such as demand and supply position, competitor pricing, landed cost of imports, levels of Inventory, freight from producing point to consuming point, and market position for customers' end products.

International Operation of CPSEs

The CPSEs are increasingly engaging in 'international trade' in goods and services, which has a direct bearing on earnings and expenditure of foreign exchange. During the year 2008-09, 146 out of the 246 operating CPSEs had either foreign exchange earnings or foreign exchange expenditure. Out of the 33 CPSEs which were net foreign exchange earners, eight CPSEs, namely ONGC Videsh Ltd., NALCO, Shipping Corporation of India Ltd., Airport Authority of India Ltd., IRCON International Ltd., Cotton Corporation of India Ltd., RITES Ltd. and Kudremukh Iron Ore Co. Ltd., earned (net) foreign exchange of more than ₹ 100 crore during 2008-09.

In terms of gross foreign exchange earning during 2008-09, Indian Oil Corporation Ltd. earned ₹ 14,962.63 crore, followed by Mangalore Refinery & Petrochemicals Ltd. which earned ₹ 11,636.18 crore. Export of merchandise was the major source of foreign exchange earnings with its share in total earnings amounting to 95.15 percent (₹ 70,588.47 crores) in 2008-09. Indian Oil Corporation Ltd. also topped the list of CPSEs in terms of gross foreign exchange expenditure with expenses of ₹ 14,994.33 crore. Other CPSEs which had large gross foreign exchange expenditure during 2008-09 were BPCL, HPCL, MRPL, CPCL, ONGC, GAIL (all oil sector companies), SAIL, HAL, BHEL, RINL, SCI, BEL, RCF, NTPC, POWERGRID, BSNL and NPCIL. The expenditure was mainly on account of import of goods and services from the rest of the world.

The share of 'raw materials'/crude oil claimed the largest share (around 83.36%) of gross foreign exchange expenditure in 2008-09. Exchange rate fluctuation and change in commodity prices have been also impacting the earnings and expenditures of CPSEs.

International Finance and Investment

International finance mainly relates to external commercial borrowings and raising of resources through the equity market abroad. International investment comprises off-shore investment by CPSEs by way of joint venture, merger and acquisition and for operation of Indian subsidiaries abroad. In view of an increasing realization among Indian companies that mere organic growth is not enough to propel them towards growth, several CPSEs covering various cognate groups have formed joint ventures or have set up subsidiaries abroad for consolidating their international operations.

Delegation of Enhanced Financial Powers to CPSEs

Under the Articles of Association, the Board of Directors of CPSEs enjoy certain amount of financial powers and autonomy in respect of recruitment, promotion and other service conditions of below Board level employees. The Board of Directors of a CPSE exercises the delegated powers subject to broad policy guidelines issued by government from time to time. The government has granted enhanced powers to the Boards of Navratna, Miniratna and other profit making enterprises (Appendix-I). In August 2005, the delegated powers were substantially enhanced.

Navratna Scheme

Under the Navratna scheme, the government has delegated enhanced powers to CPSEs having comparative advantage and the potential to become global players. The powers presently delegated to the Boards of Navratna CPSEs are as under:

Capital Expenditure: The Navratna CPSEs have the powers to incur capital expenditure on purchase of new items or for replacement, without any monetary ceiling.

Technology Joint Ventures and Strategic Alliances: The Navratna CPSEs have the powers to enter into technology joint ventures or strategic alliances and obtain by purchase or other arrangements, technology and know-how.

Organizational Restructuring: The Navratna CPSEs have the powers to effect organizational restructuring including establishment of profit centers, opening of offices in India and abroad, creating new activity centers, etc.

Human Resources Management: The Navratna CPSEs have been empowered to create and wind up all posts up to E-6 level and make all appointments up to this level. The Boards of these CPSEs have further been empowered to effect internal transfers and re-designation of posts. The Board of Directors of Navratna CPSEs have the power to further delegate the powers relating to Human Resource Management (appointments, transfer, posting, etc.) of below Board level executives to subcommittees of the Board or to executives of the CPSE, as may be decided by the Board of the CPSE.

Resource Mobilization: These CPSEs have been empowered to raise debt from the domestic capital markets and for borrowings from international market, subject to condition that approval of RBI/Department of Economic Affairs, as may be required, should be obtained through the administrative Ministry.

Joint Ventures and Subsidiaries: The Navratna CPSEs have been delegated powers to establish financial joint ventures and wholly owned subsidiaries in India or abroad with the stipulation that the equity investment of the CPSE should be limited to: (i) ₹ 1000 crore in any one project, (ii) 15 per cent of the net worth of the CPSE in one project, and (iii) 30 per cent of the net worth of the CPSE in all joint ventures/subsidiaries put together.

Mergers and Acquisitions (M and A): The Navratna CPSEs have been delegated powers for Mergers and Acquisitions subject to the conditions that (i) it should be as per the growth plan and in the core area of functioning of the CPSE, (ii) conditions/limits would be as in the case of establishing joint ventures/subsidiaries, and (iii) the Cabinet Committee on Economic Affairs would be kept informed in case of investments abroad. Further, the powers relating to M&A are to be exercised in such a manner that it should not lead to any change in the public sector character of the concerned CPSE.

Creation/Disinvestment in Subsidiaries: The Navratna CPSEs have powers to transfer assets, float fresh equity and divest shareholding in subsidiaries subject to the condition that the delegation will be in respect of subsidiaries set up by the holding company under the powers delegated to the Navratna CPSEs and further to the proviso that the public sector character of the concerned CPSE (including subsidiary) would not be changed without prior approval of the government and such Navratna CPSEs will be required to seek government approval before exiting from their subsidiaries.

Tours Abroad of Functional Directors: The Chief Executives of Navratna CPSEs have been delegated powers to approve business tours abroad of functional directors up to 5 days duration (other than study tours, seminars, etc.) in emergency under intimation to the Secretary of the administrative Ministry.

The abovementioned delegation of powers is subject to the following conditions and guidelines:

(a) The proposals must be presented to the Board of Directors in writing and reasonably well in advance, with an analysis of relevant factors and quantification of the anticipated results and benefits. Risk factors, if any, must be clearly brought out.

(b) The government Directors, the Financial Directors and the concerned Functional Director(s) must be present when major decisions are taken, especially when they pertain to investments, expenditure or organizational/ capital restructuring.

(c) The decisions on such proposals should preferably, be unanimous.

(d) In the event of any decision on important matters not being unanimous, a majority decision may be taken, but at least two thirds of the Directors should be present, including those mentioned above, when such a decision is taken. The objections, dissents, the reasons for over-ruling them and those for taking the decision should be recorded in writing and minuted.

(e) No financial support or contingent liability on the part of the government should be involved.

(f) These CPSEs will establish transparent and effective systems of internal monitoring, including the establishment of an Audit Committee of the Board with membership of non-official Directors.

(g) All the proposals, where they pertain to capital expenditure, investment or other matters involving substantial financial or managerial commitments or where they would have a long term impact on the structure and functioning of the CPSE, should be prepared by or with the assistance of professionals and experts and should be appraised, in suitable cases, by financial institutions or reputed professional organizations with expertise in the areas. The financial appraisal should also preferably be backed by involvement of the appraising institutions through loans or equity participation.

(h) The exercise of authority to enter into technology joint ventures and strategic alliances shall be in accordance with the government guidelines as may be issued from time to time.

(i) The Boards of these CPSEs should be restructured by inducting at least four non-official Directors as the first step before the exercise of the enhanced delegation of authority.

(j) These public sector enterprises shall not depend upon budgetary support or government guarantees. The resources for implementing their programmes should come from their internal resources or through other sources, including the capital markets. However, wherever government guarantee is required under the standard stipulations of external donor agencies, the same may be obtained from the Ministry of Finance through the administrative Ministry. Such Government guarantee shall not affect the Navratna status. Further, budgetary support to implement government sponsored projects of national interest and government sponsored Research and Development projects will not disqualify CPSEs from retaining their Navratna status. However, for such projects, investment decisions will be taken by the government and not by the CPSE concerned

Miniratna Scheme

In October 1997, the government decided to grant enhanced autonomy and delegation of financial powers to some other profit making companies, called Miniratnas, subject to certain eligibility conditions and guidelines to make them efficient and competitive. CPSEs which have made profit in the last three years continuously, have a pre-tax profit or ₹ 30 crore or more in at least one of the three years, and have a positive net worth are called Category-I Miniratna companies. CPSEs that have made profit for the last three years continuously and have a positive net worth are called Category-II Miniratna companies. Both the categories of Miniratna companies are eligible for the enhanced delegated powers provided they have not defaulted in the repayment of loans/interest payment on any loans due to the government.

The Miniratna companies shall not depend upon budgetary support or government guarantees. The Boards of these CPSEs should be restructured by inducting at least three non-official Directors as the first step before the exercise of enhanced delegation of authority. The administrative Ministry concerned shall decide whether a Public Sector Enterprise fulfilled the requirements of a Category-I/Category-II company before the exercise of enhanced powers. The delegation of decision-making authority available at present to the Boards of these Miniratna CPSEs is as follows:

Capital Expenditure: The power to incur capital expenditure on new projects, modernization, purchase of equipment, etc., without government approval is upto ₹ 500 crore or equal to net worth, whichever is less, for Category-I. For Category-II, government approval is not required for amounts upto ₹ 250 crore or equal to 50 per cent of the networth, whichever is less.

Joint Ventures and Subsidiaries: Category-I CPSEs: The power to establish joint ventures and subsidiaries in India with the stipulation that the equity investment of the CPSE in any one project should be limited to 15 per cent of the networth of the CPSE or ₹ 500 crore for Category-I (₹ 250 crore for Category-II), whichever is less. The overall ceiling on such investment in all projects put together is 30 per cent of the networth of the CPSE.

Mergers and Acquisitions (M and A): The Board of Directors of Miniratna CPSEs have the powers for M&A, subject to the conditions that (a) it should be as per the growth plan and in the core area of functioning of the CPSE, (b) conditions/limits would be as in the case of establishing joint ventures/subsidiaries, and (c) the Cabinet Committee on Economic Affairs would be kept informed in case of investments abroad. Further, the powers relating to M&A are to be exercised in such a manner that it should not lead to any change in the public sector character of the concerned CPSEs.

Scheme for HRD: To structure and implement schemes relating to personnel and human resource management, training, voluntary or compulsory retirement schemes, etc. the Board of Directors of these CPSEs have the power to further delegate the powers relating to Human Resource Management, viz. appointments, transfer, posting, etc. of below Board level executives to subcommittees of the Board or to executives of the CPSE, as may be decided by the Board of the CPSE.

Tour Abroad of Functional Directors: The Chief Executives of these CPSEs have the power to approve business tours abroad of functional directors up to 5 days duration (other than study tours, seminars, etc.) in emergency, under intimation to the Secretary of the administrative Ministry.

Technology Joint Ventures and Strategic Alliances: The power to enter into technology joint ventures, strategic alliances and to obtain technology and know-how by purchase or other arrangements, subject to government guidelines as may be issued from time to time.

Creation/Disinvestment in Subsidiaries: To transfer assets, float fresh equity and divest shareholding in subsidiaries subject to the condition that the delegation will be in respect of subsidiaries set up by the holding company under the powers delegated to the Miniratna CPSEs and further to the proviso that the public sector character of the concerned CPSE (including subsidiary) would not be changed without prior approval of the government, and such Miniratna CPSEs will be required to seek government approval before exiting from their subsidiaries.

The above delegation of powers is subject to similar conditions as are applicable to Navratna CPSEs.

Other Profit-making CPSEs

Those CPSEs which have earned profit in each of the 3 preceding accounting years and have a positive net worth are categorized as 'other profit-making CPSEs'. These CPSEs have been delegated enhanced powers as under:

Capital Expenditure: These CPSEs have the power to incur capital expenditure up to ₹ 150 crore or equal to 50 per cent of the net worth, whichever is less. The above delegation is subject to: (a) inclusion of the project in the approved Five Year and Annual Plans and outlays provided for the same; (b) the required funds can be found from the Internal Resources (IR) of the company or from Extra Budgetary Resources (EBR), and the expenditure is incurred on schemes included in the capital budget approved by the government.

Tours Abroad of Functional Directors: The Chief Executives of these CPSEs have the power to approve business tours abroad of functional directors up to 5 days duration (other than study tours, seminars, etc.) in emergency, under intimation to the Secretary of the administrative Ministry. In all other cases including those of Chief Executive, tours abroad would continue to require the prior approval of the Minister of the Administrative Ministry/ Department.

Maharatna Scheme

The current criteria for grant of Navratna status are size neutral. Over the years, some of the Navratna companies have grown very big and have considerably larger operations than their peers. The CPSEs which are at the higher end of the Navratna category and have potential to become Indian Multinational Companies (MNCs) are being recognized as a separate class, i.e. Maharatna. It is hoped that the new categorization will act as an incentive for other Navratna companies, provide brand value and facilitate delegation of enhanced powers to CPSEs.

The main objective of the Maharatna scheme is to empower Mega CPSEs to expand their operations and emerge as global giants. The scheme will empower big sized CPSEs to expand their operations and emerge as global giants. The eligibility criteria for CPSEs to be considered for Maharatna status is:

(a) Having Navratna status,

(b) Listed on Indian stock exchange with minimum prescribed public shareholding under SEBI regulations,

(c) An average annual turnover of more than ₹ 25,000 crore during the last three years,

(d) An average annual net worth of more than ₹ 15,000 crore during the last three years,

(e) An average annual net profit after tax of more than ₹ 5,000 crore during the last three years, and

(f) Should have significant global presence/international operations.

The procedure for grant of Maharatna status as well as their review is similar to that in vogue for the grant of Navratna status. The Boards of Maharatna CPSEs, in addition to exercising all powers to Navratna CPSEs, will exercise enhanced powers in the area of investment in joint ventures/subsidiaries and creation of below Board level posts up to E-9 level. The Boards of Maharatna CPSEs will have powers to (a) make equity investment to establish financial joint ventures and wholly owned subsidiaries in India or abroad and (b) undertake mergers and acquisitions, in India or abroad, subject to a ceiling of 15 per cent of the net worth of the concerned CPSE in one project, limited to an absolute ceiling of ₹ 5,000 crore. The overall ceiling on such equity investments and mergers and acquisitions in all projects put together will not exceed 30 per cent of the net worth of the concerned CPSE.

Revival and Restructuring of Sick/Loss Making CPSEs

Sickness in CPSEs has been the continuing concern of the Government as some of the CPSEs have been incurring losses continuously for the last several years. The accumulated loss in many of these cases has exceeded their net worth. However, over the years, there has been significant improvement in the overall condition of these enterprises. In comparison to 105 loss making CPSEs in March 2002, there were 54 loss-making CPSEs in March 2009.

Table 3: Loss making CPSEs (2002-03 to 2008-09)

Year	*No. of Loss making CPSEs, during the year*	*Aggregate Loss, during the year (₹ in crore)*	*No. of sick CPSEs**	*No. of sick CPSEs***	*Accumulated losses of sick CPSEs** (₹ in crore)*
2002-03	105	10,972	–	111	76,721
2003-04	89	8,522	–	100	73,487
2004-05	73	9,003	81	90	82,352
2005-06	63	6,845	75	81	83,554
2006-07	61	8,526	83	74	89,064
2007-08	52	10,257	78	67	93,781
2008-09	54	14,424	73	65	85,968

Note: *As per the definition of BRPSE; ** As per the definition of BIFR.

Reasons for Sickness

The reason for sickness varies from enterprise to enterprise. In some cases, the cause of sickness is historical, for example, textile companies which were taken over from the private sector on social consideration for protecting employment of workers in early seventies could not be modernized quickly. British India Corporation, Bird Jute and Exports and NTC belong to this group. Besides theses textile companies, there have been other enterprises that were taken over from the private sector but could not be modernized. These include engineering and refractory enterprises like Andrew Yule and Co., Bharat Wagons and Engineering, Biecco Lawrie, Praga Tools, Burn Standard, Braithwaith and Co., Richardsan and Crudass Ltd., drug companies like Bengal Chemicals and Pharmaceuticals Ltd., transportation/shipping companies like Hooghly Dock and Port Engineering Ltd., Central Inland Water Transport Corporation and consumer goods companies like Tyre Corporation of India and Hooghly Printing Co. Ltd.

The other group of sick companies (other than those taken over) is greenfield companies. These CPSEs became sick, over the years, on account of high manpower cost, high cost of production due to inefficiencies and competition from private sector. These include fertilizer companies like Fertilizer

Corporation of India, Hindustan Fertilizer Corporation, Pyrites, Phosphates and Chemicals Ltd., chemicals and drugs companies like Indian Drugs and Pharmaceuticals Ltd., Hindustan Insecticides Ltd., and Hindustan Antibiotics Ltd.

The third group of loss-making CPSEs is those which have had macro-economic objectives to serve like development of backward areas, providing remunerative prices to farmers, etc. Some of these companies are the Nagaland Pulp and Paper Company Ltd., Manipur State Drugs and Pharmaceuticals Ltd., and North Eastern Regional Agricultural Marketing Corporation Limited, etc.

In addition to these reasons, most sick and loss-making CPSEs have been facing common problems like adverse market/ stiff competition, obsolete technology/machines, high manpower costs, weak marketing strategies and slow decision making process. Attempts have, therefore, been made to overcome 'sickness' in these CPSEs through various policy initiatives including the Statement on Industrial Policy (1991).

Strategies for Revival/Restructuring

Some of the strategies that have been adopted for restructuring/revival of sick CPSEs are:

Financial Restructuring: The government has made investment in CPSEs through equity participation, providing loan (plan/non-plan) grants and/or write-off of past losses as well as changing the debt equity ratio. Measures such as waiver of loan/interest/penal interest, conversion of loan into equity, conversion of interest including penal interest into loan, moratorium on payment of loan/ interest, government guarantee, sale of fixed assets including excess land, sacrifices by State Government, one-time settlement with banks/financial institutions, etc.

Business Restructuring: On a case to case basis, the government has undertaken measures like change of management, hiving off viable units from CPSEs for formation of separate company, closure of unviable units, formation of joint ventures by induction of partners capable of providing technical, financial and marketing inputs, change in product mix, improving marketing strategy, etc.

Manpower Rationalization: Since salaries and wages are often a major component of cost for an enterprise, CPSEs have often resorted to Voluntary Retirement Scheme (VRS) from time to time to shed excess manpower. Voluntary Separation Scheme (VSS) has also been introduced in case of CPSEs which are found unviable and where a decision has been taken to close the unit. However, retrenchment of employees is adopted only as the last resort and in exceptional circumstances.

Revival Packages: In 2005-06, the government granted revival packages amounting to ₹ 5,221.65 crore. In 2006-07, the package amounted to ₹ 2,438.89 crore, in 2007-08 it was ₹ 769.94 crore, and in 2008-09 it was ₹ 6,698.49 crore in 2008-09. These packages have helped the sick and loss making enterprises in a big way in improving their conditions. Some of them have even turned around and recorded profit during the last two years.

Sick Industrial Companies (Special Provisions) Act, 1985 (SICA)

When expenditure (including depreciation, interest, taxes, extraordinary items, prior period adjustments but before providing appropriations to reserves) of a company is more than operating income, a company is said to have occurred 'net loss'. When an enterprise incurs 'net loss' along with 'provision for depreciation', it is termed 'cash loss', usually considered a fit case for recommending closure.

The CPSEs were brought under the purview of Sick Industrial Companies (Special Provision) Act, 1985 (SICA) which was subsequently amended in 1991 and made effective from 1992. Under the provisions of Sick Industrial Companies (Special Provisions) Act, 1985 (SICA), the industrial CPSEs whose accumulated losses are equal to or have exceeded their net worth, may be referred to the Board for Industrial and Financial Reconstruction (BIFR). The BIFR may either sanction suitable revival/rehabilitation schemes (in case of enterprises which are viable) or recommend winding up/closure (in respect of enterprises considered unviable).

During the seventeen years period from 1992-93 to 2008-09, 65 CPSEs have been referred to the BIFR. Out of which, the BIFR has already disposed of 48 cases of CPSEs either through sanctioning revival schemes (11 cases), or recommending winding up (21 cases) or declaring 'no longer sick' (3 cases) or dropping due to net worth becoming positive (5 cases) or dismissing the cases as non-maintainable (4 cases). The BIFR is yet to take any view on 17 cases of CPSEs.

The delay in decision is due to several reasons. Firstly, the process of appointment of Official Liquidator (OL) for winding up of CPSEs has been slow. Second, the process of sanctioning of revival/rehabilitation schemes has been slow on account of involvement of multiple agencies, delay in finalization of revival schemes, lack of funds, lack of adequate powers with BIFR, lack of proper monitoring of sanctioned revival schemes, delay in winding up of sick companies, etc.

Board for Reconstruction of Public Sector Enterprises (BRPSE)

The Board for Reconstruction of Public Sector Enterprises (BRPSE) was set up in December, 2004 to advise the government, *inter alia*, on the measures to restructure/revive, both industrial and non-industrial CPSEs. The Board comprises a part-time Chairman in the rank of Minister of State, three part-time Non-Official Members and three part-time Official Members including Secretary, Department of Expenditure, Secretary, Department of Disinvestment and Secretary, Department of Public Enterprises (DPE). In addition, Chairman, Public Enterprises Selection Board, Chairman, Standing Conference on Public Enterprises and Chairman, Oil and Natural Gas Corporation Limited are permanent invitees to the meetings of BRPSE. Secretaries to the government in the Administrative Ministry/Department concerned with the CPSE under consideration by the Board are Special Invitees.

The BRPSE has a full-time Secretary in the level/rank of Additional Secretary to the Government of India. The Board is located in the Department of Public Enterprises (DPE). The DPE provides necessary secretarial assistance to the Board.

The concerned administrative Ministries/Departments are required to send proposals of their CPSEs identified as 'sick' for consideration of BRPSE. Other loss making CPSEs may be considered by the Board either *suo moto* or upon reference by the administrative Ministry, if it is of the opinion that revival/ restructuring is necessary for checking the incipient sickness (incurring loss for two consecutive years) and making the CPSE profitable, keeping the industry specific business environment in view. The Board is expected to make its recommendations within two months of the date of receipt of the complete proposal from the administrative Ministry/Department.

For the purpose of making reference to BRPSE, a company is considered 'sick' if it has accumulated losses in any financial year equal to 50 per cent or more of its average net worth during four years immediately preceding such financial year, and/or a company which is a sick company within the meaning of Sick Industrial Companies (Special Provisions) Act, 1985 (SICA).

Up to September 2009, cases of 64 sick CPSEs have been referred to BRPSE; out of which the Board has made recommendations in respect of 58 cases. Out of these 58 cases, the government has approved revival proposals in respect of 36 cases of CPSEs and winding up of two enterprises, namely Bharat Opthalmic Glass Limited and Bharat Yantra Nigam Ltd. The restructuring/revival proposals approved by the government involved a total expenditure of ₹ 16,253.36 crore including ₹ 2,920.71 crore as cash assistance and ₹ 12,332.65 crore as non-cash assistance.

In addition, the Board has also recommended to the government to accord "in principle" approval for rescinding of its earlier decision to close the units of Fertilizers Corporation of India (FCIL) and Hindustan Fertilizers Corporation Ltd. (HFCL) and to explore various options for their revival.

Performance of Public Sector Insurance Companies

The insurance sector was opened up in 1999 with the enactment of Insurance Regulatory Development Act. Since then, the number of participants in the sector has steadily increased from six insurers in the year 2000 to 42 insurers operating in the life, non-life and reinsurance segments as in October 2008. This has created much greater competition in the market.

The seven insurance companies (life and non-life insurance) which are functioning as public sector enterprises are the Life Insurance Corporation of India, the New India Assurance Company Limited, the National Insurance Company Limited, the Oriental Insurance Company Limited, the United India Insurance Company Limited, the General Insurance Corporation of India and the Agriculture Insurance Company of India Limited. These insurers offer a variety of insurance policies ranging from Life insurance to Crop insurance.

Life Insurance Corporation of India (LIC)

The Life Insurance Corporation of India (LIC) was established in 1956 as a Statutory Corporation under Section 3 of the Life Insurance Act, 1956 to carry out life insurance business. The LIC has its Central Office in Mumbai and eight Zonal Offices at Mumbai, Kolkata, Delhi, Chennai, Hyderabad, Kanpur, Bhopal and Patna. The Corporation also transacts business abroad and has branch offices in Fiji, Mauritius and United Kingdom.

LIC also operates in overseas insurance markets through Joint Venture companies namely Life Insurance Corporation (International) BSC(C), registered in Bahrain, Kenindia Assurance Company Ltd. registered in Nairobi, Life Insurance Corporation (Nepal) Ltd. registered in Kathmandu, in collaboration with Vishal Group Ltd, Nepal and Life Insurance Corporation (Lanka) Ltd. registered in Colombo, in partnership with M/s Bartleet Transcapital Pvt. Ltd., Sri Lanka.

An offshore company, Life Insurance Corporation (Mauritius) Offshore Ltd. registered in Nairobi is a Joint Venture Company between LIC of India and GIC of India with focus on non-life reinsurance business with active participation of GIC. LIC along with Life Insurance Corporation (International) BSC (C), Bahrain, New India Assurance Company Ltd. and Al Hokair group of Saudi Arabia have registered a Joint Venture Company, namely Saudi Indian Company for Co-operative Insurance in the

Kingdom of Saudi Arabia to transact both Life and Non-Life Insurance business.

Through International Operations, LIC covered a total number of 62,840 policies and also generated a total premium income worth ₹ 725.75 crores in the F.Y. 2008-09. The Life Fund of LIC as on 31.3.2009 amounts to ₹ 8,07,317.43 crore. During 2008-09 the Corporation made payments of ₹ 5,962 crore under Death Claim cases, ₹ 34,744 crore under Maturity Claims and ₹ 2,812 crore under Annuities. Under *Varishtha Pension Bima Yojana*, the Corporation made payments of ₹ 103.92 crore under Death Claim and ₹ 641.12 crore under Annuities.

Some of the prominent schemes of LIC are *Janashree Bima Yojana* (launched on 10 August 2000) and *Aam Admi Bima Yojana* (launched on 2 October 2007). The Corporation has a market share of 70.52 per cent in terms of number of Policies with 13,44,856 Agents as on 31.3.2009.

General Insurance Corporation of India (GIC)

The General Insurance Corporation of India (GIC) was set up as a government company under the General Insurance Business (Nationalisation) Act, 1972 for the purpose of superintending, controlling and carrying on the business of 'General Insurance'. The GIC was authorized to carry out the general insurance business through its four subsidiaries, viz. National Insurance Company Ltd., New India Assurance Company Ltd., Oriental Insurance Company Ltd., and United India Insurance Company Ltd. However, the supervisory role of the GIC over its subsidiaries ended with the enactment of General Insurance Business (Nationalisation) Amendment Act, 2002. The ownership of these subsidiaries companies now rests with the Government of India. The Act also designated the GIC as the 'Indian Reinsurer'. The Registered Office of the Corporation is in Mumbai and its liaison/area offices are in New Delhi, Kolkata and Chennai.

The Corporation has its presence in foreign reinsurance business through its Branch offices in Dubai and London, and a Representative Office in Moscow. Apart from reinsurance business, GIC Re continues to participate in the share capital of Kenindia Assurance Company Ltd (Kenya), India International Insurance Pte Ltd., Singapore, LIC (Mauritius) Offshore Limited, Asian Reinsurance Corporation, Bangkok, and East Africa Reinsurance Company Ltd., Kenya.

In domestic business too, GIC Re has a dominant presence primarily on account of the obligatory cessions. The compulsory cessions have been gradually reduced to 10 per cent from 20 per cent. GIC Re is now competing for business on the basis of price, service and expertise. It has diversified its area of operation by accepting new lines such as life reinsurance, off-shore energy and liability business. Risk management and assessment capabilities are being enhanced to provide value added services to clients.

The Profit before tax of the Corporation was ₹ 1,812 crore as on 31st March 2009, while the total assets and net worth was ₹ 30,019 crore and ₹ 7,784 crore respectively with paid up capital of ₹ 430.00 crores.

Agricultural Insurance Company of India Limited (AICIL)

Agriculture Insurance Company of India Limited (AICIL) commenced its business with effect from 1.4.2003 with the transfer of Crop Insurance Business from General Insurance Corporation of India. AICIL is registered under the Companies Act 1956, with equity participation from General Insurance Corporation of India (35%), NABARD (30%), four Public Sector Insurance Companies (i.e. National, New India, Oriental & United India combined 30% @8.75% each). The paid up share capital of company is ₹ 200 crore against an authorized share capital of ₹ 1500 crore.

The AICIL has been set up to implement various Crop Insurance Schemes and other insurance products relating to agriculture. The company enjoys the distinction of being the largest crop insurance provider in the world in terms of the number of farmers insured annually. During 2008-09, the Company insured around 195 lakh farmers constituting 16 per cent of the total farm holdings in the country.

The Gross Direct Premium of the Company was ₹ 833.44 crore and net premium was ₹ 776.53 crore during financial year 2008-09, while net incurred claims during the year was ₹ 530 crore. The net worth of the company stood at ₹ 733 crore during 2008-09.

National Agricultural Insurance Scheme: The main product of AICIL i.e. National Agricultural Insurance Scheme (NAIS) is being implemented from Rabi 1999-2000 season replacing Comprehensive Crop Insurance Scheme (CCIS) and is presently implemented in 25 States and 2 Union Territories. The Company is making efforts to bring the remaining States/ UTs into the fold of NAIS.

AICIL is implementing the scheme on the behalf of the Ministry of Agriculture. NAIS is available to all the farmers both, loanee and non loanee irrespective of the size of their holding. The main objective of the scheme is to protect the farmers against the losses suffered due to crop failure on account of natural calamities, such as drought, flood, hailstorm, cyclone, fire, pest/diseases, etc., so as to indemnify the losses and to restore the credit worthiness of the loanee farmers for the ensuing season. The Scheme envisages coverage of all crops including cereals, millets, pulses, oilseeds and annual commercial and horticulture crops in respect of which past yield data is available. At present 70 different food and oilseed crops are covered during Kharif and Rabi seasons.

At present, 10% subsidy in premium is allowed for small and marginal farmers, shared equally by central and state government. The Scheme operates on the basis of 'Area Approach' for widespread calamities. The unit of insurance may be Gram Panchyat, Mandal, Hobli, Circle, Phirka, Block, Taluka, etc. to be decided by the respective State/UT Government.

Since the inception of the scheme and until Rabi 2008-09 about 1347 lakh farmers have been insured, covering an area of 211 million hectare for a sum insured value of ₹ 1,48,265 crore, against a premium of ₹ 4,426 crore. Claims to the tune of about ₹ 14,782 crore have been reported so far benefitting nearly 356 lakh farmers. Claims are automatically calculated based on shortfall in the current season yield obtained from crop cutting experiments conducted by State Governments under General Crops Estimation Survey (GCES) as compared to threshold yield and settled through the rural banking network.

Weather Based Crop Insurance Scheme (WBCIS): A Pilot Weather Based Crop Insurance Scheme (WBCIS) has been introduced as proposed in Union Budget 2007-08. The Scheme operates on an actuarial basis with an element of subsidy from Union and State Governments. AICIL has since implemented the scheme in various States during Kharif and Rabi seasons. WBCIS is a parametric insurance product designed to provide insurance protection to the cultivator against adverse weather incidence during the cultivation period, such as deficit and excess rainfall, frost, heat (temperature), relative humidity, wind speed, etc., which are deemed to adversely impact the crop yield.

The payouts are made on the basis of adverse variations in the current season's weather parameters as measured at Reference Weather Station (RWS). Claim under WBCIS is area based and automatic. During 2008-09, 3,33,000 farmers were covered for a sum insured of 739 crore against the premium of ₹ 68 crore in which farmers contribution was ₹ 17 crore, rest being government subsidy.

Besides the two government-sponsored schemes—National Agricultural Insurance Scheme (NAIS) and Weather Based Crop Insurance Scheme (WBCIS)—AICIL has designed and is implementing various crop insurance products to cater to the diverse needs of farming community of India. These are Apple Insurance, Bio-Fuel Insurance, Cardamom Insurance, Coconut Insurance, Grapes Insurance, Mango Weather Insurance, Potato Contract Farming Insurance, Pulpwood Tree Insurance, Rainfall Insurance Scheme-Coffee (RISC), Rabi Weather Insurance, Rubber Insurance, *Varsha Bima*/Rainfall Insurance.

Future Strategies

In a globalized economy as of today, cost-cutting strategic acquisitions and mergers are vital for facing international competition. CPSEs should be given full autonomy and functional powers to take investment decisions and to take advantage of the opportunities offered by the competitive international market. There is a need to constitute an independent Advisory Board to look after the government's interests in the CPSEs and leaving them to manage the corporation with the help of strong independent directors.

Although substantial progress has been made in the revival of sick CPSEs, close monitoring is needed to ensure that the restructuring plans are successfully implemented. While considering the revival of the remaining sick CPSEs, greater caution is necessary as it has been observed that a few of the rehabilitated units are not performing in accordance with expectations.

Further, there is a need to review the investment behaviour of the large profit-making CPSEs. It is because several CPSEs appear to prefer investing in financial assets or reducing their debt burden instead of investment which would contribute to capital formation. The government has set up a special mechanism of an Empowered Committee of Secretaries in Ministries of Petroleum and Natural Gas, Ministry of Finance, and DPE for considering projects in the oil sector involving financial decisions above a certain threshold. The recommendations of this Empowered Committee are submitted to the CCEA directly for approval. The supervisory body (that is, independent Advisory Board) suggested above could also be given the task of guiding and facilitating the investment decisions in all profit-making CPSEs.

The system of MoUs between CPSEs and the government has proved to be ineffective and dysfunctional. While the CPSEs are expected to perform in accordance with the norms, the government's commitments are marginal and not effectively monitored. Hence, there is a need to review and overhaul the system to ensure effective operational autonomy and functioning of the CPSEs. Financial delegations, particularly of the profit-making CPSEs, also need to be enhanced.

Profitability alone could not be a judge of public sector enterprises. Growth with social justice is the laudable objective of public sector. They have served as pace setters in the technological advancement and industrial growth of the country.

They have also acted as instrument of social change. By better utilization of their capacities, they may act as model enterprises in the country.

APPENDIX-I

LIST OF MAHARATNA, NAVRATNA AND MINIRATNA CPSEs

As per available information
(as on 24th May, 2010)

Maharatna CPSEs

1. Indian Oil Corporation Limited
2. NTPC Limited
3. Oil & Natural Gas Corporation Limited
4. Steel Authority of India Limited

Navratna CPSEs

1. Bharat Electronics Limited
2. Bharat Heavy Electricals Limited
3. Bharat Petroleum Corporation Limited
4. Coal India Limited
5. GAIL (India) Limited
6. Hindustan Aeronautics Limited
7. Hindustan Petroleum Corporation Limited
8. Mahanagar Telephone Nigam Limited
9. National Aluminium Company Limited
10. NMDC Limited
11. Oil India Limited
12. Power Finance Corporation Limited
13. Power Grid Corporation of India Limited
14. Rural Electrification Corporation Limited
15. Shipping Corporation of India Limited

Miniratna Category-I CPSEs

1. Airports Authority of India
2. Balmer Lawrie & Co. Limited

3. Bharat Dynamics Limited
4. BEML Limited
5. Bharat Sanchar Nigam Limited
6. Bongaigaon Refineries and Petrochemicals Limited
7. Central Warehousing Corporation
8. Central Coalfields Limited
9. Chennai Petroleum Corporation Limited
10. Cochin Shipyard Limited
11. Container Corporation of India Limited
12. Dredging Corporation of India Limited
13. Engineers India Limited
14. Ennore Ports Limited
15. Garden Reach Shipbuilders and Engineers Limited
16. Goa Shipyard Limited
17. Hindustan Copper Limited
18. Hindustan Latex Limited
19. Hindustan Newsprint Limited
20. Hindustan Paper Corporation Limited
21. Housing and Urban Development Corporation Limited
22. India Tourism Development Corporation Limited
23. Indian Railway Catering and Tourism Corporation Limited
24. IRCON International Limited
25. Kudremukh Iron Ore Company Limited
26. Mazagaon Docks Limited
27. Mahanadi Coalfields Limited
28. Manganese Ore India Limited
29. Mangalore Refinery and Petrochemicals Limited
30. Mishra Dhatu Nigam Limited
31. MMTC Limited
32. MSTC Limited
33. National Fertilizers Limited

34. Neyveli Lignite Corporation
35. NHPC Limited
36. Northern Coalfields Limited
37. Numaligarh Refinery Limited
38. Rashtriya Chemicals and Fertilizers Limited
39. Rashtriya Ispat Nigam Limited
40. RITES Limited
41. Satluj Jal Vidyut Nigam Limited
42. Security Printing and Minting Corporation of India Limited
43. South Eastern Coalfields Limited
44. State Trading Corporation of India Limited
45. Tehri Hydro Development Corporation Limited
46. Telecommunications Consultants (India) Limited
47. Western Coalfields Limited

Miniratna Category-II CPSEs

48. Broadcast Engineering Consultants (I) Limited
49. Central Mine Planning and Design Institute Limited
50. Educational Consultants (I) Limited
51. Engineering Projects (I) Limited
52. Ferro Scrap Nigam Limited
53. HMT (International) Limited
54. HSCC (India) Limited
55. India Trade Promotion Organization
56. Indian Medicines Pharmaceuticals Corporation Limited
57. MECON Limited
58. National Film Development Corporation Limited
59. PEC Limited
60. Rajasthan Electronics and Instruments Limited
61. Water & Power Consultancy (India) Limited

Source: http://dpe.nic.in/newsite/navmini.htm

APPENDIX-II

SCHEDULE-WISE LIST OF CENTRAL PUBLIC SECTOR ENTERPRISES

As on 31st January, 2010

Schedule - A

1. Airports Authority of India
2. Bharat Bhari Udyog Nigam Ltd.
3. BEML Ltd.
4. Bharat Electronics Ltd.
5. Bharat Heavy Electricals Ltd.
6. Bharat Petroleum Corporation Ltd.
7. Bharat Sanchar Nigam Ltd.
8. Central Warehousing Corporation
9. Coal India Ltd.
10. Container Corporation of India Ltd.
11. Dedicated Freight Corridor Corporation of India Ltd.
12. Electronics Corporation of India Ltd.
13. Engineers India Ltd.
14. Fertilizers and Chemicals (Travancore) Ltd.
15. Food Corporation of India
16. GAIL (India) Ltd.
17. Heavy Engineering Corporation Ltd.
18. Hindustan Aeronautics Ltd.
19. Hindustan Copper Ltd.
20. Hindustan Paper Corporation Ltd.
21. Hindustan Petroleum Corporation Ltd.
22. HMT Ltd.
23. Housing and Urban Development Corporation Ltd.
24. ITI Ltd.
25. Indian Oil Corporation Ltd.
26. IRCON International Ltd.

27. Konkan Railway Corporation Ltd.
28. Kudremukh Iron Ore Company Ltd.
29. MMTC Ltd.
30. Mahanagar Telephone Nigam Ltd.
31. Mazagon Dock Ltd.
32. MECON Ltd.
33. Mumbai Railway Vikas Corporation Ltd.
34. National Aluminium Company Ltd.
35. National Aviation Company of India Ltd.
36. National Building Construction Corporation Ltd.
37. National Fertilizers Ltd.
38. NHPC Ltd.
39. National Mineral Development Corporation Ltd.
40. National Textiles Corporation Ltd.
41. NTPC Ltd.
42. Neyveli Lignite Corporation Ltd.
43. North Eastern Electric Power Corporation Ltd.
44. Oil and Natural Gas Corporation Ltd.
45. Oil India Ltd.
46. Power Finance Corporation
47. Power Grid Corporation of India Ltd.
48. RITES Ltd.
49. RailTel Corporation of India Ltd.
50. Rail Vikas Nigam Ltd.
51. Rashtriya Chemicals and Fertilizers Ltd.
52. Rashtriya Ispat Nigam Ltd.
53. Rural Electrification Corporation Ltd.
54. Satluj Jal Vidyut Nigam Ltd.
55. Security Printing and Minting Corporation of India Ltd.
56. Shipping Corporation of India Ltd.
57. State Trading Corporation of India Ltd.

58. Steel Authority of India Ltd.
59. Telecommunications Consultants (India) Ltd.

Schedule - B

1. Andrew Yule and Company Ltd.
2. Balmer Lawrie and Company Ltd.
3. Bharat Coking Coal Ltd.
4. Bharat Dynamics Ltd.
5. Bharat Heavy Plate and Vessels Ltd.
6. Bharat Pumps and Compressors Ltd.
7. Brahmaputa Crackers and Polymers Ltd.
8. Brahmaputra Valley Fertilizer Corporation Ltd.
9. Braithwaite and Company Ltd.
10. BBJ Construction Ltd.
11. Bridge and Roof Company (India) Ltd.
12. British India Corporation Ltd.
13. Burn Standard Company Ltd.
14. Cement Corporation of India Ltd.
15. Central Coalfields Ltd.
16. Central Electronics Ltd.
17. Central Mine Planning and Design Institute Ltd.
18. Chennai Petroleum Corporation Ltd.
19. Cochin Shipyard Ltd.
20. Cotton Corporation of India Ltd.
21. Dredging Corporation of India Ltd.
22. Eastern Coalfields Ltd.
23. Engineering Projects (India) Ltd.
24. Ennore Port Ltd.
25. Fertilizer Corporation of India Ltd.
26. Garden Reach Shipbuilders and Engineers Ltd.
27. Goa Shipyard Ltd.
28. Handicrafts and Handlooms Export Corporation Ltd.

29. Hindustan Cables Ltd.
30. Hindustan Fertilizer Corporation Ltd.
31. HLL Lifecare Ltd.
32. Hindustan Newsprints Ltd.
33. Hindustan Organic Chemicals Ltd.
34. Hindustan Shipyard Ltd.
35. Hindustan Steelworks Construction Company Ltd.
36. Hindustan Vegetable Oils Corporation Ltd.
37. HMT (International) Ltd.
38. HMT Machine Tools Ltd.
39. HMT Watches Ltd.
40. India Tourism Development Corporation Ltd.
41. India Trade Promotion Organisation
42. Indian Drugs and Pharmaceuticals Ltd.
43. Indian Railway Catering and Tourism Corporation Ltd.
44. Indian Railway Finance Corporation Ltd.
45. Indian Rare Earths Ltd.
46. Indian Renewable Energy Development Agency Ltd.
47. Instrumentation Ltd.
48. MSTC Ltd.
49. Madras Fertilizers Ltd.
50. Mahanadi Coalfields Ltd.
51. Mangalore Refinery and Petrochemicals Ltd.
52. Manganese Ore (India) Ltd
53. Mineral Exploration Corporation Ltd.
54. Mishra Dhatu Nigam Ltd.
55. National Jute Manufacturers Corporation Ltd.
56. National Projects Construction Corporation Ltd.
57. National Small Industries Corporation Ltd.
58. Northern Coalfields Ltd.
59. Numaligarh Refinery Ltd.

60. ONGC Videsh Ltd.
61. PEC Ltd.
62. Pawan Hans Helicopters Ltd.
63. Projects and Development India Ltd.
64. Scooters India Ltd.
65. South Eastern Coalfields Ltd.
66. Tehri Hydro Development Corporation Ltd.
67. Tyre Corporation of India Ltd.
68. Uranium Corporation of India Ltd.
69. WAPCOS Ltd.
70. Western Coalfields Ltd.

Schedule - C

1. Andaman and Nicobar Islands Forest and Plantation Development Corporation Ltd.
2. Artificial Limbs Mfg. Corporation of India
3. Bengal Chemicals and Pharmaceuticals Ltd.
4. Bharat Petro Resources Ltd.
5. Bharat Refractories Ltd.
6. Bharat Wagon and Engineering Company Ltd.
7. Biecco Lawrie and Co. Ltd.
8. Broadcast Engineering Consultants India Ltd.
9. Central Cottage Industries Corporation of India Ltd.
10. Central Inland Water Transport Corporation Ltd.
11. Central Railside Warehouse Company Ltd.
12. Educational Consultants (India) Ltd.
13. FCI Aravali Gypsum and Minerals (India) Ltd.
14. Ferro Scrap Nigam Ltd.
15. Hindustan Antibiotics Ltd.
16. Hindustan Insecticides Ltd.
17. Hindustan Photo Films Manufacturing Company Ltd.
18. Hindustan Salts Ltd.

19. HMT Bearings Ltd.
20. HMT Chinar Watches Ltd.
21. Hooghly Dock and Port Engineers Ltd.
22. HSCC (India) Ltd.
23. Hotel Corporation of India Ltd.
24. Jute Corporation of India Ltd.
25. Nagaland Pulp and Paper Company Ltd.
26. National Backward Classes Finance and Development Corporation
27. National Film Development Corporation Ltd.
28. National Handicapped Finance and Development Corporation
29. National Handloom Development Corporation Ltd.
30. National Minorities Development and Finance Corporation
31. National Research Development Corporation of India
32. National Safai Karamcharis Finance and Development Corporation
33. National SC Finance and Development Corporation
34. National ST Finance and Development Corporation
35. National Seeds Corporation Ltd.
36. NEPA Ltd.
37. North Eastern Handicrafts and Handloom Development Corporation Ltd.
38. North Eastern Regional Agricultural Marketing Corporation Ltd.
39. Rajasthan Electronics and Instruments Ltd.
40. Richardson and Cruddas (1972) Ltd.
41. STCL Ltd.
42. Sponge Iron India Ltd.
43. State Farms Corporation of India Ltd.
44. Triveni Structurals Ltd.
45. Tungabhadra Steel Products Ltd.

Schedule - D

1. Hindustan Fluorocarbons Limited
2. Hindustan Prefab Ltd.
3. Indian Medicines Pharmaceutical Corporation Ltd.
4. Karnataka Antibiotics and Pharmaceuticals Ltd.
5. Orissa Drugs and Chemicals Ltd.
6. Rajasthan Drugs and Pharmaceuticals Ltd.

Others - Uncategorised

1. Akaltara Power Ltd.
2. AIL Airport Services Ltd.
3. Air India Air Transport Services Ltd.
4. Air India Charters Ltd.
5. Air India Engineering Services Ltd.
6. Airline Allied Services Ltd.
7. Antrix Corporation Ltd.
8. Assam Ashok Hotel Corporation Ltd.
9. BEL Optronic Devices Ltd.
10. Balmer Lawrie Investments Ltd.
11. Bharat Immunological and Biologicals Corporation Ltd.
12. Bharatiya Nabhikiya Vidyut Nigam Ltd.
13. Bhartiya Rail Bijlee Company Ltd.
14. Bharat Petro Resources JDPA
15. Bihar Drugs and Organic Chemicals Ltd.
16. Birds, Jute and Exports Ltd.
17. Bokaro Kodarma Maithon Transmission Company Ltd.
18. Brushware Ltd.
19. Certification Engineers International Ltd.
20. Coastal Karnataka Power Ltd.
21. Coastal Maharashtra Mega Power Ltd.
22. Coastal Tamil Nadu Power Ltd.

23. CREDA–HPCL Biofuel Ltd.
24. Donyi Polo Ashok Hotel Corporation Ltd.
25. East-North Interconnection Co. Ltd.
26. Export Credit Guarantee Corporation of India Ltd.
27. Fresh and Healthy Enterprises Ltd.
28. GAIL Gas Ltd.
29. Ghogarpalli Integrated Power Company Ltd.
30. Hooghly Printing Company Ltd.
31. IDPL (Tamil Nadu) Ltd.
32. IL Power Electronics Ltd.
33. India Infrastructure Finance Co. Ltd.
34. Indian Oil Technologies Ltd.
35. Indian Vaccine Corporation Ltd.
36. Instrumentation Control Valves Ltd.
37. Instrumentation Digital Control Ltd.
38. Jagdishpur Paper Mills Ltd.
39. J&K Mineral Development Corporation Ltd.
40. Kanti Bijlee Utpadan Nigam Ltd.
41. Karnataka Trade Promotion Organisation
42. Kumarakuppa Frontier Hotels (P) Ltd.
43. Madhya Pradesh Ashok Hotel Corporation Ltd.
44. Maharashtra Elektrosmelt Ltd.
45. Millenium Telecom Ltd.
46. Narmada Hydroelectric Development Corporation Ltd.
47. National Informatics Centre Services Incorporated
48. NLC Tamil Nadu Power Ltd.
49. North Karanpura Transmission Company Ltd.
50. NTPC Electric Supply Co Ltd.
51. NTPC Hydro Ltd.
52. NTPC Vidyut Vyapar Nigam Ltd.
53. Nuclear Power Corpn. of India Ltd.

54. Orissa Integrated Power Ltd.
55. PFC Consulting Ltd.
56. Pondicherry Ashok Hotel Corporation Ltd.
57. Punjab Ashok Hotel Company Ltd.
58. Ranchi Ashok Bihar Hotel Corporation Ltd.
59. REC Power Distribution Company Ltd.
60. REC Transmission Projects Co. Ltd.
61. Sakhigopal Integrated Power Company Ltd.
62. Sambhar Salts Ltd.
63. Sethusamudram Corporation Ltd.
64. Talcher-II Transmission Company Ltd.
65. Tamilnadu Trade Promotion Organisation
66. Utkal Ashok Hotel Corporation Ltd.
67. Vignyan Industries Ltd.

Source: http://dhi.nic.in/HeavyIndustry_inside_eng_2009-2010.pdf

Disinvestment in Central Public Sector Enterprises

13

The Public Enterprises have played a vital role in the development of India's economy. The nature and role of these enterprises was conceived at a time when the technological landscape and the national and international economic environment were very different. Today, the private sector in India has come of age and it substantially contributes to the nation-building process. In the scenario, both the public sector and private sector are mutually complementary parts of the national sector. Hence, there arose a need to assess and change the role of public sector in a highly competitive market. The intense pressure on public finances also compelled the Centre as well as State Governments to embark on a programme of disinvestment.

The policy on 'Disinvestment in CPSEs', i.e. disinvestment of government equity in CPSEs began in 1991-92. The policy of the government on disinvestment gradually evolved since then can be divided into two phases. The period until 1997-98 is generally considered the initial phase while the period starting from 1998-99 is considered the second phase of disinvestment. From 1991-92 to 1996-97, disinvestment in CPSEs was handled by the Department of Public Enterprises. Subsequently, the Department of Economic Affairs, Ministry of Finance took over the task of disinvestment in CPSEs.

The Initial Phase

The policy, as enunciated in the interim Budget 1991-92 presented by the Chandrashekhar Government, was to disinvest up to 20 per cent of the government equity in selected PSEs, in favour of mutual funds and financial or investment institutions in the public sector. The objective of the policy was stated to be to broad base the equity, improve management and enhance the availability of resources for the PSEs. The disinvestment was expected to yield ₹ 2,500 crores to the exchequer in 1991-92.

Industrial Policy Statement of 24 July 1991

The Industrial Policy Statement of 24 July 1991 stated that the government would disinvest part of its holdings in selected PSEs in order to provide further market discipline to the performance of public enterprises. However, the policy statement did not place any cap on the extent of disinvestment. Nor did it restrict disinvestment in favour of any particular class of investors.

In his Budget speech of 1991-92, the Finance Minister reinstated cap of 20 per cent for disinvestment in selected public sector undertakings and the eligible investors' universe was again modified to consist of mutual funds and investment institutions in the public sector and the workers in these firms. The objectives too were modified and stated to be "to raise resources, encourage wider public participation and promote greater accountability". In the budget speech of 1992-93, the cap of 20 per cent was re-instated and the list of eligible investor was enlarged to include FII's, employees and OCB's.

Thus, disinvestment of the government's equity in CPSUs started in 1991-92, when minority shareholding of the Central Government in 30 individual CPSUs was sold to selected financial institutions (LIC, GIC, UTI) in bundles, in order to ensure that along with the attractive shares, not so attractive shares also got sold. Subsequently, shares of individual CPSUs were sold and the category of eligible buyers was gradually expanded to include individuals, NRIs and registered FIIs. By 1997, sale through the GDR route was also initiated and MTNL (1997-98), VSNL (1998-99) and GAIL (1999-2000) all used the opportunity to access the GDR market.

Rangarajan Committee Report of April 1993

The report of the Committee on the Disinvestment of Shares in PSEs headed by Dr. C. Rangarajan presented in April 1993 emphasised the need for substantial disinvestment. The report stated that the percentage of equity to be divested could be up to 49 per cent for industries explicitly reserved for the public sector. It recommended that in exceptional cases such as the enterprises which had a dominant market share or where separate identity had to be maintained for strategic reasons, the target public ownership level could be kept at 26 per cent, that is, disinvestment could take place to the extent of 74 per cent. In all other cases, it recommended 100 per cent divestment of government stake. Holding of 51 per cent or more equity by the government was recommended only for six Schedule industries, namely Coal and lignite; Mineral oils; Arms, ammunition and defence equipment; Atomic energy; Radioactive minerals; and Railway transport.

The United Front Government and Disinvestment Commission

The Common Minimum Programme of the United Front Government in 1996 said: "The question of withdrawing the public sector from non-core strategic areas will be carefully examined subject, however, to assuring the workers and employees of job security or, in the alternative, opportunities for retraining and redeployment. The United Front Government will establish a Disinvestment Commission to advise the government on these steps. Any decision to disinvest will be taken and implemented in a transparent manner". No disinvestment objective was, however, mentioned in the policy statement.

Pursuant to the above policy, the United Front Government constituted a Public Sector Disinvestment Commission on 23 August 1996, for a period of three years, as an independent, non-statutory, advisory body with G.V. Ramakrishna as full-time Chairman, four other Members (part-time) and a full-time Member-Secretary. The Commission gave its recommendations on 58 PSEs in Feb. 1997. The recommendations indicated a shift from public offerings to strategic/trade sales, with transfer of management. In case of PSEs involving change in ownership/management, the Commission recommended strategic sale of 29

PSEs and trade sale of eight PSEs. In cases involving no change in ownership/management, the Commission recommended offer of shares of five PSEs. In cases where there is no change, the Commission deferred disinvestment of eleven PSEs and no disinvestment of one PSE. The Commission recommended closure/ sale of assets of four PSEs. The Commission did not take up examination of the cases of six CPSEs which were registered with the Board for Industrial and Financial Reconstruction (BIFR).

The Second Phase

In its first budgetary pronouncement, the new National Democratic Alliance Government in 1998-99 decided to bring down government shareholding in the PSUs to 26 per cent in the generality of cases, thus facilitating ownership changes, as was recommended by the Disinvestment Commission. It however, stated that the government would retain majority holdings in PSEs involving strategic considerations and that the interests of the workers would be protected in all cases.

Subsequently, the government announced that its strategy for 1999-2000 towards public sector enterprises will continue to encompass a judicious mix of strengthening strategic PSUs, privatizing non-strategic PSUs through gradual disinvestment or strategic sale and devising viable rehabilitation strategies for weak units. A highlight of the policy was that the expression 'privatisation' was used for the first time.

Strategic and Non-strategic Classification

On 16 March 1999, the government classified the Public Sector Enterprises into strategic and non-strategic areas for the purpose of disinvestment. It was decided that the Strategic Public Sector Enterprises would be those in the areas of:

- Arms and ammunitions and the allied items of defence equipment, defence aircraft and warships;
- Atomic energy (except in the areas related to the generation of nuclear power and applications of radiation and radio-isotopes to agriculture medicine and non-strategic industries); and
- Railway transport.

All other Public Sector Enterprises were to be considered non-strategic. For the non-strategic Public Sector Enterprises, it was decided that the reduction of government stake to 26 per cent would not be automatic and the manner and pace of doing so would be worked out on a case-to-case basis. Further, any decision in regard to the percentage of disinvestment, i.e. government stake going down to less than 51 per cent or to 26 per cent, would be taken on the basis of: (i) Whether the industrial sector requires the presence of the public sector as a countervailing force to prevent concentration of power in private hands, and (ii) Whether the industrial sector requires a proper regulatory mechanism to protect the consumer interests before Public Sector Enterprises are privatised.

Department for Disinvestment

The government also established a new Department for Disinvestment under the Ministry of finance on 10 December 1999 to introduce a systematic policy approach to disinvestment and privatisation and to give a fresh impetus to the strategic sales of identified PSUs. The Department of Disinvestment was given the following functions:

(a) (i) All matters relating to disinvestment of Central Government equity in CPSEs; (ii) All matters relating to sale of Central Government equity through offer for sale or private placement, in the erstwhile CPSEs.

(b) Decisions on the recommendations of the Disinvestment Commission on the modalities of disinvestment, including restructuring.

(c) Implementation of disinvestment decisions, including appointment of advisers, pricing of shares, and other terms and conditions of disinvestment.

(d) Matters relating to Disinvestment Commission.

(e) Issues relating to CPSEs for purposes of disinvestment of government equity only.

(f) Financial policy in regard to the utilization of the proceeds of disinvestment, channelised into the National Investment Fund.

All other post-disinvestment matters, including those relating to and arising out of the exercise of 'call-option' by the Strategic Partner in the erstwhile CPSEs, were to be continued to be handled by the administrative Ministry (or Department concerned), where necessary, in consultation with the Department of Disinvestment. The Department was later elevated in 2001 and became the Ministry of Disinvestment. Subsequently from 2004, it has once again been turned into a Department of the Ministry of Finance.

Disinvestment Policy for 2000-01

The highlights of the policy for the year 2000-01 as enunciated in Budget speech 2000-01 were that for the first time the government made the statement that it was prepared to reduce its stake in the non-strategic PSEs even below 26 per cent if necessary, that there would be increasing emphasis on strategic sales and that the entire proceeds from disinvestment/privatisation would be deployed in social sector, restructuring of PSEs and retirement of public debt. The main elements of the government's clear and unambiguous policy towards the public sector were:

1. To restructure and revive potentially viable PSEs;
2. To close down PSEs which cannot be revived;
3. To bring down government equity in all non-strategic PSEs to 26 per cent or lower, if necessary;
4. To fully protect the interests of workers;
5. To put in place mechanisms to raise resources from the market against the security of PSEs' assets for providing an adequate safety-net to workers and employees;
6. To establish a systematic policy approach to disinvestment and privatisation and to give a fresh impetus to this programme, by setting up a new Department of Disinvestment;
7. To emphasize increasingly on strategic sales of identified PSEs;
8. To use the entire receipt from disinvestment and privatisation for meeting expenditure in social sectors, restructuring of PSEs and retiring public debt.

During 1998-2000, the government approved restructuring of 20 PSUs. As a result, many PSUs were able to restructure their operations, improve productivity and achieve a turn around in performance. In 2000, the government also approved a comprehensive package for restructuring of SAIL, a Navaratna PSU. However, in order to secure the presence of the public sector as a countervailing force, the government on 23 June 2000 took the decision of not going for disinvestment of GAIL, IOC and ONGC, and retaining them as flagship companies.

The government found that resources under the National Renewal Fund are not sufficient to meet the cost of Voluntary Separation Scheme (VSS) for PSUs which need to be closed down as they are sick and not capable of being revived. It was also realized that if the assets of those PSUs are unbundled and realized, then they can be used for funding VSS. In view of the situation, the government decided to put in place mechanisms to raise resources from the market against the security of these assets and use these funds to provide an adequate safety-net to workers and employees.

The government, further, affirmed that equity in all non-strategic PSUs will be reduced to 26 per cent or less while fully protecting the interests of the workers. The government added that the entire receipt from disinvestment and privatisation will be used for meeting expenditure in social sectors, restructuring of PSUs and retiring public debt.

Disinvestment Policy for 2001-02

The government's approach to PSEs was also outlined in the address by the President to Parliament during the Budget Session, February 2001. The threefold objective was: revival of potentially viable enterprises; closing down of those PSUs that cannot be revived; and bringing down government equity in non-strategic PSUs to 26 per cent or lower. The President added "that the interests of workers will be fully protected through attractive VRS and other measures. The government has decided to disinvest a substantial part of its equity in enterprises such as Indian Airlines, Air India, ITDC, IPCL, VSNL, CMC, BALCO, Hindustan Zinc, and Maruti Udyog. Where necessary, strategic partners would be selected through a transparent process."

In the Budget Speech 2001-02, it was announced that the process of disinvestment was in the advanced stage in many of the PSUs. A receipt of ₹ 12,000 crore was expected from disinvestment during the financial year. Out of this amount, ₹ 7,000 crore was to be used for providing restructuring assistance to PSUs, safety net to workers and reduction of debt burden. The remaining sum of ₹ 5000 crore was to be used to provide additional budgetary support for the Plan primarily in the social and infrastructure sectors. This additional allocation for the Plan was to be contingent upon realisation of the anticipated receipts.

The Public Sector Disinvestment Commission was re-constituted on 24 July 2001 with Dr. R.H. Patil as Chairman (part-time) along with four other Members (part-time) and a full time Member-Secretary. The then Ministry of Disinvestment had informed the Commission on 23 January 2002 that all non-strategic CPSUs, including subsidiaries, but excluding IOC, ONGC and GAIL, stood referred to the Commission for it to prioritize, examine and make recommendations in the light of the government policies articulated earlier on 16 March 1999 and the budget speeches of Finance Ministers from time to time. The reconstituted Commission submitted its reports on 41 CPSEs, including review cases of earlier Commission's recommendations on 4 CPSEs. The term of the Commission expired on 31 October 2004 and the Commission was wound up.

Disinvestment Policy for 2002-03

The government decided in September 2002 that CPSEs and Central Government owned cooperative societies, where government's ownership is 51 per cent or more, should not be permitted to participate as bidders in the disinvestment of other CPSEs as bidder unless specifically approved by the Core Group of Secretaries on Disinvestment (CGD). In December 2002, on the basis of a proposal of the Department of Fertilizers, it was decided that Multi State Cooperative Societies under the Department of Fertilizers be allowed to participate in the disinvestment of fertilizer CPSEs including National Fertilizers Limited.

In a *suo motu* statement made in both Houses of Parliament on 9th December, 2002, by the then Minister of Disinvestment, the government reiterated the policy as:

> The main objective of disinvestment is to put national resources and assets to optimal use and in particular to unleash the productive potential inherent in our public sector enterprises. The policy of disinvestment specifically aims at:
>
> - Modernization and upgradation of Public Sector Enterprises;
> - Creation of new assets;
> - Generating of employment; and
> - Retiring of public debt.
>
> Government would continue to ensure that disinvestment does not result in alienation of national assets, which, through the process of disinvestment, remain where they are. It would also ensure that disinvestment does not result in private monopolies. In order to provide complete visibility to the Government's continued commitment of utilisation of disinvestment proceeds for social and infrastructure sectors, the Government would set up a Disinvestment Proceeds Fund. This Fund would be used for financing fresh employment opportunities and investment, and for retirement of public debt. For the disinvestment of natural asset companies, the Ministry of Finance and the Ministry of Disinvestment would work out guidelines. The Ministry of Finance would also prepare for consideration of the Cabinet Committee on Disinvestment a paper on the feasibility and modalities of setting up an Asset Management Company to hold, manage and dispose the residual holding of the Government in the companies in which the Government's equity has been disinvested to a strategic partner.

Disinvestment Policy for 2003-04

In the budget speech for 2003-04, the government announced that details regarding the already announced Disinvestment Fund and Asset Management Company, to hold residual shares post disinvestment, would be finalized early in 2003-04. Subsequently, on 25 April 2003, the then Ministry of Disinvestment issued guidelines regarding Management-Employee Bids in Strategic Sale to encourage and facilitate the participation of employee participation in strategic sales.

Policy of UPA Government

The National Common Minimum Programme (NCMP) adopted by the United Progressive Alliance (UPA) Government in May 2004 outlined the policy of the government with respect to the public sector as mentioned below:

> The UPA Government is committed to a strong and effective public sector whose social objectives are met by its commercial functioning. But for this, there is need for selectivity and a strategic focus. The UPA is pledged to devolve full managerial and commercial autonomy to successful, profit-making companies operating in a competitive environment. Generally profit-making companies will not be privatized.
>
> All privatizations will be considered on a transparent and consultative case-by-case basis. The UPA will retain existing 'navratna' companies in the public sector while these companies raise resources from the capital market. While every effort will be made to modernize and restructure sick public sector companies and revive sick industry, chronically loss-making companies will either be sold-off, or closed, after all workers have got their legitimate dues and compensation. The UPA will induct private industry to turn around companies that have potential for revival.
>
> The UPA Government believes that privatization should increase competition, not decrease it. It will not support the emergence of any monopoly that only restrict competition. It also believes that there must be a direct link between

privatization and social needs—like, for example, the use of privatization revenues for designated social sector schemes. Public sector companies and nationalized banks will be encouraged to enter the capital market to raise resources and offer new investment avenues to retail investors.

In conformity with the policy enunciated in NCMP, it was decided in February 2005 to formally call off the process of disinvestment through Strategic Sale of profit making Central Public Sector Enterprises (CPSEs), as enumerated below:

Table 1: List of Strategic Sale Cases Called-off

S. No.	*Name of the CPSE*	*Percentage of equity which was earlier proposed to be sold through Strategic Sale*
1	Manganese Ore India Limited	51%
2	Sponge Iron India Limited	100%
3	Shipping Corporation of India Limited	54.12% (51% through Strategic Sale and 3.12% to Employees)
4	National Aluminium Company Limited	61.15% (10% Domestic Issue, 20% ADR Issue, 29.15% Strategic Sale, 2% to Employees)
5	National Building Construction Corporation Limited	74%
6	National Fertilizers Limited	53% (51% through Strategic Sale and 2% to Employees)
7	Rashtriya Chemicals and Fertilizers Limited	53% (51% through Strategic Sale and 2% to Employees)
8	Hindustan Petroleum Corporation Limited	39.01% (34.01% through Strategic Sale and 5% to Employees)
9	Engineers India Limited	61% (51% through Strategic Sale and 10% to Employees)
10	Balmer Lawrie and Company Limited	61.8%
11	Engineering Projects India Limited	74%
12	Hindustan Paper Corporation Limited	74%
13	State Trading Corporation of India Limited	75% (65% through Strategic Sale and 10% to Employees)

The Budget Speech 2004-05 (July 2004) said disinvestment and privatization are useful economic tools, which will be selectively employed by the government, consistent with the declared policy. Further, the government will establish a Board for Reconstruction of Public Sector Enterprises (BRPSE) to advise the government on the measures to be taken to restructure

PSEs, including cases where disinvestment or closure or sale is justified. The disinvestment revenues will be part of the Consolidated Fund of India.

In January 2005, the government approved, in principle, the following:

1. Listing of currently unlisted profitable CPSEs, each with a net worth in excess of ₹ 200 crore, through an Initial Public Offering (IPO) either in conjunction with a fresh equity issue by the CPSE concerned or independently by the Government on a case to case basis, subject to the residual equity of the government remaining at least 51 per cent and the government retaining management control of the CPSE;
2. Sale of minority shareholding of the government in listed and profitable CPSEs either in conjunction with a Public Issue of fresh equity by the CPSE concerned or independently by the government subject to the residual equity of the government remaining at least 51 per cent and the government retaining management control of the CPSE; and
3. Constitution of a National Investment Fund (NIF) into which the realisation from sale of minority shareholding of the government in profitable CPSUs would be channelised.

In November 2005, the government reiterated its decision, in principle, to list large, profitable CPSEs on domestic stock exchanges and to selectively sell small portions of equity in listed, profitable CPSEs other than the Navratnas.

National Investment Fund

The NIF is to be maintained outside the Consolidated Fund of India and the income from NIF would be used for two broad investment objectives: (i) 75 per cent of annual income of NIF to be used as investment in social sector projects which promote education, health care and employment; and (ii) The rest 25 per cent of annual income to be used to meet the capital investment in selected profitable and revivable Public Sector Enterprises that yield adequate returns in order to enlarge their capital base to finance expansion/diversification.

The corpus of the National Investment Fund is to be of a permanent nature. The Fund is to be professionally managed to provide sustainable returns to the government, without depleting the corpus. Select public sector Mutual Funds have been entrusted with the management of the corpus of the Fund.

Fund Managers: The following Public Sector Mutual Funds have been appointed (initially) as Fund Managers to manage the funds of NIF under the 'discretionary mode' of Portfolio Management Scheme which is governed by SEBI guidelines, namely: (i) the UTI Assets Management Company Ltd. (ii) the SBI Funds Management Company (Pvt.) Ltd., and (iii) the Jeevan Bima Sahayog, Asset Management Company Ltd.

Corpus of NIF: The corpus of the Fund through the proceeds from the disinvestment in Power Grid Corporation of India Limited and Rural Electrification Corporation stood at ₹ 1814.45 crore. While the pay out on NIF, in the first year, stood at ₹ 84.81 crores, it was ₹ 206.21 crores in the second year. (Average income worked out to 8.47 per cent in the first year and 10.02 per cent in the second year). The average income for the two years, therefore, worked out to 9.245 per cent, against the hurdle rate of 9.25 per cent.

Notable Disinvestment in CPSEs under UPA Government

Several notable disinvestments were made in CPSEs during the first term of Prime Minister Manmohan Singh. The government approved disinvestment of 5.25 per cent equity of National Thermal Power Corporation Limited (NTPC) on 12th July, 2004 out of government's shareholding in conjunction with the IPO by the Company. The IPO that was completed in October 2004 fetched an amount of ₹ 2684.07 crore.

Subsequently on 25th November, 2005, the government decided, in principle, to list large, profitable CPSUs on domestic stock exchanges and to selectively sell small portions of equity in listed, profitable CPSUs, other than the Navratna CPSEs. The government sold 8 per cent equity in Maruti Udyog Limited

(MUL) in January 2006 out of its residual shareholding of 18.28 per cent to public sector financial institutions (FIs) and public sector banks through a differential pricing method. The government realized, in the process, ₹ 1567.60 crore from this sale. Subsequently in March 2006, 0.01 per cent equity of the Company was sold to the employees and the government realized an amount of ₹ 2.08 crore. On 21 December 2006, the government decided to disinvest its entire residual shareholding of 10.27 per cent in Maruti Udyog Limited. The shareholding of 10.27 per cent was finally disinvested in May 2007 through the differential pricing method to Indian public sector FIs, public sector banks and Indian Mutual Funds. The government realized in the process ₹ 2277.62 crore from this disinvestment.

In February, 2007, the government decided to piggy-back with an 'Offer-for-Sale' of 10 per cent, 5 per cent and 5 per cent of the pre-issue paid-up capital of REC, PGCIL and NHPC respectively. The IPO of PGCIL was completed in October 2007 and the government realized an amount of ₹ 994.82 crore. The IPO of REC was completed in March 2008 and the government realized an amount of ₹ 819.63 crore. The IPO of NHPC was completed in August 2009 and the government realized an amount of ₹ 2012.85 crore.

In August 2007, the government approved disinvestment of 10 per cent equity in Oil India Ltd, out of its shareholding along with fresh issue of equity of 11 per cent of the post-issue paid-up capital of Oil India Limited and simultaneous disinvestment of 10 per cent equity of government in favour of IOC, HPCL and BPCL in the ratio of 2:1:1, at the market discovered price. The IPO was completed in September 2009 and the government realized an amount of ₹ 2247.046 crore.

Receipts from Disinvestment

Starting from 1991-92 when the government began disinvesting till 30 September 2009, the total receipts have been to the tune of ₹ 57,682.93 crore (See Annexure I). Out of this, the majority receipts of ₹ 39,617.91 have been through sale of minority shareholding. Receipts from sale of residual shareholding in disinvested CPSEs/companies has been ₹ 6,398.27 crore while receipts through Strategic Sale has been ₹ 6,344.35 crore. Other earnings have been through receipts from other related transactions (₹ 4,005.17 crore) and receipts through sale of majority shareholding of one CPSE to another CPSE (₹ 1,317.23 crore).

Understanding the Strategic Sale Agreements

In the strategic sale of a company, the transaction has two elements: transfer of a block of shares to a Strategic Partner, and transfer of management control to the Strategic Partner. The transfer of shares by government may not necessarily be such that more than 51 per cent of the total equity goes to the Strategic Partner for the transfer of management to take place. In the case of PSEs, in order that the company no longer has the character of a government company, the transfer of shares involves bringing down governments shareholding below 51 per cent.

As per the Companies Act, 1956 a 'Government Company' is a company in which the government holds more that 51%. The Act does not define what a PSE is. Once the governments' shareholding goes below 51 per cent, it ceases to be a government company and hence, it requires changes in the Articles of Association of the company especially in relation to the Presidential directives, etc. The Strategic Partner, after the transaction, may hold less percentage of shares than the government but the control of management would be with him. For instance, if in a PSU the shareholding of government is 51 per cent and the balance is dispersed in public holdings, then government may go in for a 25 per cent strategic sale and pass on management control, though the government would post-transfer have a larger share holding (26%) than the Strategic Partner (25%).

In Company Law, the number 26 per cent has a special significance because at least three-fourths majority is required in a general meeting to get a special resolution passed, and the 26 per cent block acts as a check. Special resolutions are required under law in case of certain critical decisions by the company such as reduction of capital, alteration in Articles of Association and Memorandum of Association, winding up of the company, issue of share with variation of rights of special classes of shareholders, etc. However, in case of strategic sale of PSEs, government typically has affirmative rights on several issues, which are much wider in scope than what is provided in Company Law for special resolutions. In fact, the Agreements can be structured such that these rights are exercisable even when government holding goes below 26 per cent. The other critical number in Company Law is 10 per cent shareholding because below it one loses voting rights unless specially provided.

The Strategic Sale agreements assume great significance in the case of strategic sale of PSEs since the shareholders mutually agree to certain rights and obligations which may by dint of the Agreement between the parties assign certain special rights and obligations on the shareholders to which they would normally not be bound through the provisions of the Company Law. However, the government has to ensure that the Agreements signed with the Strategic Partner adequately safeguard the governments/nation's interests, the interests of the company and finally those of the employees. Therefore, these documents have to be carefully structured.

Environment of the Sale

In a strategic sale the various stakeholders involved in the transaction are the PSE itself, the Government of India, Strategic Partner, Employees, Other Shareholders, Company Law, SEBI, and Environment issue. While the government and the Strategic Partner are the obvious stakeholders, the transaction affects the other shareholders and the employees. The shareholders are directly affected as the value of the shared held by them depends on the success of the transaction.

Transfer of shares is generally governed by the provisions of the Companies Act, 1956 (Sections 108, etc). In case of listed companies, however, the interest of the small investors is taken care of by SEBI through its various regulations. The SEBI Takeover Code gets triggered when a person acquires more than 15 per cent of the voting equity shares of the company. Then, the person taking over these shares is required to make a public offer to purchase shares not less than 20 per cent of the equity of the company. This provision has a great impact on the strategic sale transaction as the transaction size more than doubles, which in big PSEs may mean enormous sums of money. When the deal size goes up, it reduces the number of players and hence competition. The other impact it can have is that it reduces the floating stock, which can at times go even below 10 per cent, resulting in de-listing of the company. Reduction in floating stock affects trading and hence impacts the value of the residual shareholding of the government. Apart from the immediate effect the transaction would have on the share prices, the other shareholders also get affected depending upon whether the Strategic Partner enhances corporate value and hence their earnings or not.

The employees also equally as from the security of the public sector work environment they would find themselves in a new atmosphere of increased competition, demand for higher productivity and accountability. They would, therefore, logically try not to let go the protections presently enjoyed by them. government, in a welfare state, also would like to look after the employees' interest. There obviously has to be a trade off, however, between the protection that the employees can be given and providing to the Strategic Partner a degree of freedom to run the company. These competing interests have to be carefully balanced in drafting the Agreements.

The PSU is an important player that gets affected by the transaction as when it is passed on to the hands of a serious Strategic Partner, its worth goes up. But the reverse could also happen.

The Strategic Partner, perhaps, has the highest stakes because in case the deal does not work out right he loses money and reputation in the market. On the other hand, in case the assessment made by the strategic partner about the potential of the company, its assets/liabilities position and his ability to implement a good business plan is right, he gains money, reputation and goodwill.

Typically, industries would have environmental issues, especially for manufacturing units. They may not be very relevant, however, in Consultancy Companies or Software Companies. Therefore, the Agreements have to, at times, address the environmental issues clearly, e.g. which party takes what part of the risk in regard to responsibilities for actions taken/not taken prior to disinvestment. All these would govern the structure of the Agreements. These concerns of the various stakeholders are taken care of through the transaction documents such as Shareholders Agreement, Share Purchase Agreement, and Parent Guarantee Agreement, etc.

Shareholders Agreement

The shareholders agreement defines the relationship between the Strategic Partner and the government (the shareholders) once the company is transferred to the Strategic Partner. Broadly, it addresses issues such as Exit mechanism, Raising of capital, Affirmative rights, Deadlock, Termination, Arbitration, etc.

Exit Mechanism: When a company is being taken over by a Strategic Partner, both the Strategic Partner and the government would like to know upfront about the exit mechanisms. Normally, there is a lock-in period for the Strategic Partner before which he cannot sell whole/part of purchased shares, typically three to five years. This is because government would not like to encourage a fly-by-night operator take over a crucial government asset. Once the bidders know that government wants a stable and serious minded partner in the business, only serious parties would come. Similarly, in case of the bidder coming through an SPV, it is important to stipulate a lock-in period (matching with the lock-in period for the company shares) for the holding of the Strategic Partner in the SPV. Otherwise the lock in period in case of the PSU shares becomes meaningless, as the bidder can exit out of the SPV and the government may be left with an undesirable partner.

Once a party has decided to exit, the other party should have the right of first refusal. This can act against government at times because, in future, when government wants to disinvest further, no serious offers may come as those parties would be aware of the right of first refusal provision in favour of the Strategic Partner. Right of first refusal is normally reciprocal. Usually, the Agreement would also provide for tag-along rights to the parties in case they do not exercise their right of first refusal, i.e. in case the Strategic Partner is selling its shares to a third party, the government can require that the government's shareholding be also sold along with the Strategic Partner's share at the same price.

For the government, there could also be a lock-in period after which it can exit from the balance holding at any time. This may be desirable in some cases where the Strategic Partner may like to have government as a partner for some time at least, during which period, using the government's presence, some issues (licenses, land issues, etc.) involving dealings with the government can be resolved quickly. Government would then have a 'put' option exercisable after a certain period of time (say 1 year). The Strategic Partner may also look for a 'call' option to buy out the government but this should typically get triggered after some period of time (3-5 years depending upon the PSU). The general idea is that the Strategic Partner is there to stay and, depending upon the situation, government would exit. After sometime, the Strategic Partner should have the freedom to go it alone and buy out government because, in any case, the policy is for government to ultimately quit from the commercial venture.

Raising of Capital: On takeover, the Strategic Partner would in all likelihood have to immediately inject funds into the company for capital expenditure or to meet pending revenue expenditure. This would be required in the case of sick PSUs and may even be required in profit making PSUs as well. Therefore, the government may agree to the Strategic Partner bringing in funds at the time of takeover, itself, in which case provision in the Agreement has to be made for such 'contribution' shares. In other cases, the Strategic Partner may like to first take over the management and then look to raising capital. The Agreement has to clearly provide for such situations. Capital raised can be either as equity or as a loan. Equity capital can be raised through the Rights issue, IPO, or Preferential Allotment.

However, there has to be some restrictions on the Strategic Partner raising capital in the form of equity or loan as government would not be in any position to contribute to the capital requirements, any equity subscription would mean that the percentage holding of the government would be going down. If the post transfer holding of government were 26 per cent, then this would imply that government holding would go below 26 per cent and government would lose control as vested in the special resolution provisions of the Companies Act. The one safeguard is that even if the government holding goes below 26 per cent, if the affirmative rights survive, government's interest vis-à-vis asset stripping, employee protection, etc. remain as the government can always block such a proposal being passed in the Board meeting/general meeting. But a situation may arise that within the first few months government's share holding can go below the stipulated 15 per cent/10 per cent limit beyond which the Agreement itself does not survive. Therefore, it may be necessary that there would be a period of moratorium (say 1 year) on proposals for raising capital through equity. Or, alternatively, the agreement may provide that for the lock-in period (3/5 years) even if agreement terminates government will have affirmative vote on select items (say asset stripping, employees) as long as government has one share.

Affirmative Rights: The government cannot just handover the reigns of the company to the Strategic Partner and then take no interest in the running of the company. It has to ensure that the Strategic Partner is following the Agreement both in letter and spirit. It has to make sure that the assets of the company are not being misused or quietly disposed of or that the employees are not being adversely treated or that the Strategic Partner is not taking any action detrimental to the interest of the company. One way of ensuring this is the section on Board Representation, i.e. through its nominees the government gets the progress report from the company in each Board meeting. Another way is for the Agreement to provide for veto rights to the government in certain important matters, called Affirmative

Rights of government. These rights are included to ensure that the Strategic Partner fulfills the desired intention of the strategic sale by the government and utilize the assets in enhancing the value of the existing business and ensure growth and not misutilise or harm the assets, including the employees.

The items on which affirmative vote of the government nominee on the board would be required, may *inter alia*, cover asset stripping, non-changeable line of business, guarantee exposures beyond a certain limit cannot be taken, change in service condition of employees or decision for retrenchment, opening new line of business, winding up of the company, reduction of share capital/share buy-back, etc. It would, however, depend from case to case on what items government would like to reserve this right. It should not be so restrictive as to frustrate the efforts of the Strategic Partner or be so liberal as to give an absolute license to the Strategic Partner to do whatever he likes.

Deadlock: Deadlock occurs when government holds back consent in a Board meeting on any affirmative right issue. Deadlock is first tried to be resolved through mutual discussion of senior representatives of parties. If discussion fails, then government could have a 'put' option at higher of FMV or unit sale price (at the time of deadlock the Strategic Partner can hold more than the shares transferred at the time of strategic sale) plus interest minus dividend paid. The logic behind providing this option is that in case of minor issues, if government thinks fit, the government can let the Strategic Partner run the Company by quitting through the 'put' option at a premium as a deadlock would mean that the partners are not able to carry on together and their continuing would harm the Company. If it is major issues say asset stripping, then government would not utilize this 'put' option and the Strategic Partner would have to live with the situation.

Termination: Termination would typically take place by mutual agreement, company becoming bankrupt, or when either party owns less than x per cent (e.g. 10%/15%/25%) of the outstanding and issued voting equity share, and/or either party owns more than x per cent (75% is relevant usually) of voting shares. In some extremely sensitive cases government can insist that the Agreement does not terminate till government holds even one share. Covenants on confidentiality, indemnity, etc., however, have to survive termination. In case government wants protection to the employees not to terminate with the Agreement then this should be taken care of also and this should be included amongst items that would survive termination. Similarly, the affirmative rights of the government would also seize once the Agreement terminates. On the termination of the Agreement, however, the parties are not released of the liabilities accrued prior to the termination.

Arbitration: Arbitration clauses are incorporated in Agreements to take care of disputes concerning interpretation of the agreement or application or rights and obligations. Generally, Indian Arbitration and Conciliation Act, 1996, govern arbitration.

Valuation Methodologies

Based on the recommendations of the Disinvestment Commission and in keeping with the best market practices the four methodologies that are being used for valuation of PSUs are: Discounted Cash Flow (DCF) Method, Balance Sheet Method, Transaction Multiple Method, and Asset Valuation Method.

Discounted Cash Flow Method

The Discounted Cash Flow (DCF) methodology expresses the present value of a business as a function of its future cash earnings capacity. This methodology works on the premise that the value of a business is measured in terms of future cash flow streams, discounted to the present time at an appropriate discount rate. It is used to determine the present value of a business on a going concern assumption. It recognizes that money has a time value by discounting future cash flows at an appropriate discount factor. The DCF methodology depends on the projection of the future cash flows and the selection of an appropriate discount factor.

When valuing a business on a DCF basis, the objective is to determine a net present value of the free cash flows (FCF) arising from the business over a future period of time called the explicit forecast period. FCF include all inflows and outflows associated with the project prior to debt service such as taxes, amount invested in working capital and capital expenditure. Under the DCF methodology, value must be placed both on the explicit cash flows and the ongoing cash flows a company will generate after the explicit forecast period. The latter value, also known as terminal value, is also to be estimated.

The discount rate applied to estimate the present value of explicit forecast period free cash flows as also continuing value, is taken at the Weighted Average Cost of Capital (WACC). One of the advantages of the DCF approach is that it permits the various elements that make up the discount factor to be considered separately, and thus, the effect of the variations in the assumptions can be modelled more easily. The principal elements of WACC are cost of equity (which is the desired rate of return for an equity investor given the risk profile of the company and associated cash flows), the post-tax cost of debt and the target capital structure of the company (a function of debt to equity ratio). In turn, cost of equity is derived, on the basis of capital asset pricing model (CAPM), as a function of risk-free rate, Beta (an estimate of risk profile of the company relative to equity market) and equity risk premium assigned to the subject equity market.

The DCF methodology is considered to be the best methodology for valuation the world over because it takes into account all the factors relevant for valuation. It takes into consideration all the cash flows available to stakeholders of a firm and the necessary outflows, as estimated for the future. Further, the net present value takes into account the cost of debt, cost of equity and target capital structure. It also takes into account the risks to which the enterprise is exposed. The discount rate (i.e. the average expected return on capital employed) is based on the overall risk perception of the business. It also takes into account the value of the non-core assets of the company.

For a going concern, various intangibles like brand equity, market share, competition, etc. have a significant bearing on the valuation of the company. These factors have no financial value of their own that can be measured in money terms. Hence, there is no way of evaluating them in any other methodology. DCF is the only methodology, which takes into account these factors by incorporating them intrinsically in estimated cash flows. In calculating DCF, different assumptions will be made of market share, competition from imports, etc., which are translated into financial terms.

In a strategic sale, the bidders take into account not only DCF valuation, but also a premium for management control—a subjective item for each bidder—which will be reflected in the competitive bids. Therefore, the seller, while calculating the Reserve Price, should not incorporate this premium in the valuation amount separately. Since there is no scientific method to quantify the control premium, it may be arbitrary to add control premium while arriving at the Reserve Price.

Balance Sheet Method

The Balance sheet or the Net Asset Value (NAV) methodology values a business on the basis of the value of its underlying assets. This is relevant where the value of the business is fairly represented by its underlying assets. The NAV method is normally used to determine the minimum price a seller would be willing to accept and, thus serves to establish the floor for the value of the business. This method is pertinent where the value of intangibles is not significant, or where the business has been recently set up.

This method takes into account the net value of the assets of a business or the capital employed as represented in the financial statements. Hence, this method takes into account the amount that is historically spent and earned from the business. This method does not, however, consider the earnings potential of the assets and is, therefore, seldom used for valuing a going concern. The above method is not considered appropriate, particularly in cases where the financial statement sheets do not reflect the true value of assets, or where intangibles such as brand, goodwill, marketing infrastructure, and product development capabilities, etc., form a major part of the value of the company, or where due to the changes in industry, market or business environment, the assets of the company have become redundant and their ability to create net positive cash flows in future is limited.

Market Multiple Method

This method takes into account the traded or transaction value of comparable companies in the industry and benchmarks it against certain parameters, like earnings, sales, etc. Although this method captures most value elements of a business, it is based on the past/current transaction or traded values and does not reflect the possible changes in future of the trend of cash flows being generated by a business, neither takes into account the time value of money adequately. At the same time, it is a reflection of the current view of the market and hence is considered as a useful rule of thumb, providing reasonable checks to valuations arrived at from other approaches. Accordingly, one may have to review a series of comparable transactions to determine a range of appropriate capitalisation factors to value a company as per this methodology.

EBITDA Multiple: Two commonly used parameters in this method are: Earnings before Interest, Taxes, Depreciation and Amortisations (EBITDA) multiple, and Sales multiple. The EBITDA multiple or the earnings method is based on the premise that the value of a business is directly related to the quantum of its gross profits. The net profits are adjusted to reflect the operating recurring profits of the business on a stand-alone basis, i.e. after deducting extraordinary or unusual items, or items of a non-recurring nature. Further, the profits are adjusted for non-cash items, including depreciation and amortisation and other factors, such as interest and taxation (which vary from business to business) to derive EBITDA.

Sales Multiple: The sales multiple techniques in the market multiple method are based on a similar analysis of relevant acquisitions and are the ratio of Enterprise Value to the current sales, i.e. net of excise duty, sales tax and non-recurring extra-ordinary income.

The Transaction Multiple methodology, however, does not consider actual money required to earn the maintainable profits/

sales of the business as a going concern, for instance, future capital expenditure. This methodology does not take into account the time value of money. Notwithstanding these limitations, these multiples are widely used by investors to arrive at benchmark values for a company.

Asset Valuation Methodology

The asset valuation methodology essentially estimates the cost of replacing the tangible assets of the business. The replacement cost takes into account the market value of various assets or the expenditure required to create the infrastructure exactly similar to that of a company being valued. Since the replacement methodology assumes the value of business as if we were setting a new business, this methodology may not be relevant in a going concern. Instead it will be more useful in case of liquidation/closure of the business. In this case, certain adjustments may have to be made to the equity value arrived at by this method including settlement of all borrowings on the company's balance sheet on the date of valuation and settlement of employee dues. These adjustments should include all the process related cost involved in closure and liquidation.

The asset valuation approach suffers from certain very serious limitations. Practically, it is extremely difficult to determine the exact replacement cost of the assets owned by a company. This is so on account of number of reasons, such as changes in technology over a period of time, absence of a marketplace where such assets are or can be traded, inability of the seller to be able to actually realize the value of assets in one go, changes in the duty structure, etc. Secondly, the asset valuation approach also does not take into account the very purpose for which a company acquired the assets, i.e. for future economic benefits. Hence, the historical or replacement cost of a particular asset may tend to convey a wrong picture of the value that the buyer may perceive in the asset. Thirdly, this approach also tends to overlook the intangible assets that a company, over a period of its existence tends to build such as goodwill, brands, distribution network, customer relationships, etc. all of which are very important to determine its true intrinsic value.

The Current Policy

The current policy on disinvestment emanate from the President's Address to the Joint Session of both the Houses of Parliament (4 June 2009) where it was stated: "Our fellow citizens have every right to own part of the shares of public sector companies while the Government retains majority shareholding and control. My Government will develop a roadmap for listing and people-ownership of public sector undertakings while ensuring that Government equity does not fall below 51 per cent".

Furthermore, in the Budget Speech delivered on 6 July 2009, it was announced that the "Public Sector Undertakings (PSUs) are the wealth of the nation, and part of this wealth should rest in the hands of the people. While retaining at least 51 per cent Government equity in our enterprises, I propose to encourage people's participation in our disinvestment programme. Here, I must state clearly that public sector enterprises, such as, banks and insurance companies will remain in the public sector and will be given all support, including capital infusion, to grow and remain competitive". The Minster added that "the Department of Disinvestment, Ministry of Finance, in consultation with Ministries/Departments will accordingly identify cases for disinvestment in select CPSEs. The focus will first be on profitable CPSEs that are listed with less than 10 per cent public shareholding (and make them compliant through Follow-on Public Offerings). Profitable unlisted companies will be also listed on stock exchanges through Offer-for-Sale or through Issue of Fresh Equity by the companies or both in conjunction."

Advantages of Listing: There are inherent advantages in the listing of shares of profitable CPSEs on the stock exchanges. Besides enhancing shareholder's value in such CPSEs, the process bestows the following benefits on these listed companies:

(a) Higher disclosure levels bring greater transparency, liquidity and credibility to their stocks;

(b) Enhance corporate governance through induction of 'independent directors' on the Boards of these CPSEs, which is mandatory for listed companies;

(c) Higher levels of public scrutiny enforce ethical conduct of business in these CPSEs and thus improve corporate culture;

(d) Expectations of investors/shareholders bring pressure upon the management to perform and to unlock the true value of these enterprises;

(e) Listing enables wider shareholding of CPSE stocks, and people-ownership of CPSEs.

Future Strategy

Engineers India Limited (EIL): Engineers India Limited is a Public Sector Undertaking under the Ministry of Petroleum and Natural Gas is engaged in providing engineering and related technical services for petroleum refineries and other industrial projects. Government of India is holding 90.40 per cent paid up equity capital of the company and the balance is held by the general public. The shares of the company are listed on the stock exchanges with less than 10 per cent mandatory public shareholding.

The Cabinet Committee on Economic Affairs (CCEA) on 14 January 2010 decided to disinvest 10 per cent paid up equity capital of Engineers India Limited, out of government's shareholding of 90.40 per cent, in the domestic market through Public Offering. After this disinvestment government shareholding in the company would come down to 80.40 per cent. It has also been decided that before the Public Offering the company will take the following steps: (a) Issue bonus two shares for every one share; (b) Split one share of the face value of ₹ 10 into two at the face value of ₹ 5 each; and (c) Declare special dividend of 1000 per cent of the paid up equity capital.

Steel Authority of India Ltd. (SAIL): The CCEA on 8 April 2010 approved the proposal for raising additional equity by the Steel Authority of India Ltd. (SAIL) to the extent of 10 per cent of the paid up equity and disinvestment of a portion of Government of India's shareholding in SAIL by an extent of 10 per cent through offer for sale, to be carried out in two separate tranches.

The further public offering (FPO) would comprise the first tranche of the fresh issue of 5 per cent pre-issue paid up equity of the company and offer for sale of 5 per cent of government equity in SAIL. The CCEA has accorded permission for affecting the first tranche and the second tranche, similar to the first, would be issued at an appropriate time depending on prevailing market conditions. The further offerings along with disinvestment would be carried out as per SEBI regulations and procedure adopted by the Department of Disinvestment which is the nodal agency for handling of disinvestment of government public sector units.

As a result of the further public offer, there would be enhanced public holding in SAIL from the present level of 14.2 per cent to 31 per cent and it is expected that the enhanced holding would lead to greater public accountability leading to greater depth in the market. As a result of the secondary offering and equity dilution, there would thus be larger public ownership of the company, leading to greater public oversight and increased accountability.

The disinvestment of government's equity in SAIL is in line with the overall policy of the government that ownership of CPSEs would be shared with the public. The proceeds from fresh issue of equity by SAIL would help in filling the resource gap in availability for funding SAIL's capital expenditure emerging from the increased pressure on steel prices and diminished margins. SAIL is presently amidst massive expansion plans for increasing its installed hot metal production capacity from existing 13.82 million tonnes per annum (MTPA) to 23.46 MTPA in the current phase.

Hindustan Copper Limited (HCL): The paid up equity capital of Hindustan Copper Limited (HCL) is ₹ 462.61 crore. Government of India is holding 99.59 per cent paid up equity capital of the Company at present. The face value of the share is ₹ 5 each. The CCEA on 15 June 2010 approved the proposal for disinvestment of 10 per cent paid up equity capital of HCL out of Government of India's shareholding along with issue of fresh equity of equal size by the Company in the domestic market. The divestment will be done in the following manner:

(i) Issue of fresh equity by HCL to the extent of 10 per cent of the pre-issue paid up capital of the company equivalent to 9,25,21,800 shares of face value of ₹ 5 each in the domestic market as per SEBI rules and regulation.

(ii) In conjunction with the issue of fresh equity as at (i) above; government to disinvest its 10 per cent of pre issue paid up capital of the company, equivalent to 9,25,21,800 shares of face value of ₹ 5 each.

(iii) Reservation of shares for employees of HCL will be on a discount of 5 per cent, which will also be available to retail investors as per the guidelines of SEBI.

Coal India Limited (CIL): Coal India Ltd. (CIL), a Central Public Sector Enterprise, is a Navratna Company engaged in production and marketing of coal and coal products. At present, the paid up equity capital of the company is ₹ 6316.36 crore and the Government of India holds 100 per cent of the equity in the company.

The CCEA on 15 June 2010 gave its approval to divest 10 per cent equity of the CIL out of its holding of 100 per cent through book building process in the domestic market. One per cent of the equity will be offered to the employees of CIL and its eight subsidiaries. The CCEA has also decided to allow 5 per cent price concession to the retail investors in order to encourage greater public ownership of the public sector companies. The CCEA also approved a 5 per cent concession to the employees of the company and its subsidiaries to encourage their becoming stakeholders in the company. After this disinvestment, Government of India's shareholding in the company would come down to 90 per cent.

Power Grid Corporation of India Limited (PGCIL): Power Grid Corporation of India Limited (PGCIL) went for a maiden Initial Public Offering (IPO) of equity shares consisting of issue of fresh equity shares with 10 per cent of paid up capital and disinvestment of Government of India equity holding of 5 per cent of paid up capital in October 2007 through the book building process and the issue was subscribed 64.50 times. The shares of the PGCIL got listed in the National Stock Exchange and Bombay Stock Exchange on 5.10.2007. PGCIL raised

₹ 2984 crore at the issue price of ₹ 52/- per share out of which ₹ 995 crore was paid to the Government of India towards the disinvestment proceeds and the balance amount, after meeting the issue expenses, was utilized for capital expenditure of identified projects during the financial year 2007-08 and 2008-09.

The CCEA on 22 July 2010 approved the Follow-on Public Offer (FPO) of PGCIL of 84,17,68,246 Equity shares of ₹10 each constituting 20 per cent of existing paid-up capital. This comprises fresh issue of 42,08,84,123 Equity Shares (10 % of existing paid-up capital) and offer for Sale (Disinvestment) of 42,08,84,123 Equity Shares (10% of existing paid-up capital).

Additional resources generated through the issue of an FPO will be utilized by PGCIL in its investment programmes. PGCIL will be required to approach the capital market for raising funds through issue of fresh equity for funding its investment programme commencing from Financial Year 2010-11. The requirement of funds to be raised through issue of fresh equity for funding the capital expenditure for the balance Eleventh Plan period will be in the order of ₹ 4200 crore. The fresh issue of FPO would result in the PGCIL meeting with the CERC allowed norms of 30 per cent equity contributions during the Eleventh Plan period.

Manganese ORE (India) Ltd. (MOIL): At present, the Central Government holds 81.57 per cent of the equity of Manganese Ore India Ltd. (MOIL), a Miniratna Central Public Sector Enterprise. The balance is held by the State Governments of Maharashtra and Madhya Pradesh to the extent of 9.62 per cent and 8.81 per cent respectively. MOIL is engaged in production of manganese ore, which is the raw material for manufacturing of alloys, an essential input for steel making and dioxide ore for manufacturing dry batteries.

The CCEA on 9 September 2010 approved the disinvestment of 10 per cent of total paid up equity of MOIL out of its holding through Initial Public Offering (IPO). The State Governments of Maharashtra and Madhya Pradesh have also decided to divest 5 per cent each of total paid up equity in MOIL out of their shareholding along with the Government of India. This will lead to MOIL listing its shares in the Stock Exchanges. The CCEA has also approved to allow 5 per cent price discount to the employees of the company under employees reservation quota to encourage their becoming stakeholders in the company. The CCEA has further decided to allow this 5 per cent price discount to retail investors as well as to encourage the development of people-ownership.

Concluding Remarks

India's recent history of big public sector offers, both initial public offerings (IPOs) like CIL's and follow-on public offerings (FPOs) like SAIL's, has involved the significant participation of another government organization, the Life Insurance Corporation of India (LIC). Both in case of NMDC FPO and NTPC IPO, LIC saved the day, as high net-worth individuals (HNIs) and retail investors bid for only about a fifth of their allotments, while the interest of foreign institutional investors (FIIs) was nominal. In such a scenario, the question arises whether such an exercise can be truly called disinvestment. No doubt, the government achieves its objective of getting the money, but it is doubtful whether there has been any price discovery or whether the ownership has become wider. In any case, it is not in anybody's interest to have such a large holding in one entity.

The question also arises whether there was any need to have an FPO because the government can just place the shares with LIC, which can then gradually offload the shares into the market. If the response to disinvestment is poor and issues list below their offer price, investors will keep shying away. Traditionally, some degree of underpricing has been the norm in many countries. The retail investor prefers to stay out unless convinced of a significant underpricing. On the other hand, for the government, underpricing and equity offer will be tantamount to transferring taxpayers' wealth to investors who constitute less than 5 per cent of the population.

Since the proportion or retail investors vis-à-vis institutions is already quite high in India compared to the US, the government can afford to stop worrying about retail investors. Instead, it can be aggressive in pricing public offers. Also, there are vested interests in overpricing. Promoters set a fund-raising target with an objective to dilute as little of the stake as possible. Merchant bankers set an unofficial price-per-share target with the promoters. The bankers too prefer a higher price as they often forgo fees. Also, reputation and size count while tallying public sector IPOs in end-of-year rankings. So, the bigger the issue, the better, which leads to a bias toward higher pricing.

In the meantime, the Securities and Exchange Board of India (SEBI) has tweaked the rules, confusing the situation. While it suggested the French auction system for the NTPC issue, it went back to the traditional book-building route for NMDC issue. SEBI has also mandated that qualified institutional buyers, which include foreign institutional investors, will have to put 100 per cent of the bid amount on application instead of the 10 per cent at present. While this is yet to take effect, it is feared that liquidity problems may temper the response to IPOs.

Disinvestment remains one of the trump cards for the government in managing fiscal deficit. However, the ambiguity over the pace of disinvestment and the absence of any visible progress in disinvestment has led to uncertainty over willingness of the government to play the disinvestment card. However, the recent announcement that all profitable listed PSEs to have minimum 10 per cent public ownership gives the much needed traction to the disinvestment programme. The expected public offers for SAIL and CIL will determine the success of the Indian Government's efforts to raise billions of dollars through disinvestment.

Unlike Brazil and China, where the government budget does not hang in the balance, in India, the Finance Minister is using disinvestment to balance his books. He has received a pat on the back from Standard & Poor's, which has raised its outlook for India to stable. But that outlook could easily be reversed if the disinvestment plans and the fiscal deficit do not meet targets.

As India is moving from a \$1 trillion economy to a \$2 trillion one, it has appetite to absorb these massive investments mainly due to the 38 per cent savings rate. PSE divestment has created value for investors in the long run. Taking this into consideration, several mutual funds have launched PSU Funds which would tend to benefit from the PSU divestments.

APPENDIX-I: SUMMARY OF RECEIPTS FROM DISINVESTMENT: 1991-92 to 30.9.2009

Year	Budgeted receipt (₹. crore)	Receipts through sale of minority shareholding	Receipts through sale of majority share-holding of one CPSE to another CPSE (₹ crore)	Receipts through Strategic sale (₹ crore)	Receipts from other related transactions (₹ crore)	Receipts from sale of residual shareholding in disinvested CPSEs/ companies (₹ crore)	Total receipts (₹ crore)	Transacations
1991-92	2,500	3,037.74	-	-	-	-	3,037.74	Minority shares sold in Dec. 1991 and Feb, 1992 by auction method in bundles of "very good", "good" and "average" companies
1992-93	2,500	1,912.51	-	-	-	-	1,912.51	Shares sold separately for each company by auction method.
1993-94	3,500	-	-	-	-	-	-	Equity of 6 companies sold by auction method but proceeds received in 1994-95.
1994-95	4,000	4,843.10	-	-	-	-	4,843.10	Shares sold by auction method.
1995-96	7,000	168.48	-	-	-	-	168.48	Shares sold by auction method.
1996-97	5,000	379.67	-	-	-	-	379.67	GDR -VSNL
1997-98	4,800	910.00	-	-	-	-	910.00	GDR -MTNL
1998-99	5,000	*5371.11	-	-	-	-	5,371.11	GDR-VSNL; Domestic offerings of CONCOR and GAIL; Cross purchase by 3 Oil sector companies i.e. GAIL, ONGC and IOC.
1999-00	10,000	**1479.27	-	105.45	275.42	-	1,860.14	GDR-GAIL; Domestic offering of VSNL; capital reduction and dividend from BALCO; Strategic sale of MFIL.
2000-01	10,000	-	1,317.23	554.03	-	-	1,871.26	Sale of KRL, CPCL and BRPL to CPSEs; Strategic sale of BALCO and LJMC.
2001-02	12,000	-	-	3,090.09	2,567.60	-	5,657.69	Strategic sale of CMC, HTL, VSNL, IBP, PPL, hotel properties of ITDC and HCI, slump sale of Hotel Centaur

(Contd.)

(Contd. Appendix-I)

								Juhu Beach, Mumbai and leasing of Ashok Bangalore; Special dividend from VSNL, STC and MMTC; sale of shares to VSNL employees.
2002-03	12,000	-	-	2,252.72	1,095.26	-	3,347.98	Strategic sale of HZL, IPCL, hotel properties of ITDC, slump sale of Centaur Hotel Mumbai Airport, Mumbai; Premium for renunciation of rights issue in favour of SMC; Put Option of MFIL; Sale of shares to employees of HZL and CMC.
2003-04	14,500	12,741.62	-	342.06	-	2,463.73	15,547.41	Strategic sale of JCL; Call Option of HZL; Offer for Sale of MUL, IBP, IPCL, CMC, DCI, GAIL and ONGC; Sale of shares of ICI Ltd.
2004-05	4,000	2,700.06	-	-	64.81	-	2,764.87	Offer for Sale of NTPC and spill over of ONGC; sale of shares to IPCL employees.
2005-06	No target fixed	-	-	-	2.08	1,567.60	1,569.68	Sale of MUL shares to Indian public sector financial institutions & banks and employees.
2006-07	No target fixed	-	-	-	-	-	-	
2007-08	No target fixed	1,814.45	-	-	-	2,366.94	4,181.39	Sale of MUL (₹ 2366.94 cr) shares to public sector financial institutions, public sector banks and Indian mutual funds and sale of PGCIL (₹ 994.82 cr) and REC (₹ 819.63 cr) shares through Offer for Sale.
2008-09	No target fixed	-	-	-	-	-	-	
2009-10	No target fixed	4,259.90	-	-	-	-	4,259.90	(₹ 2012.85 - NHPC and ₹ 2247.05-OIL)
Total		**39,617.91**	**1,317.23**	**6,344.35**	**4,005.17**	**6,398.27**	**57,682.93**	

* Out of ₹ 5371.11, ₹ 4184 crore constitute receipts from cross purchase of shares of ONGC, GAIL and IOC.

** Out of ₹ 1479.27, ₹ 459.27 crore constitute receipts from cross purchase of shares of ONGC, GAIL and IOC.

Annexure–I

Report of Ad Hoc Group of Experts on Empowerment of Central Public Sector Enterprises (Deptt. of Public Enterprises, Ministry of Heavy Industries and Public Enterprises, Govt. of India, April 2005)

EXECUTIVE SUMMARY

Ownership Issues and Powers of CPSEs

1. For effective governance of Central Public Sector Enterprises (CPSEs), their ownership functions, the powers and operational procedures of the Board of Directors and their responsibilities together with suitable checks and balances for exercising control over the Management should be properly designed and implemented.

   (Para 2.1)

2. The Ad-hoc Group of Experts (AGE) recommends that any decision to reduce Government share holding to a level less than 51 per cent in case of Category I CPSEs, i.e. Navratna, Miniratnas and consistently profit making CPSEs, should be taken only with the consent of the Parliament. The Board of Directors should have all the powers to raise equity capital from the market so long as the government's share of the overall equity remains above 51 per cent. However, in case of Category II CPSEs, i.e. other than those mentioned above, Government should have full flexibility of owning or disinvesting their shares.

   (Para 2.3, Para 2.16)

3. The AGE recommends that governance of CPSEs, especially the Navratnas and Miniratnas and other profit making companies, should continue to be supervised by the three tier system, namely the Ministry concerned

representing the government, the Board of Directors and the Management, with the role, powers and functions of each of them clearly defined and codified.

(Para 2.5)

4. The AGE recommends that an institutional arrangement is required in order to ensure harmonious relations and interactions among the three tiers and to provide for the redressal of grievances of the stakeholders. To fulfill this requirement, the establishment of six overarching Supervisory Bodies, each consisting of ten members (three Ministers, five independent distinguished experts of the relevant sector and Secretary of the Ministry/Department and CMD concerned) is considered essential. The AGE has suggested the setting up of such Supervisory Bodies for six different sectors.

(Para 2.5)

5. The Supervisory Body should not give any direct instructions to the CPSEs. The Body should give its views only on matters referred to it.

(Para 2.6)

6. The Ministry should effectively perform the role of the sole/major shareholder as well as owners of the company. The Ministry should consult other Ministries, including Finance and other relevant Departments and, where necessary, obtain the approval of the Cabinet. It should assist the implementation of the projects of CPSE in its charge in line with government policy.

(Para 2.9)

7. Adverse actions like reprimand, suspension, premature termination, denial of extension of tenure, supercession of the recommendations of PESB, etc. must be referred to the Supervisory Body and the ACC should take its views into account before taking any decision on such matters. Appointments to Board level positions in CPSEs may be made for the period until superannuation instead of fixed tenures.

(Para 2.10)

8. The Ministry should not give instruction directly or indirectly to the Management. It should be the responsibility of the concerned Board of Directors. The views of the Ministry should be communicated to the Board through government Directors.

(Para 2.11)

9. If the Ministry considers it necessary to issue mandatory instruction to a CPSE, the same must be given in the form of a Presidential Directive. The issuance of such Presidential Directives should have the approval of the Cabinet.

(Para 2.12)

10. The Ministry should not normally review the functioning of the company more than twice a year. Such reviews should be based on the reports of the relevant Board of Directors and selected major performance indicators. Since the profitability of CPSEs is influenced by several factors such as the administered price mechanism and fluctuations in international price of the commodities, the Group recommends that the Ministries concerned should develop CPSE-specific criteria to determine their overall performance, independent of profitability.

(Para 2.13)

11. There should be a negative list of areas which must be kept away from the intervention of the government (except for respective jurisdiction of CAG and CVC).

(Para 2.14)

12. The current restrictions regarding capital expenditures, joint ventures, etc. need to be done away with. Such decisions should be left entirely to the Board of Directors. However, if that is not possible at one stroke, as the first step towards this desirable goal, enhanced powers should be given to Navratna/Miniratna and other profit making companies in respect of Capital expenditure, setting up of Joint Ventures (JVs)/Subsidiaries, subsequent investment in JVs. JVs between Navratnas, merger and acquisition, appointment of Directors in subsidiaries and JVs, etc.

The Chief Executive of CPSE concerned should be a member of Search Committee for selection of non-official Directors.

(Para 2.15)

13. There should be detailed procedural guidelines including limits of financial expenditure on foreign travel of Chief Executives and Board Members, formulated by the Board of Directors of the CPSEs concerned and no reference to the government for approval should be necessary unless deviation from such guidelines is intended.

(Para 2.17)

14. The Board of Directors should be fully responsible for the supervision and control over the Management of the company.

(Para 2.18)

15. Subject to statutory requirements, government policy and regulatory guidelines issued by the RBI, the Board of Directors should have full powers of pursuing new lines of business, deciding on suitable Acquisitions and Mergers, setting up Subsidiaries and exiting from any line of business, as also of making Capital expenditure up to the levels indicated in Para 2.15, without any prior clearance from the government.

(Para 2.19)

16. No more than two officers should be nominated as Board Members by the government on the Board of Directors of Navratna, Miniratna or other profit making CPSEs. The performance of government Directors must be suitably reflected in their personal CRs. An appraisal system for performance review of Independent Directors should be formulated.

(Para 2.20)

17. The Chief Executives and the Functional Directors should also be entitled to performance linked bonus/incentive within the permissible limit of 5 per cent of distributable profit. The Compensation Committee of the Board as

constituted under the 'Listing Agreement' should have the authority to decide on the quantum of such performance-linked incentives on the basis of individual's performance and contribution during the year under review. Such bonus/incentive would, however, be governed by the limits prescribed in the Companies Act.

(Para 2.21)

18. The Chief Executive should be entirely responsible for the day-to-day management and operation of the company under the overall supervision of the Board of Directors.

(Para 2.22)

19. The Management should be free to exercise all powers explicitly delegated by the Board of Directors. It should function under the supervision of the Chief Executive and Functional Directors on the Board.

(Para 2.23)

20. The Management should be responsible for implementation of the decisions of the Board of Directors, and compliance of all statutory requirements as well as policy guidelines.

(Para 2.24)

Audit of Government Companies

21. The AGE has made various suggestions for streamlining of the present system of test/supplementary/transaction audit of CPSEs in order to save time and to avoid duplications.

(Para 3.4)

Article 12 of the Constitution and CPSEs

22. The AGE has suggested that the issue relating to amendment of Article 12 of the Constitution could be revisited by the policymakers at an appropriate time.

(Para 4.5)

Parliamentary Accountability

23. The AGE has made some suggestions in regard to Parliamentary accountability of CPSEs in order to enable

them to focus on their business and to avoid disclosure of commercially sensitive information.

(Para 5.5)

Vigilance Management in CPSEs

24. The AGE, after taking into account suggestions made by Arvind Pande Committee, has made several recommendations in regard to Vigilance related issues concerning CPSEs.

(Para 6.12)

CHAPTER 1: INTRODUCTION

1.1 The last couple of decades have witnessed an accelerated pace of political and economic integration across the world and the increasing interdependence between economies of different countries. This phenomenon, which is broadly called 'globalisation', has been reinforced in the last decade by an increasing impact of the multilateral trade regime ushered in by the formation of the World Trade Organization in 1994. Another phenomenon that has assumed tremendous significance is the technological revolution, including information technology, that is sweeping the world forcefully in an all pervasive manner. Any failure to respond to this can only lead to obsolescence, in the total sense of the term. Technology, information and ideas are no longer confined within the boundaries of a sovereign state. All the above-mentioned factors have also caused institutional changes, including modifications in the policy, industrial organization and administration of laws and regulations that govern the behaviour of economic agents.

1.2 The response of India to this changing world environment has resulted in far-reaching economic reforms initiated more comprehensively since the beginning of the 1990s. Fiscal and monetary policies, trade and export-import policies, industrial policies, etc. have all been aligned with the new reforms and initiatives.

1.3 With increasing competition from the domestic private sector as well as foreign companies in the wake of liberalization and globalisation, the need to empower Central Public Sector Enterprises (CPSEs) with greater financial and operational powers was realized in order to enable them to effectively face increasing levels of competition. To delegate these powers, the concept of Navratna and Miniratna was introduced in July and October 1997. The powers delegated were related to incurring Capital expenditure, formation of Joint Ventures/ Subsidiaries/strategic alliances, implementation of HRD policies including VRS, etc. Later, certain powers for incurring Capital expenditure were also delegated to other profit making CPSEs. The professionalization of Boards of Directors was made a precondition to ensure that the enhanced powers were used prudently. Professionals were inducted in the Boards of Directors of these CPSEs and audit committees were also set up. These measures have helped in more objective and quicker decision-making by the Boards of Directors of CPSEs, with the independent Directors bringing in fresh thinking. The National Common Minimum Programme of the UPA Government has mandated devolution of full managerial and commercial autonomy to successful and profit making CPSEs operating in a competitive environment. Such measures are expected to motivate the Management and the employees of the Navratna and Miniratna CPSEs to perform better. These would also motivate other CPSEs to improve their performance in order to achieve the coveted status of being either a Navratna or Miniratna.

1.4 The first delegation of powers to Navratnas/Miniratnas in 1997 has certainly contributed to the improved performance of some of those Enterprises. But the fast changing world economic environment and the mandate of the National Common Minimum Programme now call for some bold and new thinking, and not mere incrementalism in empowerment. The last decade or so has witnessed perceptible performance improvements in a number of companies, whether it be GE or Motorola elsewhere in the world or Bajaj Auto, Infosys or Wipro at home. The managements of these companies did not believe in incrementalism of performance; and the quantum leaps in their performance have been the result of fully accountable but fully empowered management teams. Repeating/inducing such success in the CPSEs will require more than incremental empowerment. In a deregulated, fast changing and competitive economy, and with gradual dismantling of tariff barriers as envisaged in the non-agricultural market access negotiations in WTO, a company which is not adaptive and not growing fast enough will definitely cease to exist. The rigour of these new challenges is equally matched by unprecedented opportunities in the new world order which are such that a determined management can take its company to new levels of success much more quickly and effectively than in the past. Such opportunities can, however, be exploited fully by CPSEs only if certain specific areas are addressed in respect of autonomy accompanied by accountability. They are:

- Issues of ownership by the government and delegation of administrative and financial powers to CPSEs
- Audit of government companies
- Constitutional issues
- Parliamentary accountability
- Vigilance issues

CHAPTER 2: OWNERSHIP ISSUES AND POWERS OF CPSEs

2.1 The question of the autonomy of CPSEs essentially relates to the issues of ownership, control and management. Ownership is usually associated with the overall control of the enterprise for the long-term value creation of the company and achieving its medium and long-term objectives. The shareholders who are the owners seldom get involved in controlling the day-to-day operations of the company. For that, the companies have their Board of Directors, who are responsible for reviewing and overseeing the effectiveness of operations and management at periodic intervals. The Management, in turn, is in the charge of the Chief Executive of the company assisted by other functional Directors. In order to ensure effective governance of the company, it is necessary to properly design and implement the ownership functions, the powers and operational procedures of the Board of Directors and the responsibilities together with suitable checks and balances for exercising control over the Management.

2.2 For maintaining the overall control of the company, it is not necessary that the owner should own 100 per cent of the shares. A majority of shareholding is in most cases sufficient for all purposes and even a minority shareholding in a widely held company may often let the owners have basic control of the company operations, necessary to ensure the maintenance and improvement of the value of the assets of the company, as well as implementation of the programmes for realizing its basic objectives.

2.3 The National Common Minimum Programme (NCMP) of the UPA Government affirms commitment to a strong and effective public sector. To facilitate better commercial functioning of the successful and profit-making CPSEs which are operating in a competitive environment, the NCMP has pledged to devolve full managerial and commercial autonomy. It is also mentioned in the NCMP that generally profit-making CPSEs will not be privatized.

The Ad-hoc Group of Experts (AGE), therefore, felt that the government, as the principal owner of the CPSEs, should have complete flexibility of owning or disinvesting its shares to obtain the maximum value for their assets through sale and purchase or disinvestment and reinvestment of the shares. The Group was of the view that this issue has to be dealt with differentially by dividing the CPSEs in two categories: Navratnas, Miniratnas and other consistently profit-making CPSEs (those CPSEs which have been making profits for the past three consecutive years and have a positive net worth) in Category I and the other CPSEs in Category II.

In keeping with the letter and spirit of the NCMP, the Group was of the view that a decision, if any, to privatize a Category I CPSE by reducing government shareholding to a level less than 51 per cent in it should be taken only with the consent of the Parliament, as the ultimate representative of the people. However, in case of other CPSEs (Category II), the government should have full flexibility of owning or disinvesting their shares. The Board of Directors of both categories of CPSEs should also have the power to raise equity capital from the market, so long as the government's share of the overall equity remains above 51 per cent.

2.4 The Ministry in charge of the company should recognize the fact that they are not the owners of the company but are only exercising the functions of ownership as a custodian on behalf of the government and the public at large. The Group felt that the current system of the Ministry being in overall charge of a CPSE, facilitating its functions and looking after its interests has been quite useful and should therefore be continued, subject to certain suggestions which have been made in the subsequent paragraphs. However, it must be ensured that the Ministry takes into account not only the interest of the government as a whole but also of the non-governmental shareholders, who are equally interested in safeguarding the value of their asset. This is particularly important as many of the CPSEs are now listed in the stock markets, with their shares held by members of the public at large as well as financial/non-financial institutions. Furthermore, it also must be ensured that the government in discharging the functions of ownership does not get involved in controlling the details of operations and the day-to-day management of the company. Finally, as far as the listed CPSEs are concerned, the government should also facilitate the fulfillment of the provisions of Clause 49 of listing agreement, in conformity with the guidelines of the market regulator, SEBI.

2.5 The Group considered several models of ownership of companies and an arms-length relationship of government with the Board of Directors and the Management and came to the view that the governance of CPSEs, and especially the Navratnas and Miniratnas and other profit making companies should continue to be supervised by the three tier system, namely, the Ministry concerned representing the government, the Board of Directors, and the Management, with the role, powers and functions of each of them clearly defined and codified. After studying the working of all the three tiers involved, the Group was strongly of the view that an institutional arrangement is required in order to ensure harmonious relations and interactions among the three tiers and to provide for the redressal of grievances of the stakeholders. To fulfill this requirement, the Group recommends the establishment of six overarching sectoral Supervisory Bodies, consisting of ten members each, with the following composition:

Permanent Members

Minister of Finance
Minister in charge of DPE – Convener
Five independent distinguished experts of the relevant sector

Agenda Specific Members

Minister of Administrative Ministry of the concerned CPSE
Secretary of Administrative Ministry of the concerned CPSE
Chief Executive of the concerned CPSE

The five independent expert members representing diverse, professional and non-political interests from the relevant sector should be nominated for a fixed term by the Prime Minister.

Separate Supervisory Bodies should be set up for the sectors indicated below. These six sectors have been suggested to ensure that these bodies are not ministry-specific but cover a broad and diverse group of CPSEs.

Energy
Manufacturing
Infrastructure
Trading and Services
Food and Agriculture
Social Sector

The Role of the Supervisory Body

2.6 The Supervisory Body will undertake the following responsibilities:

- To take an overview of the conformity of corporate strategy to the Vision and the Mission of the CPSE.
- To periodically review interactions between the administrative Ministry and the CPSE.
- To be the arbiter of ethics; in particular, to review all allegations against the members of the Board of Directors and make appropriate recommendation to the concerned authority.
- To recommend continuation/separation of Functional Directors in case of difference between recommendations of the Public Enterprises Selection Board (PESB) and the Ministry concerned.
- To monitor redressal of stakeholder grievances.
- To consider any other issue to promote independent, efficient and cohesive functioning of the concerned Board of Directors.

The Supervisory Body should not give any direct instructions to the CPSEs. It should give its views only on matters referred to it. The Supervisory Body would also provide a formal grievance redressal system for the Board Members of CPSEs.

2.7 There are some issues related to Vigilance. Details of the same along with the suggested role of Supervisory Body in the resolution of such issues are dealt with in Chapter 6 under the heading 'Vigilance Management in Public Sector Enterprises'.

2.8 In all other matters, whenever there is a difference of views between the Ministry and the Management, the advice of the Supervisory Body must be sought prior to deciding any course of action by the government.

The Role of the Ministry

2.9 The Ministry should effectively perform the role of the shareholders and owners of the company. The Ministry should consult other ministries, including finance and other relevant departments and, where necessary, obtain the approval of the cabinet. It should facilitate the implementation of the projects of the company in conformity with overall government policy.

2.10 The Ministry, in exercising the function of ownership, is responsible for the appointment of the Chief Executive as well as the Functional Directors of the company. It should follow the established guidelines with regard to these appointments, based on the recommendation of PESB. Although the Ministries have the power to recommend the termination of their services to the PESB, in the case of appointment and termination (except in case of Schedule 'C' & 'D' CPSEs where the Ministry concerned is competent for such approvals if the same are in line with the PESB recommendations), the decisions of the Ministry concerned must continue to be subject to the approval of the Appointments Committee of the Cabinet. In the case of adverse actions like reprimand, suspension, premature termination, denial of extension of tenure, superseding the recommendations of PESB, etc., the case should be referred to the new Supervisory Body and ACC should take its views into account before taking any decision. It is further suggested that considering the benefits of continuity in leadership positions, the appointments to the Board level positions in CPSEs may be made for the period up to superannuation instead of shorter fixed tenure. In any case, the current system has a provision for premature termination in case of non-performance.

2.11 The views of the Ministry should be communicated for consideration by the Board of Directors through the government Directors, who would take up these matters at the meetings of the Board of Directors. The Ministry should not give instruction directly or indirectly to the management. That should be the prerogative of the Board of Directors.

2.12 The government Director(s) should interact with the companies only as Members of the Board, where decisions in general should continue to be taken by a consensus or a majority. If the government Director(s) feel that the Board of Directors has not appropriately taken into account the views of the Ministry on a given subject, they ought to refer the matter back to the Ministry, which after consulting the Supervisory Body, can instruct the Board of Directors and the Management to follow its directions. But such instructions must be given in the form of Presidential Directives. The issuance of such Presidential Directives should have the approval of the Cabinet.

2.13 The Ministry should not normally review the functioning of a CPSE more than twice a year. Such review should be based on reports of the Board of Directors and selected major performance indicators. These indicators, numbering not more than five, may be chosen from among the indicators agreed upon in the MoUs and considered appropriate by the Cabinet Secretariat and other agencies. The Ministry should be able to assess the performance of the company in terms of these indicators and also consider the fulfillment and non-fulfillment of the obligations of both the management of the company and of the government departments concerned as spelt out in the MoUs. A special review may, however, take place in addition to the half-yearly session, if the concerned Ministry wishes to take stock of any issue of outstanding importance referred by it to a CPSE.

Since the profitability of CPSEs is influenced by several factors such as the administered price mechanism and fluctuations in international price of the commodities, the Group recommends that the Ministries concerned should develop CPSE-specific criteria to determine their overall performance, independent of profitability.

2.14 The Group felt that to increase the autonomy of the CPSEs the government must accept the difference between ownership and management and ensure that CPSEs are run by the Boards of Directors and not by the owner. The procedures of governance suggested above should ensure such autonomy. However, in order to make the whole relationship clear and transparent, the Group recommends that there should be a negative list of areas which must be kept away from the intervention of the government (except for respective jurisdiction of CAG and CVC). That list should, *inter alia*, include:

- Decisions relating to Pricing/Distribution policy
- Decisions on Exports/Imports
- Appointment of dealers and agents
- Appointment/promotion/transfer/suspension of below Board level employees
- Award of Contracts and procurement decisions
- Selection of Consultants and Joint Venture partners
- Issuance of directive or guideline restricting the authority of the Board of Directors [empowerment once provided to the Board of Directors should not be diluted without the approval of the authority which had originally sanctioned it]
- Insistence on CPSEs furnishing information considered commercially sensitive by the Board of Directors in answers to questions raised in the Parliament and its Committees
- Issuance of instructions for intervening in any manner in the business or administrative decisions of the CPSEs

- Withholding of implementation of recommendations of PESB in respect of tenure extensions of Board Members
- Non observance of SEBI stipulations for listed companies regarding appointment of non-official Directors.

2.15 In regard to the investments of the company and the ceilings that currently exist for Joint Ventures and other Capital expenditures for the Navratna and Miniratna companies, the Group is of the view that these decisions should be left entirely to the Board of Directors and owners should only review the implementation of these decisions in light of the MoU-related performance indictors mentioned above. In case, there is any difficulty in implementing this recommendation immediately, it is suggested that the same could be executed in two steps.

As the first step, the Group recommends the delegation of authority to the Board of Directors of the Navratna, Miniratna and other profit-making CPSEs be raised as mentioned hereunder.

A. Investments for Capital Expenditure

For Navratnas

The Board of Directors to continue to enjoy the powers to approve investments in their own projects without any limits.

For Miniratnas-I

The delegation may be increased from the existing ₹ 300 cr. to Rs. 500 cr. or an amount equivalent to their net worth, whichever is less.

For Miniratnas-II

The delegation may be increased from the existing ₹ 150 cr. to ₹ 250 cr. or an amount equivalent to 50 per cent of their net worth, whichever is less.

For other Profit-making CPSEs

The delegation may be increased to ₹ 150 cr. or an amount equivalent to 50 per cent of their net worth, whichever is less.

B. Investments in Joint Ventures and Subsidiaries

For Navratnas

Keeping in view the increasingly large size of infrastructure projects and in order to achieve better economies of scale, Navratna delegation to invest equity in Joint Venture Companies/ Subsidiaries needs to be enhanced from ₹ 200 crore (up to a maximum of 5 per cent of Net Worth) in one project to at least ₹ 1000 crore or 15 per cent of Net Worth, whichever is less, in one Joint Venture/Subsidiary. Further, the present overall ceiling of equity investment up to 15 per cent of Net Worth in all Joint Ventures/Subsidiaries put together also needs to be increased to at least 30 per cent of the Net Worth.

For Miniratnas-I

Miniratna-I delegation to invest equity in Joint Venture Companies/Subsidiaries needs to be enhanced to ₹ 500 crore or 15 per cent of Net Worth, whichever is less, in one Joint Venture/Subsidiary. Further, the overall ceiling of equity investment in all Joint Ventures/Subsidiaries put together also needs to be increased to at least 30 per cent of Net Worth.

For Miniratnas-II

Miniratna-II delegation to invest equity in Joint Venture Companies/Subsidiaries needs to be enhanced to ₹ 250 crore or 15 per cent of Net Worth, whichever is less, in one Joint Venture/Subsidiary. Further, the overall ceiling of equity investment in all Joint Ventures/Subsidiaries put together also needs to be increased to at least 30 per cent of Net Worth.

For Other Profit-making CPSEs

These CPSEs may be delegated the powers to invest equity in Joint Venture Companies/Subsidiaries up to ₹ 100 crore or 15 per cent of Net Worth, whichever is less, in one Joint Venture/Subsidiary. Further, the overall ceiling of equity investment in all Joint Ventures/Subsidiaries should be 30 per cent of Net Worth.

However, if the Board of Directors feels it necessary to exceed the levels of investment limits recommended above in a given case, it may refer the matter to the Ministry for an appropriate decision in cases deserving of special consideration on individual merit.

C. Creation and Disinvestment of Subsidiaries

The Board of Directors may be empowered to create Subsidiaries for existing/new activities with equity investments within the overall limits specified for creating Subsidiaries. The Board of Directors may be further empowered to transfer assets to such subsidiaries from the parent company. The Board of Directors may also be empowered to float fresh equity and divest their shareholding in such Subsidiaries complying with SEBI guidelines. However, in case any existing fixed assets of the holding company have been transferred to a Subsidiary, then such subsidiary may not be allowed to transfer these assets to anyone other than the parent CPSE. Also, disinvestment in such a subsidiary company to an extent of more than 50 per cent, if proposed at a later date by the holding CPSE, would require the approval of the Government.

D. Subsequent Investments in Successful JVs

The above mentioned limits may be applicable only for initial investments in these joint ventures. In case the JV Company is operating successfully for a defined period, say two years, any further investment in such successful and profitable Joint Ventures may not have any limitations prescribed.

E. JVs between Navratnas

While there is no restriction on Capital investment that a Navratna company can make in its own projects/ventures, there is a restriction on the amount of investment it can make when two or more Navratna CPSEs take up a project/venture together. It would therefore be in the fitness of things that Navratna CPSEs should have powers to make equity investments without any limit in Joint Ventures with other Navratna CPSE(s).

F. Mergers and Acquisitions

As per existing Delegation of Powers, Navratna and Miniratna companies can enter into Joint Venture arrangements within the parameters laid down in the respective circulars.

However, for equity participation in existing companies or acquiring stake in existing/new companies or for deciding on mergers and acquisitions for promoting further business, prior approval of Government is required. The powers to decide on mergers, acquisitions and acquiring minority or majority stakes in existing or new companies should be delegated to the Boards of Directors of Navratna and Miniratna CPSEs where such decisions are necessary to facilitate business promotion within ceilings as proposed for Joint Ventures.

G. Investment Approvals where Budgetary Support is Involved

At present the Navratnas, Miniratnas and other profit making CPSEs are not permitted to avail of Budgetary Support even for expansion, diversification or other developmental purposes without losing their Navratna/Miniratna status. The Group recommends that these restrictions may be relaxed so that Budgetary Support to implement planned developmental activities should not result in disqualifying the CPSEs from retaining their Navratna/Miniratna status.

H. Investment Approval for Projects Involving Government Guarantees

The Boards of Directors of Navratna, Miniratna and other profit making CPSEs should be given powers to approve Capital expenditure without the requirement of seeking PIB/CCEA approvals even in case of projects involving government guarantees, as funding by multilateral agencies invariably involves government guarantee. However, this should be subject to ceilings, if any, prescribed for investment delegations.

I. Appointment of Functional Directors in Subsidiaries and JVs by the Board of Directors of the Holding Company

CPSEs have been entering new business fields to add value to their core business. Sometimes they choose to do so through a JV or a Subsidiary with the intention to bring in the required technological/managerial expertise as well as to protect the parent balance sheet from the business risks of the new venture. Such new ventures can succeed only when they work in a seamless manner with the parent organization to leverage the parent's strength. Also, complete accountability of the management of the Joint Venture/Subsidiary to the parent organization is absolutely essential for the new venture to progress and add value to the core business of the parent organization. Company law provides for the placement of Functional Directors in the subsidiaries by the holding company. However, Government of India (Transaction of Business) Rules, 1961 provide for the appointment of Functional Directors by the government. The Group recommends that full-time Board level appointments in Joint Ventures/Subsidiaries may be made by the Board of Directors of the holding Company in line with provisions of Sections 255, 256 and 257 of the Companies Act for partly owned Government companies.

J. Chief Executive to be Member in the Search Committee for Independent Directors

The guidelines of DPE and SEBI require CPSEs to have some Independent Directors on their Board of Directors. With the market becoming more complicated, performance and survival of the CPSEs require the wise counsel and directions by eminent persons with good stature in the industry and the market. To identify and induct such eminent persons, there is a need to adhere strictly to the prescribed qualification requirements without any dilution. Also, Search Committees formed to identify Independent Directors should include the Chief Executive of the concerned CPSE as a Member.

The Group further recommends that the restrictions contained in the interim delegation by way of the first step towards autonomy of successful CPSEs as described above, should be removed as the next and final step within a period of three years from now, whereafter investment decisions should be entirely left to the Board of Directors.

2.16 The Board of Directors already have the full authority to raise short-term or long-term loans from the market without any prior approval from the Government, subject to existing rules and procedures laid down by regulatory authorities like the RBI or SEBI. In the same manner, the Board of Directors should have the power to raise equity capital from the market, so long as the government's share of the overall equity remains above 51 per cent. Raising such equity may require enhancement of the authorized capital, for which government permission would be necessary. It may be stipulated that such permission for expanding the authorized capital would be given in a time-bound manner provided the government's shareholding does not fall below 51 per cent. At the time of granting such approval, the government may decide to extinguish a part of its shareholding at the price which the company shares command in the market. If the government does extinguish some shares in this manner it would amount to disinvestment in a transparent market-determined way. But if the government does not extinguish any share, the proportion of the government's shareholding would come down without giving up the ownership or control over the company.

2.17 Finally, there are certain issues like foreign travel of the Chief Executive and the Functional Directors, which are currently referred to the Ministry for approval. The Group felt that there should be detailed procedural guidelines including limits of financial expenditure in this regard formulated by the Board of Directors of the CPSE concerned, and accordingly recommends that no reference to the Government for approval should be necessary unless deviation from guidelines approved by the Board is intended.

The Role of the Board of Directors

2.18 The Board of Directors should be fully responsible for the control and supervision of the Management of the company. It should be responsible for placement and promotion of senior personnel, formulation of company's policy for creation/abolition/up-gradation of posts, rewards and incentives for meritorious performance and out-of-turn promotions, and on all matters relating to human resource development.

2.19 The Board of Directors, subject to statutory requirements, government policy and regulatory guidelines issued by RBI, should have the powers to pursue new lines of business, make suitable acquisitions of companies, set up JVs/ Subsidiaries and exit a line of business, and to make Capital expenditure up to levels as indicated in Para 2.15 without prior approval of the government.

2.20 No more than two officers should be nominated as Board Members by the government on the Board of Directors for Navratna, Miniratna or other profit-making CPSEs. The performance of government Directors on Board of Directors of CPSEs must be suitably reflected in their Confidential Reports. Furthermore, it is suggested that a suitable appraisal system for performance review of non-official Independent Directors may also be developed.

2.21 Existing DPE guideline for CPSEs permits 5 per cent of distributable profit to be allocated to employees as performance-linked bonus/incentive. Functional Directors of CPSEs serve on contract/covenant and their compensation is governed by the terms and conditions of the appointment. However, keeping in mind the significance of the role played by the leadership (the Chief Executive and the Functional Directors) in the success of the organization, the Group is of the view that the Chief Executive and the Functional Directors should also be entitled to performance linked bonus/incentive within the permissible limit of 5 per cent of distributable profit. The Group recommends that the Compensation Committee of the Board as constituted under the 'Listing Agreement' may decide the quantum of such performance linked incentives, on the basis of the individual's performance and contributions during the year under review. The Compensation Committee may also devise CPSE-specific norms for determination of such incentives. Such bonus/ incentives would, however, be governed by the limits prescribed in the Companies Act.

The Role of the Management

2.22 The Chief Executive should be entirely responsible for the day-to-day management and operation of the company under the overall supervision of the Board of Directors. The appointment of the Chief Executive should be made strictly in accordance with the procedures laid down for this purpose.

2.23 The Management should be free to exercise all powers explicitly delegated by the Board of Directors. It should function under the supervision of the Chief Executive and Functional Directors on the Board.

2.24 It should be responsible for implementation of the decisions of the Board of Directors and compliance of all statutory requirements as well as policy guidelines.

CHAPTER 3: AUDIT OF GOVERNMENT COMPANIES

3.1 Pursuant to Section 19(1) of Comptroller and Auditor General's (CAG) Duties, Powers and Conditions of Service Act, 1971, audit of the accounts of government companies is conducted by the Comptroller and Auditor General in accordance with the provisions of the Companies Act, 1956. Under Section 619 of the Companies Act, 1956, the Auditor (Chartered Accountant) of a government company is appointed or re-appointed by CAG. It is further stipulated that CAG shall have the power to (a) direct the auditor to conduct the audit in a specified manner, (b) give instructions on any matter relating to the performance of his functions, (c) conduct himself a supplementary or test audit of the company's accounts and (d) comment upon or supplement the audit report in such manner as he (CAG) thinks fit. The comments of CAG are to be placed before AGM along with Auditor's Report.

3.2 As regards the present status of audit in CPSEs, CAG appoints the statutory auditor of government company. The statutory auditor audits the account of the CPSEs in accordance with the provisions of Companies Act and other applicable statutes. CAG has issued directions to statutory auditors of government companies requiring them to furnish to CAG a detailed report covering various items specified in the questionnaire, in addition to the normal auditor's report under Companies Act, 1956, within three weeks from the date of signing their Auditors' Report. After the receipt of certified accounts and Auditor's Report, CAG conducts supplementary or test audit based on which the comments of CAG upon the report of Statutory Auditors or a supplementary report by him may be issued. These comments form part and parcel of Auditor's Report. CAG also does a transaction/propriety audit in addition to supplementary/test audit. In some CPSEs there are resident audit parties who conduct concurrent audit. Under such audit, the propriety of the transaction is also subjected to scrutiny. The authority of such audit is not specified as far as Companies Act, 1956 is concerned.

3.3 CONCERNS OF CPSEs

Test/Supplementary Audit

The basic concern of CPSEs regarding test/supplementary audit of CAG is that it leads to delay in finalization of audit of accounts resulting in non-compliance of directives of SEBI regarding publication of audited results and quarterly results.

Since statutory audit is conducted by statutory auditor appointed by the CAG in the manner directed by him, it is felt that the test/supplementary audit is duplication of audit work already done by statutory auditor.

Transaction/Test Audit

The main focus of such audit is to bring to light the mistakes made in the past. On account of the benefit of hindsight, circumstances/compulsions under which such business decisions were taken tend to get glossed over or ignored by the auditor.

Such audit highlights only isolated deficiencies of CPSEs which damage their corporate image in the public to the detriment of their commercial interests.

Such audit also leads to a defensive attitude on the part of corporate executives leading to delay in decisions which may not be in the best commercial interests of the Company.

3.4 The requirement of transaction audit is perhaps borrowed from the system of audit in government. CPSEs, being commercial entities, have their own system of internal audit which requires compliance in conformity with standards laid down by the Institute of Chartered Accountants of India, disclosure guidelines of SEBI (for listed companies) and compliance to the observations of Audit Committees and Statutory Audit.

Keeping in view the above statutory requirements and concerns of CPSEs, the Group makes the following suggestions which may be considered for implementation.

Test/Supplementary Audit

- CAG may consider issuance of revised guidelines to statutory auditors and rely mainly on their report.
- Test/supplementary audit may be resorted to only in exceptional cases rather than as a routine exercise.
- Appointment of Statutory Auditors may be made at the earliest in the beginning of financial year.
- Appointment of Branch auditors may be dispensed with. Only those firms of Chartered Accountants which are capable of making Head Office as well as Branch Office audit may be considered for appointment.
- CAG may also consider giving suitable directions for consultations with Statutory Auditors at appropriate levels to minimize the need for supplementary audit.
- CAG may consider making its audit concurrent with the audit by statutory auditors so as to complete it along with the audit by the statutory auditors. Normally statutory auditors conduct their audit in two phases

i.e. one up to December which is completed before end of the year and next phase after year end. CAG may also like to adopt similar practice.

Transaction/Test Audit

After considerable deliberation, the Group was of the view that only malafide intentional mistakes, frauds, gross negligence or willful ignorance of advice/suggestions should form part of Audit Observation. However, bonafide errors of judgment may be mentioned by the audit only as suggestions for improvement of performance in future. Overall performance should be the guiding criterion rather than review of individual commercial decision. Otherwise the Executives will be apprehensive of making commercial judgements and decisions, which will be detrimental to the commercial interest of CPSEs.

CHAPTER 4: ARTCLE 12 OF THE CONSTITUTION AND CPSEs

4.1 Some judicial pronouncements have declared public enterprises to be an extension or arm of the State under Article 12 of the Constitution. Under Article 12, 'State', unless the context otherwise requires, includes the government and Parliament of India and the governments and Legislature of each of the states and all local or other authorities within the territory of India or under the control of the Government of India. Although Article 12, in so many words, does not provide that CPSEs fall within the definition of the 'State', they still are deemed as being included in the category 'other authorities' and therefore, covered under the definition of 'State' as pronounced by different Courts including the Apex Court.

4.2 In the competitive environment in the wake of liberalization/globalization, this situation undermines the entrepreneurial and commercial functioning of public enterprises and puts them at a disadvantageous position vis-à-vis their private sector counterparts and competitors. This negation of the essential distinction between government *per se* and public enterprise—a distinction conceived by Parliament and embodied in the Industrial Policy Resolution of 1956—has led to a situation where any aggrieved employee or contractor can move the court against the management of public enterprises calling in question individual actions or decisions in the same way as against the State. This would seem to imply that government enterprises can function only as government departments and in accordance with the modalities, procedures and styles similar to government administration. This impedes decision-making in CPSEs, particularly in the competitive environment in the wake of liberalization/globalization. Indeed, it is precisely because business cannot be run efficiently in the normal governmental style and in accordance with government procedures that public enterprises have been organized in the corporate form.

4.3 It was brought to the notice of the Group that the matter was considered by the Committee of Secretaries in 1987 and, based on its decision, the same was referred to the Ministry of Law suggesting that the possibility of inserting an explanation below the Article 12 may be examined. The suggested insertion was as under: "A statutory corporation, a company formed and registered under the Companies Act, 1956 or a society under the Societies Registration Act shall not be considered as 'State' for the purpose of this Article".

4.4 The Ministry of Law placed the issue before the Law Commission which looked into various possibilities but could not find a solution. In its 145th Report submitted in 1992, the Law Commission concluded as follows:

> Such an amendment would not be a proper or necessary measure to be adopted for dealing with the difficulties that may be experienced by public sector undertakings in the matter of award of contracts, rejection of tenders, service matters and the like arising out of the present applicability of Article 12 to such undertakings.

Having regard to the Preamble and total philosophy of the Constitution, even if such an amendment is made, some of the problems experienced by the public sector undertakings would still survive under the ordinary law.

In particular, judicial intervention in the form of injunctions issued under the ordinary law cannot be ruled out, even after the suggested amendment.

It is highly doubtful whether, in the light of the theory of non-amenability of the basic features of the Constitution as at present recognized, such an amendment will pass muster on the Constitution level.

4.5 While taking note of the deliberations on the subject in the past, one should still consider the dynamic changes that are taking place in the business and economic environment on account of globalization. Global competition is cutting into the margins and market shares of Indian corporates, including CPSEs, facilitated by crumbling tariff barriers. The far-reaching mandatory legal implications of Article 12 inhibit the functioning of CPSEs as commercial entities like similar companies in the private sector. In consideration of the foregoing position, the Group recommends that this issue could be revisited by the policy makers at an appropriate time in future.

CHAPTER 5: PARLIAMENTARY ACCOUNTABILITY

5.1 In India, government companies are governed by the provisions of Indian Companies Act 1956. Under Section 620 of the Act, the Central Government has a right to exempt partly or wholly the application of any provision of the Act to the government companies except Sections 618, 619(A). The audit and accountability to Parliament is prescribed under Sections 619 and 619(A) of the Companies Act which relate to audit and admission of annual report.

5.2 Public enterprises are accountable to the people through their elected representatives. Parliament exercises surveillance of a general nature over them and makes major legislative decisions about the policies relating to public enterprises. Parliament also authorizes budgetary allocations for investment and other needs of public enterprises where required. The property, assets, powers and functions of public enterprises emerge directly or indirectly from one or another legislation passed by the Parliament. Public enterprises, while enjoying autonomy in financial matters, are ultimately accountable to Parliament for investments made in them from the Consolidated Fund of India.

5.3 Currently, Parliament exercises control over the CPSEs in the following manner:

- Members of the Parliament can ask questions to the concerned Minister on the working of public enterprises under his charge.
- Members of Parliament can discuss the affair of the public enterprises when the House takes up demands for grants for discussion and vote.
- Parliament can examine the working of selected enterprises through its committees.
- Parliament receives every year a comprehensive appraisal of the working of selected public enterprises done by the Audit Board.
- Public enterprises are required to present to Parliament their annual report together with a copy of the audit report made by the CAG of India.
- Oral Evidence of CPSEs before Parliamentary Committees is also required to be given from time to time.

5.4 The Chief Executives of Navratna CPSEs were given an opportunity to express their views before the Group. Their views are summarized below:

- Accountability to Parliament may be deemed as complied with through Annual Reports.

- Questions on sensitive operational matters need to be avoided in the interest of business confidentiality and competitiveness of CPSEs.
- Screening Committee may be set up for Parliament Questions so as to avoid submission of voluminous data and sensitive business information.
- Instead of various Parliamentary Committees, there should be only one Committee which should cover all aspects.
- Obligations should be the same for public and private sector in the interest of level playing field.
- Independent body should be created to exercise all ownership rights of the Government.
- Parliament should focus mainly on the review of performance of CPSEs.

5.5 On the basis of the above cited presentations and discussions, the Group would suggest the following for the consideration of appropriate authorities:

- Day-to-day affairs of CPSEs may not be taken up in the Parliament
- Conduct of Chief Executive and Functional Directors may not be discussed in the Parliament as there are other fora available for this purpose.
- It is essential to distinguish between accountability to Parliament and involvement of the Government in day to day functioning, personnel related matters etc. of CPSEs.
- Control points and occasions could be few, effective and concerned with major aspects of public enterprise policy. Their focus should be on enabling the enterprises to fulfill the norms of accountability expected of them.
- Profitability and working could be tested from time to time by the Parliament in enterprises where production and expansion are taking place since it involves government expenditure.

- Appropriate competent authorities in the government and the Parliament may therefore like to consider setting up of a screening committee to screen Parliament questions from the angle mentioned above as well as the need for confidentiality of business decisions.

CHAPTER 6: VIGILANCE MANAGEMENT IN PUBLIC SECTOR ENTERPRISES

6.1 The Central Vigilance Commission (CVC) was set up by the Government of India by its Resolution dated 11.2.1964 in pursuance of the recommendations of the Santhanam Committee. The Commission acts as the apex body for exercising general superintendence and control over vigilance matters with a view to ensuring probity in public administration. It is vested with the authority of initiating investigations/enquiries into cases involving corruption, malpractices and lack of integrity. The CVC possesses statutory status by virtue of the Central Vigilance Commission Bill passed by the Parliament which received assent of the President on 11 September 2003. The aim of the Act is to provide for the constitution of CVC to inquire into offences alleged to have been committed under the Prevention of Corruption Act, 1988 by certain categories of public servants including those of public enterprises.

6.2 Section 8(1)(h) of the Act provides that the Commission shall exercise superintendence over the administration of various Ministries of the Central Government or Corporations established by or under any Central Act, Government Companies, Societies and Local Authorities owned or controlled by the Government. Executives on the Board of Directors of CPSEs and two levels below the Board of Directors fall within the purview of CVC, as important decision making in most of the CPSEs is limited to two levels below the Board level. The Commission tenders appropriate advice to the concerned disciplinary authorities in all matters of corruption, malpractices, misconduct, lack of integrity, etc.

6.3 **Special Chapter on Vigilance Management in CPSEs:** CVC in consultation with the Department of Personnel and Training (DoPT) and some other bodies had issued a Special Chapter on Vigilance Management in CPSEs and the role and functioning of CVC. It covers the entire gamut of vigilance principles and procedures to regulate vigilance management in CPSEs to deal with any complaints of corruption, gross negligence, misconduct, recklessness, lack of integrity or other kinds of malpractices on the part of public servants.

Present Vigilance Set Up in CPSEs

6.4 A study was conducted by Department of AR&PG on vigilance set-up in respect of CPSEs. It prescribed a Model Vigilance Structure at different levels (Corporate/ Unit/Regional) in CPSEs to deal with investigations, disciplinary proceedings, anti-corruption work and preventive vigilance with adequate personnel to carry out all necessary functions to prevent possibilities of corruption. Guidelines have been issued to the CPSEs for necessary compliance as per the size of the organization. Under Section 8(1)(h) of the Act Central Vigilance Commission has issued instructions to the CPSEs to encourage a culture of honesty, greater transparency in administration, speedy departmental inquiries, transparent decision-making on NITs, etc.

6.5 **Appointment of Chief Vigilance Officers:** To provide for adequate vigilance apparatus in CPSEs, appointment of Chief Vigilance Officer (CVO) with concurrence of Central Vigilance Commission has to be made along with a number of vigilance officers with desired manpower requirements of skilled and trained vigilance personnel. The CVO acts as a link with the CVC and CPSEs. He functions as the principal vigilance aide to the Chief Executive and as the focal point in respect of the entire work relating to vigilance. The role of the Chief Vigilance Officer is both preventive and punitive.

6.6 CPSEs having full-time posts of CVOs fill up such posts as per the procedure prescribed for appointments under the Central Staffing Scheme. DoPT requests the Cadre Controlling Authority of various organized services to offer officers of proven integrity for these posts. The names so received are forwarded along with bio-data of the officers concerned and their ACR dossiers to the Commission for approval. The DoPT maintains a panel of names approved by the Commission, which are operative for a period of one year. The Commission then prepares a panel of names and recommends it to the administrative Ministry/Department concerned for making appointment.

In case of CPSEs which do not have full-time posts of CVOs, one of the officers from a panel of three senior officers forwarded to CVC by the PSE is selected by the Commission as the CVO.

6.7 **Examinations/Investigations of Complaint against Board Level Appointees:** CVC has issued necessary instructions in the matter of dealing with complaints against the Board Level Appointees. If the CVO of an administrative Ministry asks for a factual report against a Board level appointee from the CVO of the PSE, the latter sends the same to the CVO of the Ministry, after endorsing a copy of the report to the CMD to keep him informed of the development. However, if the CMD himself is the subject matter of the investigation, the CVO of the PSE need not endorse a copy of the report to him. In such cases it is the responsibility of the CVO of the Ministry to obtain the version of CMD at the appropriate time. The CVO of the Ministry has to make a reference to the CVC after collecting all the relevant facts and following the prescribed procedure.

6.8 **Investigations by the CBI-Constitution of Central Advisory Board:** The special chapter on Vigilance Management issued by CVC provides as under:

Considering the complexities involved in commercial decisions of the PSE, the CBI may find it worthwhile to obtain the benefit of expert advice from various disciplines before registration of PE/RC. A Central Advisory Board may be constituted to assist CBI for this purpose. Appointments on the Board may be made from the panel of names approved by the CVC. The Board should give its considered opinion within one month from the date of reference before registration of PE/RC, failing which the CBI would be competent to decide the matter without advice. Advice of the Board should not be binding on the CBI.

6.9 **Strengthening of Vigilance Machinery in CPSEs:** CVC has been issuing necessary instructions to strengthen vigilance set-up in the CPSEs. The CVOs of the level of Joint Secretaries to the Govt. of India and above in the Schedule 'A' and 'B' Companies have been given status equivalent to that of a Functional Director with other facilities and perquisites available to the Functional Directors in these companies. CVC has also recommended creation of the post of CVO at the level of Functional Director in Schedule 'A' companies, which has hitherto been acted upon only in the Navratna CPSEs.

Concerns/Suggestions of Chief Executives of CPSEs

6.10 The current business environment calls for speedy decision making amid a welter of factors and changes induced by globalization, liberalization, technology changes and continuously increasing competition. Public Sector Enterprises are being evaluated as commercial entities and are expected to take business decisions in a dynamic scenario. There is need to empower these CPSEs by providing mechanisms which would enable speedier decision making in a changing business environment with all the inherent risks.

6.11 During the discussions with Chief Executives of some of the Navratna central public sector enterprises, certain points relating to vigilance administration in CPSEs were brought to the notice of the Ad Hoc Expert Group. Views were expressed to the effect that the role of CBI/CVC should be restricted and CPSE executives may be protected against misconceived and unnecessary vigilance action based on lack of full appreciation of business related decisions. It was suggested that necessary measures may be recommended in this regard so that executives in CPSEs do not shy away from taking business decisions on account of fear of vigilance action. This is particularly significant for improving the commercial functioning of CPSEs in the competitive environment in the wake of liberalization/globalization.

6.12 CVC had constituted a Committee under the Chairmanship of Shri Arvind Pande, ex-Chairman, SAIL to study the vigilance administration in the Public Sector Enterprises and to recommend measures to strengthen it. The Committee has since submitted its report to the Commission and the recommendations made therein are under consideration of the Commission in consultation with concerned Ministries/Departments for a final decision on the report. Some of the recommendations of Arvind Pande Committee are relevant to the issues raised by the Chief Executives of some Navratna CPSEs before the Expert Group. Keeping the committees recommendations in mind, the Group recommends the following:

- The CVC and the CPSEs need to adopt an approach of capacity building that can integrate better with the modern day requirements of risk management, security management, and financial controls and compliance. This effort will add discernible value to the competitiveness of the enterprise apart from promoting probity, and integrity amongst public officials and supporting, synergizing and fostering corporate governance.
- The coverage of CVC's jurisdiction should be restricted to executives of E-8, E-9 levels and Functional Directors (including the Chief Executive) of all companies. This ensures parity going by the pay scales of Schedule-D companies' directors and the E-8. However, the CVC

may consider making specific exemptions in the case of select Navratnas, which have in place internal systems, controls, and procedures that would demonstrably meet the preset standards evolved by the CVC. In case of such exceptions, the CVC's jurisdiction could be limited to the Director level only. However, it is recommended that this empowerment should be earned by the respective organizations by meeting quality standards and subject to withdrawal of the privilege should their systems fall short of the standards in future.

- Anonymous and pseudonymous complaints forwarded by Hon'ble MPs or MLAs should be verified by the concerned CVOs or official. Where the complainant is identifiable, it could be suggested to the MP or MLA concerned to obtain the complainant's signature and name, failing which the case may be proceeded with as if the Hon'ble MP or MLA is the complainant.
- The CVC may consider issuing guidelines specifically allowing CPSEs to initiate proceedings under the relevant sections of the IPC and the CrPC in all cases wherein complaints have delayed strategic decisions and are ultimately found to be unfounded, malicious and false.
- The process of vigilance clearance may be simplified in the case of PSE officials aspiring for Board appointments. The CVO concerned should be empowered to verify the records, make enquiries, and furnish the assessment without countrywide scrutiny through various CBI offices. It is also recommended that a period of 5 years should be the periodicity of reverification, unless there is good reason to do so at a shorter interval.
- Prior approval of the government in the concerned Ministry is required for launching criminal prosecution against officers above a designated rank working with the Ministry. The employees of PSEs who are equivalent

in rank to that level should be treated on par with the latter as CPSEs are treated as government and its employees as public servants.

- Furthermore, the vigilance cases against Board members of CPSEs need to be referred to the 'Advisory Board' of CVC (similar to the one constituted for the Banking sector) as envisaged in para 3.3.29 of Pande Committee Report to determine whether a given decision was *bona fide* or *mala fide*. The decision of the Advisory Board should be binding on the investigating agency.
- If as a result of the inquiry it is proposed to launch prosecution, then the sanctions/permissions for initiating prosecution or suspension of the Board level incumbents should be granted after fully consulting the Supervisory Body. The recommendation of the Supervisory Body should normally be accepted by the prosecuting agencies, unless there are strong reasons for a contrary view.
- The CVOs should be trained more frequently and intensively, and should be adequately equipped with knowledge of management audit, decision making processes, domain issues of particular industries, financial analysis and transaction, risk management, control systems, coordination abilities, etc.
- The vigilance set up of Subsidiaries of CPSEs should be under the vigilance administration of the holding company and need not have direct interface with the CVC.
- Decision on suspension of Board level officials by the Ministry must be taken after obtaining the concurrence of the Supervisory Body. In case of other officials below Board-level concurrence of the sub-committee of the Board must be obtained.

No. 18(24)/2003-GM
Government of India
Ministry of Heavy Industry & Public Enterprises
Department of Public Enterprises

Block No. 14, CGO Complex,
Lodhi Road, New Delhi 110003

Dated the 11th November, 2004

Subject: Constitution of an Ad-hoc Group of experts to consider issues relating to autonomy, delegation of financial powers, etc. of Central Public Sector Undertakings.

It has been decided to set up an Ad-hoc Group of expert to consider issues like autonomy, greater delegation of financial powers, corporate governance, R&D, technological upgradation, effective functioning in a competitive environment, etc. related to the Central Public Sector Undertakings in the context of the mandate under the National Common Minimum Programme.

2. The composition of the Group is as under:

(i) Dr. Arjun Sengupta, Chairman
(ii) Shri Anwarul Hoda, Member, Planning Commission
(iii) Dr. Adarsh Kishore, Secretary to Government, Department of Public Enterprises, Convenor
(iv) Dr. Nitish Sengupta
(v) Shri Moosa Raza
(vi) Shri Prabir Sengupta
(vii) Shri Subir Raha, CMD, ONGC Ltd.
(viii) Shri C.P. Jain, CMD, NTPC Ltd. and Chairman, SCOPE
(ix) Shri A.K. Rath, Joint Secretary, DPE

3. Detailed Terms of Reference of the Group shall be notified separately.

4. The Ad-hoc Group will submit its recommendations to the government within one month's time.

(G.S. Bothyal)
Director
Tel. 24360218

To

Members of the Group
Copy to PS to Secretary (PE)

No. 18(24)/2003-GM
Government of India
Ministry of Heavy Industry & Public Enterprises
Department of Public Enterprises

Block No. 14, CGO Complex,
Lodhi Road, New Delhi 110003
Dated the 25th February, 2005

Subject: Constitution of an Ad-hoc Group of Experts to consider issues relating to autonomy, delegation of financial powers, etc. of Central Public Sector Undertakings.

In continuation to this Department's Notification of even number dated 11th November, 2004 on the subject mentioned above, it has now decided that Shri Priyadarshi Thakur, Secretary, Department of Public Enterprises will be a Member of the Ad-hoc Group of Experts. Dr. Adarsh Kishore, former Secretary, Department of Public Enterprises and presently OSD (Expenditure), Ministry of Finance would continue to be the Convener of the Group.

The issues with the approval of the competent authority.

(K.D. Tripathi)
Joint Secretary to the Govt. of India
Tel: 24360204

1. Dr. Arjun Sengupta, Chairman, Room No. 36, Udyog Bhawan, New Delhi-1.
2. Shri Anwarul Hoda, Member, Planning Commission, Yojna Bhawan, New Delhi-1.
3. Dr. Nitish Sengupta, Pocket 40, H.N. 135, C.R. Park, New Delhi.
4. Shri Prabir Sengupta, DG, Indian Institute of Foreign Trade, New Delhi-16.

5. Shri Moosa Raza, Move Pvt. Ltd., 5A, Atmaram Housing Society, 1, Tolstoy Marg, New Delhi-1.
6. Dr. Adarsh Kishore, OSD (Expenditure), Department of Expenditure, North Block, New Delhi-1.
7. Shri Priyadarshi Thakur, Secretary, Department of Public Enterprises, Udyog Bhawan, New Delhi.
8. Shri Subir Raha, CMD, ONGC Ltd., Jeevan Bharati Building, 124, Indira Chowk, New Delhi-1.
9. Shri C.P. Jain, CMD, NTPC and Chairman, SCOPE, Core-7, SCOPE Complex, New Delhi-3.

Annexure–II

Guidelines on Corporate Governance for Central Public Sector Enterprises – 2010 (Deptt. of Public Enterprises, Ministry of Heavy Industries and Public Enterprises, Govt. of India)

CHAPTER 1: INTRODUCTION

1.1 Corporate Governance involves a set of relationships between a company's management, its Board, its shareholders and other stakeholders. Corporate Governance provides a principled process and structure through which the objectives of the company, the means of attaining the objectives and systems of monitoring performance are also set. Corporate Governance is a set of accepted principles by management of the inalienable rights of the shareholders as a true owner of the corporation and of their own role as trustees on behalf of the shareholders. It is about commitment to values, ethical business conduct, transparency and makes a distinction between personal and corporate funds in the management of a company.

1.2 There are about 250 Central Public Sector Enterprises (CPSEs). Majority of these CPSEs, including Maharatnas, Navratnas and Miniratnas, are earning profit and have improved their financial performance over the years. In the context of the policy of the government to grant more autonomy to the CPSEs and encourage them to access the capital markets for their fund requirement, Corporate Governance has become even more important. Under the recently introduced Maharatna Scheme, CPSEs are expected to expand international operations and become global giants, for which effective Corporate Governance is imperative.

1.3 These guidelines on Corporate Governance are formulated with the objective that the CPSEs follow the guidelines in their functioning. Proper implementation of these guidelines would protect the interest of shareholders and relevant stakeholders.

1.4 The Department of Public Enterprises (DPE) had issued guidelines on composition of Board of Directors of Central Public Sector Enterprises (CPSEs) in 1992 (**Annex-I**). According to these guidelines at least one-third of the Directors on the Board of a CPSE should be non-official Directors. The Maharatna, Navratna and Miniratna schemes provide that exercise of the enhanced powers delegated to these CPSEs is subject to the condition that their Boards are professionalised by inducting adequate number of non-official Directors, with minimum of four in case of Maharatna, Navratnas and minimum of three in case of Miniratnas. The schemes for Maharatna, Navratna and Miniratna CPSEs also provide for setting up of Audit Committees.

1.5 In November 2001, DPE issued further guidelines on the composition of Board of Directors of listed CPSEs (**Annex-II**). It provided that the number of Independent Directors should be at least one-third of the Board if the Chairman is non-executive, and not less than 50 per cent if the Board has an executive Chairman. Relevant extracts of Clause 49 of the Listing Agreement with Stock Exchanges issued by Securities and Exchange Board of India (SEBI) forms part of the said guidelines.

1.6 To bring in more transparency and accountability in the functioning of CPSEs, the Government in June, 2007 introduced, for an experimental period of one year, the Guidelines on Corporate Governance for CPSEs. These Guidelines were of voluntary nature. Since the issue of these guidelines, the CPSEs have had the opportunity to implement them for the whole of the financial year 2008-09. These Guidelines have been modified and improved upon based on the experience gained during the experimental period of one year. The Government have felt the need for continuing the adoption of good Corporate Governance Guidelines by CPSEs for ensuring higher level of transparency and decided to make these Guidelines mandatory and applicable to all CPSEs.

1.7 Apart from these instructions of DPE, the CPSEs are governed by the Companies Act, 1956 and regulations of various authorities like Comptroller and Auditor General of India (CAG), Central Vigilance Commission (CVC), Administrative Ministries, other nodal Ministries, etc. The Right to Information Act, 2005 is also applicable to the CPSEs. The CPSEs fall under the definition of 'State' as provided in Article 12 of the Constitution of India. Further, some principles of Corporate Governance are already in vogue in public sector because (a) the Chairman, Managing Director and Directors are appointed independently through a prescribed procedure; (b) Statutory auditors are appointed independently by the CAG; (c) Arbitrary actions, if any, of the Management can be challenged through writ petitions; (d) Remuneration of Directors, employees, etc. are determined on the basis of recommendations of Pay Committees constituted for this purpose; etc.

CHAPTER 2: APPLICABILITY OF GUIDELINES

2.1 For the purpose of evolving Guidelines on Corporate Governance, CPSEs have been categorised into two groups, namely (i) those listed on the Stock Exchanges; (ii) those not listed on the Stock Exchanges.

CPSEs Listed on Stock Exchanges

2.2 In so far as listed CPSEs are concerned, they have to follow the SEBI Guidelines on Corporate Governance. In addition, they shall follow those provisions in these Guidelines which do not exist in the SEBI Guidelines and also do not contradict any of the provisions of the SEBI Guidelines.

Non-listed CPSEs

2.3 Each CPSE should strive to institutionalize good Corporate Governance practices broadly in conformity with the SEBI Guidelines. The listing of the non-listed CPSEs on the stock exchanges may also be considered within a reasonable time frame to be set by the Administrative Ministry concerned in consultation with the CPSEs concerned. The non-listed CPSEs shall follow the Guidelines on Corporate Governance given in the subsequent chapters, which are mandatory.

2.4 The guidelines on Corporate Governance for listed and unlisted CPSEs are being dealt in the succeeding chapters under the following headings.

- Board of Directors
- Audit Committee
- Remuneration Committee
- Subsidiary Companies
- Disclosures
- Report, Compliance and Schedule of Implementation

CHAPTER 3: BOARD OF DIRECTORS

3.1 Composition of Board

3.1.1 The Board of Directors of the company shall have an optimum combination of Functional, Nominee and Independent Directors.

3.1.2 The number of Functional Directors (including CMD/MD) should not exceed 50 per cents of the actual strength of the Board.

3.1.3 The number of Nominee Directors appointed by government/other CPSEs shall be restricted to a maximum of two.

3.1.4 In case of a CPSE listed on the Stock Exchanges and whose Board of Directors is headed by an Executive

Chairman, the number of Independent Directors shall be at least 50 per cent of Board Members; and in case of all other CPSEs (i.e. listed on Stock Exchange but without an Executive Chairman, or not listed CPSEs), at least one-third of the Board Members should be Independent Directors. The expression 'Independent Director' shall mean a part-time Director of the company who:

(a) apart from receiving Director's remuneration, does not have any material pecuniary relationship or transaction with the company, its Directors, its senior management or its holding company, its subsidiaries and associates which may affect independence of the Director;

(b) is not related to persons occupying management positions at the Board level or at one level below the Board;

(c) has not been a senior executive or managerial personnel of the company in the immediately preceding three financial years;

(d) is not a partner or an executive, or was not a partner or an executive during the preceding three years, of any of the following:

  (i) the statutory audit firm or the internal audit firm or tax audit firm or energy audit firm or management audit firm or risk audit firm or insurance audit firm that is associated with the company, and

  (ii) the panel advocate(s) or legal firm(s) or consultant(s) and consulting firm(s) or expert(s) that have a material association with the company.

(e) is not a material supplier, service provider or customer or a lessor or lessee of the company, which may affect independence of the director;

(f) is not a substantial shareholder of the company, i.e. owning two per cent or more of the block of voting shares.

Explanation

For the purposes of the sub-clause 3.1.4:

(i) "Associate" shall mean a company which is an "associate" as defined in Accounting Standard 23 (AS-23), "Accounting for Investments in Associates in Consolidated Financial Statements", issued by the Institute of Chartered Accountants of India.

(ii) "Senior management" shall mean personnel of the company who are members of its core management team excluding Board of Directors. Normally, this would comprise all members of management one level below the Functional Directors, including all functional heads.

(iii) "Relative" shall mean "relative" as defined in Section 2(41) and Section 6 read with Schedule IA of the Companies Act, 1956 (Extract from the Companies Act is at **Annex-III**).

3.1.5 Nominee Directors appointed by an institution which has invested in or lent to the company shall be deemed to be Independent Directors.

Explanation: "Institution" for this purpose means a public financial institution as defined in Section 4A of the Companies Act, 1956 or a "corresponding new bank" as defined in Section 2(d) of the Banking Companies (Acquisition and Transfer of Undertakings) Act, 1970 or the Banking Companies (Acquisition and Transfer of Undertakings) Act, 1980 [both Acts].

3.2 Part-time Directors' Compensation and Disclosures

All fees/compensation, if any, paid to part-time Directors, including Independent Directors, shall be fixed by the Board of Directors subject to the provisions in the DPE guidelines and the Companies Act, 1956.

3.3 Other Provisions as to Board and Committees

3.3.1 **Number of Board Meetings:** The Board shall meet at least once in every three months and at least four such meetings shall be held every year. Further, the time gap between any two meetings should not be more than three months. The minimum information to be made available to the Board is given in **Annex-IV**.

3.3.2 A Director shall not be a member in more than 10 committees or act as Chairman of more than five committees across all companies in which he is a Director. Furthermore, it should be a mandatory annual requirement for every Director to inform the company about the committee positions he occupies in other companies and notify changes as and when they take place.

Explanation

a. For the purpose of considering the limit of the committees on which a Director can serve, all public limited companies, whether listed or not, shall be included.

b. For the purpose of reckoning the limit under this sub-clause, Chairmanship/membership of the Audit Committee and the Shareholders' Grievance Committee alone shall be considered.

3.3.3 **Compliance of Laws to be reviewed:** The Board shall periodically review compliance reports of all laws applicable to the company, prepared by the company as well as steps taken by the company to rectify instances of non-compliances.

3.4 Code of Conduct

3.4.1 The Board shall lay down a code of conduct for all Board members and senior management of the company. The code of conduct shall be circulated and also posted on the website of the company.

3.4.2 All Board members and senior management personnel shall affirm compliance with the code on an annual basis. The Annual Report of the company shall contain a declaration to this effect signed by its Chief Executive.

3.4.3 Guidelines and policies evolved by the Central Government with respect to the structure, composition, selection, appointment and service conditions of Boards of Directors and senior management personnel shall be strictly followed.

3.4.4 There shall be no extravagance in expenditure on the part of Board members and senior management personnel. CPSEs executives shall be accountable for their performance in conformity with established norms of conduct.

Explanation: For this purpose, the term "senior management" shall mean personnel of the company who are members of its core management team, excluding Board of Directors. Normally, this would comprise all members of management one level below the Functional Directors, including all functional heads.

3.4.5 Any external/internal changes made from time to time, due to addition of or amendment to laws/regulatory rules, applicable to CPSEs, need to be dealt with carefully by the respective Boards/senior management personnel.

3.4.6 A suggested list of items to be included in the code of conduct is given at **Annex-V**. Further, to assist the CPSEs in the formulation of the code, a model Code of Business Conduct and Ethics for Board Members and Senior Management is given at **Annex-VI**.

3.5 Functional Role Clarity between Board of Directors and Management

A clear definition of the roles and the division of responsibilities between the Board and the Management is necessary to enable the Board to effectively perform its role. The Board should have a formal statement of Board Charter which clearly defines the roles and responsibilities of the Board and individual Directors. The Board of each CPSE may be encouraged to articulate its Corporate Governance objectives and approach (within the broad parameters of these guidelines and the general perception of business risk) to satisfy the expectations of its majority shareholders and other stakeholders.

3.6 Risk Management

Enterprise risk management helps management in achieving CPSE's performance and profitability targets. It helps to ensure effective reporting and compliance with laws and regulations, and helps avoid damage to the entity's reputation and associated consequences. Considering the significance of risk management in the scheme of corporate management strategies, its oversight should be one of the main responsibilities of the Board/ Management. The Board should ensure the integration and alignment of the risk management system with the corporate and operational objectives and also that risk management is undertaken as a part of normal business practice and not as a separate task at set times.

3.7 Training of Directors

The company concerned shall undertake training programme for its new Board members (Functional, Government, Nominee and Independent) in the business model of the company including risk profile of the business of company, responsibility of respective Directors and the manner in which such responsibilities are to be discharged. They shall also be imparted training on Corporate Governance, model code of business ethics and conduct applicable for the respective Directors.

CHAPTER 4: AUDIT COMMITTEE

4.1 Qualified and Independent Audit Committee

A qualified and independent Audit Committee shall be set up, giving the terms of reference.

4.1.1 The Audit Committee shall have minimum three Directors as members. Two-thirds of the members of audit committee shall be Independent Directors.

4.1.2 The Chairman of the Audit Committee shall be an Independent Director.

4.1.3 All members of Audit Committee shall have knowledge of financial matters of Company, and at least one member shall have good knowledge of accounting and related financial management expertise.

Explanation 1: The term "knowledge of financial matters of Company" means the ability to read and understand basic financial procedures and statements, i.e. balance sheet, profit and loss account, and statement of cash flows.

Explanation 2: A member will be considered to have accounting and related financial management expertise if he or she possesses experience in finance or accounting, or requisite professional certification in accounting, or any other comparable experience or background which results in the individual's financial sophistication, including being or having been a chief executive officer, chief financial officer or other senior officer with financial oversight responsibilities.

4.1.4 The Chairman of the Audit Committee shall be present at Annual General Meeting to answer shareholder queries; provided that in case the Chairman is unable to attend due to unavoidable reasons, he may nominate any member of the Audit Committee.

4.1.5 The Audit Committee may invite such of the executives, as it considers appropriate (and particularly the head of the finance function) to be present at the meetings of the Committee. The Audit Committee may also meet without the presence of any executives of the company. The Finance Director, Head of Internal Audit and a representative of the Statutory Auditor may be specifically invited to be present as invitees for the meetings of the Audit Committee as may be decided by the Chairman of the Audit Committee.

4.1.6 The Company Secretary shall act as the Secretary to the Audit Committee.

4.2 Role of Audit Committee: The role of the Audit Committee shall include the following:

4.2.1 Oversight of the company's financial reporting process and the disclosure of its financial information to ensure that the financial statement is correct, sufficient and credible.

4.2.2 Recommending to the Board the fixation of audit fees.

4.2.3 Approval of payment to statutory auditors for any other services rendered by the statutory auditors.

4.2.4 Reviewing, with the management, the annual financial statements before submission to the Board for approval, with particular reference to:

a. Matters required to be included in the Directors' Responsibility Statement to be included in the Board's report in terms of clause (2AA) of Section 217 of the Companies Act, 1956;

b. Changes, if any, in accounting policies and practices and reasons for the same;

c. Major accounting entries involving estimates based on the exercise of judgment by management;

d. Significant adjustments made in the financial statements arising out of audit findings;

e. Compliance with legal requirements relating to financial statements;

f. Disclosure of any related party transactions; and

g. Qualifications in the draft audit report.

4.2.5 Reviewing, with the management, the quarterly financial statements before submission to the Board for approval.

4.2.6 Reviewing, with the management, performance of internal auditors and adequacy of the internal control systems.

4.2.7 Reviewing the adequacy of internal audit function, if any, including the structure of the internal audit department, staffing and seniority of the official heading the department, reporting structure, coverage and frequency of internal audit.

4.2.8 Discussion with internal auditors and/or auditors any significant findings and follow up there on.

4.2.9 Reviewing the findings of any internal investigations by the internal auditors/auditors/agencies into matters where there is suspected fraud or irregularity or a failure of internal control systems of a material nature and reporting the matter to the Board.

4.2.10 Discussion with statutory auditors before the audit commences, about the nature and scope of audit as well as post-audit discussion to ascertain any area of concern.

4.2.11 To look into the reasons for substantial defaults in the payment to the depositors, debenture holders, shareholders (in case of non payment of declared dividends) and creditors.

4.2.12 To review the functioning of the Whistle Blower Mechanism.

4.2.13 To review the follow up action on the audit observations of the CAG audit.

4.2.14 To review the follow up action taken on the recommendations of Committee on Public Undertakings (COPU) of the Parliament.

4.2.15 Provide an open avenue of communication between the independent auditor, internal auditor and the Board of Directors.

4.2.16 Review all related party transactions in the company. For this purpose, the Audit Committee may designate a member who shall be responsible for reviewing related party transactions.

Explanation: The term "related party transactions" shall have the same meaning as contained in the Accounting Standard 18, issued by the Institute of Chartered Accountants of India.

4.2.17 Review with the independent auditor the co-ordination of audit efforts to assure completeness of coverage, reduction of redundant efforts, and the effective use of all audit resources.

4.2.18 Consider and review the following with the independent auditor and the management:

- The adequacy of internal controls including computerized information system controls and security, and
- Related findings and recommendations of the independent auditor and internal auditor, together with the management responses.

4.2.19 Consider and review the following with the management, internal auditor and the independent auditor:

- Significant findings during the year, including the status of previous audit recommendations

- Any difficulties encountered during audit work including any restrictions on the scope of activities or access to required information,

Explanation: If the company has set up an Audit Committee pursuant to provision of the Companies Act, the said Audit Committee shall have such additional functions/features as contained in these guidelines.

4.2.20 Carrying out any other function as is mentioned in the terms of reference of the Audit Committee.

4.3 Powers of Audit Committee

Commensurate with its role, the Audit Committee should be invested by the Board of Directors with sufficient powers, which should include the following:

(i) To investigate any activity within its terms of reference.

(ii) To seek information on and from any employee.

(iii) To obtain outside legal or other professional advice, subject to the approval of the Board of Directors.

(iv) To secure attendance of outsiders with relevant expertise, if it considers necessary.

(v) To protect whistle blowers.

4.4 Meeting of Audit Committee

The Audit Committee should meet at least four times in a year and not more than four months shall elapse between two meetings. The quorum shall be either two members or one-third of the members of the Audit Committee whichever is greater, but a minimum of two independent members must be present.

4.5 Review of Information by Audit Committee

The Audit Committee shall review the following information:

(i) Management discussion and analysis of financial condition and results of operations;

(ii) Statement of related party transactions submitted by management;

(iii) Management letters/letters of internal control weaknesses issued by the statutory auditors;

(iv) Internal audit reports relating to internal control weaknesses;

(v) The appointment and removal of the Chief Internal Auditor shall be placed before the Audit Committee; and

(vi) Certification/declaration of financial statements by the Chief Executive/Chief Finance Officer.

CHAPTER 5: REMUNERATION COMMITTEE

5.1 Each CPSE shall constitute a Remuneration Committee comprising at least three Directors, all of whom should be part-time Directors (i.e Nominee Directors or Independent Directors). The Committee should be headed by an Independent Director. CPSE will not be eligible for Performance Related Pay unless the Independent Directors are on its Board. Remuneration Committee will decide the annual bonus/variable pay pool and policy for its distribution across the executives and non unionized supervisors, within the prescribed limits.

CHAPTER 6: SUBSIDIARY COMPANIES

6.1 At least one Independent Director on the Board of Directors of the holding company shall be a Director on the Board of Directors of its subsidiary company.

6.2 The Audit Committee of the holding company shall also review the financial statements of its subsidiary company.

6.3 The minutes of the Board meetings of the subsidiary company shall be placed at the Board meeting of the holding company. The management should periodically bring to the attention of the Board of Directors of the holding company, a statement of all significant transactions and arrangements entered into by its subsidiary company.

Explanation: For the purpose of these guidelines, only those subsidiaries whose turnover or net worth is not less than 20 per cent of the turnover or net worth respectively of the Holding company in the immediate preceding accounting year may be treated as subsidiary companies.

CHAPTER 7: DISCLOSURES

7.1 Transactions

7.1.1 A statement in summary form of transactions with related parties in the normal and ordinary course of business shall be placed periodically before the Audit Committee.

7.1.2 Details of material individual transactions with related parties, which are not in the normal and ordinary course of business, shall be placed before the Audit Committee.

7.1.3 Details of material individual transactions with related parties or others, which are not on an arm's length basis should be placed before the Audit Committee, together with Management's justification for the same.

7.2 Accounting Standards

7.2.1 Where in the preparation of financial statements, a treatment different from that prescribed in an Accounting Standard has been followed, the fact shall be disclosed in the financial statements, together with the management's explanation in the Corporate Governance Report as to why it believes such alternative treatment is more representative of the true and fair view of the underlying business transaction.

7.2.2 The Companies Act, 1956 as well as many other statutes require that financial statements of an enterprise should give a true and fair view of its financial position and working results. That requirement is implicit even in the absence of a specific detailed provision to this effect. However, what constitutes a true and fair view has not been defined either in the Companies Act, 1956 or in any other statute. The Accounting Standards as well as other transactions of the Institute of Chartered Accountants of India on accounting matters seek to prescribe the accounting principles and the methods of applying these principles in preparation and presentation of financial statements so that they give a true and fair view.

7.2.3 Consolidated financial statements present financial information about the parent company, its subsidiaries, its associates and joint ventures as an economic entity to show the economic resources controlled by the group, the obligation of the group and the results the group achieved with its resources, which is not determinable from individual financial statements of parent, subsidiaries, associates and joint ventures. All CPSEs shall prepare consolidated financial statements as per Accounting Standards, namely, AS21, AS23 and AS27 issued by the Institute of Chartered Accountants of India (ICAI) in relation to the Consolidation of Financial Statements.

7.2.4 Many CPSEs provide groups of products and services or operate in geographical areas that are subject to differing rates of profitability, opportunities for growth, future prospects, and risks which may not be determinable from the aggregated data. Reporting of segment information is widely regarded as necessary for meeting the needs of users of financial statements. Hence, all CPSEs are required to publish segment wise profit and loss as per Accounting Standard 17 "Segment Reporting" issued by ICAI.

7.3 Board Disclosures—Risk Management

7.3.1 The company shall lay down procedures to inform Board members about the risk assessment and minimization procedures. These procedures shall be periodically reviewed to ensure that executive management controls risk through means of a properly defined framework. Procedure will be laid down for internal risk management also.

7.3.2 The Board should implement policies and procedures which should include:

(a) staff responsibilities in relation to fraud prevention and identification

(b) responsibility of fraud investigation once a fraud has been identified

(c) process of reporting on fraud related matters to management

(d) reporting and recording processes to be followed to record allegations of fraud

(e) requirements of training to be conducted on fraud prevention and identification.

7.4 Remuneration of Directors

7.4.1 All pecuniary relationship or transactions of the part-time Directors vis-à-vis the company shall be disclosed in the Annual Report.

7.4.2 Further the following disclosures on the remuneration of Directors shall be made in the section on the Corporate Governance of the Annual Report.

(a) All elements of remuneration package of all the directors, i.e. salary, benefits, bonuses, stock options, pension, etc.

(b) Details of fixed component and performance linked incentives, along with the performance criteria.

(c) Service contracts, notice period, severance fees.

(d) Stock option details, if any—and whether issued at a discount as well as the period over which accrued and over which exercisable.

7.5 Management

7.5.1 As part of the Directors' Report or as an addition thereto, a Management Discussion and Analysis Report should form part of the Annual Report. This Management Discussion and Analysis should include discussion on the following matters within the limits set by the company's competitive position:

(i) Industry structure and developments

(ii) Strength and weakness

(iii) Opportunities and Threats

(iv) Segment-wise or product-wise performance

(v) Outlook

(vi) Risks and concerns

(vii) Internal control systems and their adequacy

(viii) Discussion on financial performance with respect to operational performance

(ix) Material developments in Human Resources, Industrial Relations front, including number of people employed.

(x) Environmental Protection and Conservation, Technological conservation, Renewable energy developments, Foreign Exchange conservation

(xi) Corporate social responsibility

7.5.2 Senior management shall make disclosures to the board relating to all material financial and commercial transactions, where they have personal interest that may have a potential conflict with the interest of the company (e.g. dealing in company shares, commercial dealings with bodies, which have shareholding of management and their relatives, etc.)

Explanation: For this purpose, the term "senior management" shall mean personnel of the company who are members of its core management team excluding Board of Directors. Normally, this would comprise all members of management one level below the Functional Directors, including all functional heads.

CHAPTER 8: REPORT, COMPLIANCE AND SCHEDULE OF IMPLEMENTATION

8.1 Report on Corporate Governance

There shall be a separate section on Corporate Governance in each Annual Report of company, with details of compliance on Corporate Governance. The suggested list of items to be included in the report on Corporate Governance is in **Annex-VII.**

8.2 Compliance

8.2.1 The company shall obtain a certificate from either the auditors or practicing Company Secretary regarding compliance of conditions of Corporate Governance as stipulated in these Guidelines and Annexes. The aforesaid certificate with the Directors' Report, which is sent annually to all the shareholders of the company, should also be included in the Annual Report.

8.2.2 Chairman's speech in Annual General Meeting (AGM) should also carry a section on compliance with Corporate Governance guidelines/norms and should form part of the Annual Reports of the concerned CPSE.

8.2.3 The grading of CPSEs may be done by DPE on the basis of the compliance with Corporate Governance guidelines/ norms.

8.3 Schedule of Implementation

These Guidelines on Corporate Governance are now mandatory. The CPSEs shall submit quarterly progress reports, within 15 days from the close of each quarter, in the format (Annex VIII) to respective Administrative Ministries/ Departments. The Administrative Ministries will consolidate the information obtained from the CPSEs and furnish a comprehensive report to the DPE by 31 May of every financial year on the status of compliance of Corporate Governance Guidelines during the previous financial year by the CPSEs under their jurisdiction.

8.4 DPE will, from time to time, make suitable modifications to these Guidelines in order to bring them in line with prevailing laws, regulations, acts, etc., DPE may also issue clarifications to the concerned Administrative Ministries/CPSEs on issues relating to the implementation of these Guidelines.

ANNEX-I

GUIDELINES ON COMPOSITION OF BOARD OF DIRECTORS OF CPSEs

I. Composition of Board of Directors of Public Sector Enterprises

The question of Composition of the Board of Directors of PSEs has been considered from time to time and various guidelines have been issued in this regard by the Bureau of Public Enterprises. The Members of the Board of PSEs generally consist of the following three categories:

i. **Functional Directors:** These are full time operational Directors responsible for day to day functioning of the enterprise. The Economic Administrative Reform Commission (EARC) had recommended that each Board should have an adequate number of Functional Directors on it. This was considered by the Govt. and the Bureau of Public Enterprises had issued guidelines in 1984 that the posts of Director (Finance) and Director (Personnel) be created in all Schedule 'A' and Schedule 'B' enterprises and on a selective basis in Schedule 'C' Companies. Apart from these two functions, the enterprises could have representation at Board level for other disciplines such as production, marketing, project, planning etc. It is, however, observed that these guidelines are not being followed by the Administrative Ministries while constituting the Boards of PSEs. While in some cases the Boards are functioning without a single Functional Director, in others there is preponderance of such Directors.

ii. **Government Directors:** These are appointed by the Administrative Ministries and are generally the officers dealing with the concerned enterprise. In most cases, there are two such Directors on a Board; the Joint Secretary or Additional Secretary dealing with particular enterprise and the Financial Adviser of the Ministry. The question of representation of Government Directors on the Boards of PSEs was examined by the Arjun Sengupta Committee and following its recommendation, the Bureau of Public Enterprises have issued guidelines in 1986 that the Administrative Ministry concerned should not have more than one nominee Director on the Board of a PSE. In case of PSEs engaged in trading or dealing with important and exclusive items the number of Government Directors could be two. It is, however, noticed that in actual practice the number of Government Directors on the Boards of PSEs continues to be large.

iii. **Non-Official Directors:** The induction of Non-Official Directors on the Boards of PSEs has been considered essential by various Committees and Commissions in order to make the Boards more professional. They are to be drawn from the public men, technocrats, management experts and consultants, and professional managers in industry and trade with a high degree of proven ability. The Bureau of Public Enterprises have issued guidelines in 1983 that the number of such Directors on a Board should be one-third of its total strength.

This input is considered very important as it plays a complementary role in providing professional and managerial advice to the Board. It has, however, been the experience that the vacancies of these Directors are not filled up to stipulated levels in many enterprises by the Ministries.

The Department of Public Enterprises has recently considered the question of professionalization of the Boards of PSEs in pursuance of the New Industrial Policy statement made in the Parliament on 24th July, 1991 and it has been decided that the composition of the Boards of Directors in PSEs should be broadly on following lines:

(A) Functional Directors

Every Board should have some full time Functional Directors. The number of such Directors on a Board should not exceed 50 per cent of the actual strength of the Board.

i. In cases where the number of Functional Directors on the Board is more than the 50 per cent of its actual strength (not sanctioned strength), Administrative Ministries will immediately undertake a review of the strength of the Board in consultation with Department of Public Enterprises and PESB.

ii. On such Boards where the posts of Functional Directors do not exist, Administrative Ministries will take immediate steps to create such posts in accordance with the prescribed guidelines.

(B) Government Directors

The number of the Government Directors on the Board of Directors of an enterprise should not exceed one-sixth of the actual strength of the Board.

i. It will be preferable to have only one Government Director from the concerned Administrative Ministry on each Board. The choice of the nominee Director would vest with the Secretary of the concerned Department.

ii. In case of PSEs where it is considered essential to give representation on the Boards to other concerned Government agencies/Ministries/State Governments, only one representation from the Group could also be appointed on the Board as part-time Government Director.

iii. The number of Government Directors on a Board should in no case exceed two.

(C) Non-Official Directors

i. The number of Non-Official Part-time Directors on a Board should be at least one-third of its actual strength. Wherever there is under representation of such Directors on the Board, the concerned Ministries should take immediate steps to fill up the vacancies to stipulated level.

ii. A Panel of suitable persons who could be considered for appointment as Non-Official Part-Time Director on the Boards of PSEs will be maintained centrally by Department of Public Enterprises. This Panel will be prepared in consultation with PESB and the Secretary of the concerned Administrative Ministry.

(DPE O.M. No. 18 (6)/91-GM dated 16th March, 1992)

II. Composition of Board of Directors of Public Sector Enterprises

Reference is invited to this Department's O.M. of even number dated the 16th March, 1992 on the above mentioned subject. In para 2(B)(ii) of the said O.M., it was, *inter alia*, mentioned that the choice of the Nominee Director would vest with the Secretary of the concerned Department. The matter was reconsidered in this Department and it has now been decided that the choice of the Nominee Director would vest with the administrative Ministry of the concerned Department.

(DPE O.M. No. 18 (6)/91-DPE (GM)
dated 13th November, 1995)

III. *Age of Retirement of Part-Time Chairmen and Criteria for Appointment of Part-Time Non-Official Directors in Central PSUs*

The question of prescribing age of retirement for part-time Chairmen of Central Public Sector Enterprises as also laying down requisite criteria for appointment of part-time nonofficial Directors on the Boards of PSUs were under consideration of the Government.

2. Government have now decided that the age of retirement of part-time Chairmen of public enterprises should be 62 years.
3. As regards the selection and appointment of part-time non-official Directors, the following criteria will come into force forthwith:
   (a) **Qualification:** Minimum qualification for part-time non-official Directors would be graduate degree from a recognized university.
   (b) **Experience:** Not less than 10 years at the level of Joint Secretary and above in the Government; CMD/MD in Corporate Sector/PSU; Professor level in an Academic Institution or professionals of repute like eminent Chartered Accountants/Cost Accountants at the level of Directors of Institutes/Heads of Department.

   In selecting academics at the level of Professors, these academics should be in fields relevant to the company's area of operation, e.g. management, finance, marketing, technology, human resources, or law, as Professors of some other disciplines may have little to contribute.

   (c) **Age:** The age band should be between 45-65 years (minimum/maximum limit). This could however, be relaxed for eminent professionals, for reasons to be recorded, being limited to 70 years.
4. It has also been decided that the above criteria should be applied for Navratna/Miniratna enterprises in such a way as to ensure that they could be globally competitive and have a level playing field with the Corporates.

(DPE O.M. No. 18(10)/2003-GM-GL-55
dated 11th March, 2004)

IV. Criteria for Appointment of Non-Official (Independent) Directors in Central PSEs

The undersigned is directed to refer to this Department's O.M. of even number dated 11th March, 2004 wherein the criteria for appointment of part-time non-official Directors in Central PSEs were laid down.

2. The criterion relating to 'Experience' has been reviewed by the government and para 3(b) of the above referred OM has been modified as under:

   (b) **Experience:** Not less than 10 years at the level of Joint Secretary and above in the Government; CMD/MD in Corporate Sector/PSE; Professor level in an Academic Institution or professionals of repute like eminent Chartered Accountants/Cost Accountants at the level of Directors of Institutes/Heads of Department; persons of eminence with proven track record from Industry, Business or Agriculture.

3. All the administrative Ministries/Departments are requested to take note of the above modifications in the criteria for appointment of non-official (Independent) Directors for guidance and compliance.

(DPE O.M. No. 18(10)/2003-GM-GL-75
dated 10th November, 2005)

V. Turning selected Public Sector Enterprises into Global Giants—Operational and Administrative modalities—Restructuring of the Boards.

The Common Minimum Programme of the government states, *inter alia*, that government will identify public sector enterprises that have comparative advantages and support them in their drive to become global giants. In pursuance of these objectives, the government have decided to grant enhanced autonomy and delegation of powers to nine selected public sector enterprises, namely BHEL, BPCL, HPCL, IOC, IPCL, NTPC, ONGC, SAIL and VSNL.

2. The exercise of the enhanced autonomy and authority shall be exercisable only after the Boards have been restructured, as indicated below. It must be ensured that each of these PSEs inducts in the first instance at least four non-official part-time Directors of an impeccable stature and background. This number should be more for those PSEs which have a very large number of Functional Directors. It should also be ensured that within six months, the number of non-official part-time Directors is increased to reach at least 1/3rd of the total strength of the Board.
3. The above is in partial modification to the general guidelines issued by the Department of Public Enterprises vide OM No.18(6)/91-GM dated 16th March, 1992.
4. While selection of full-time Directors and part-time Government nominees Directors would continue to be done as per the existing procedures, for selection of the non-official part time Directors in these companies, a Search committee comprising Chairman-PESB, Secretary-DPE, Secretary of the Administrative Ministry and an eminent person(s) to be nominated by Industry Minister has been set up.

(DPE OM No.DPE/11(2)/97-Fin. dated 22nd July, 1997)

ANNEX-II

COMPOSITION OF BOARD OF DIRECTORS OF LISTED CENTRAL PUBLIC SECTOR ENTERPRISES

According to the existing policy, as contained in this Department's O.M. No. 18(6)/91-GM dated 16.3.1992, the Board of Directors of Public Sector Undertakings should consist of (i) Full time Functional Directors whose number should not exceed 50 per cent of the actual strength of the Board; (ii) Government Directors whose number should not exceed one-sixth of the actual strength of the Board subject to the condition that in no case the number should exceed two; and (iii) Non-official part-time Directors whose number should be at least one-third of the actual strength of the Board.

2. The Securities and Exchange Board of India (SEBI) has issued guidelines regarding Listing Agreements with Stock Exchanges, which include a new Clause 49 on Corporate Governance, an extract of which is enclosed (Annexure-I). It provides that in the cases of companies with non-Executive Chairmen at least one-third of the Board should comprise Independent Directors and in the cases of companies with Executive Chairmen at least half of the Board should comprise Independent Directors. The definition of Independent Directors is also given under the Clause 49. The SEBI has clarified that in the case of Public Sector Undertakings the government nominee Directors cannot be considered as Independent Directors for the purpose of constitution of Board of Directors. The SEBI has, however, subsequently agreed that the nominees of Financial Institutions would be treated as Independent Directors for listed public sector companies. A schedule of implementation is also enclosed (Annexure-II).
3. As all listed companies including PSUs have to comply with the SEBI guidelines, there may be a need to reconstitute the Boards of Directors of some of the listed PSUs so that the requisite number of Independent Directors is inducted in order to avoid de-listing.
4. All the administrative Ministries/Departments are, therefore, requested to take appropriate action, if not already taken, to reconstitute the Board of Directors of listed PSEs in accordance with the SEBI guidelines within the time schedule prescribed. In case there is a need to increase the maximum number of Directors permissible under the Articles of Association, the respective PSEs may be advised to take steps to amend the relevant Article suitably.

(DPE O.M. No. 18(6)/2000-GM dated 26th November, 2001)

ANNEXURE-I of O.M. dated 26.11.2001

Clause 49: Corporate Governance—Board of Directors

A. The company agrees that the board of directors of the company shall have an optimum combination of executive and non-executive directors with not less than fifty percent of the board of directors comprising of non-executive directors. The number of independent directors would depend whether the Chairman is executive or nonexecutive. In case of a nonexecutive chairman, at least one-third of board should comprise of independent directors and in case of an executive chairman, at least half of board should comprise of independent directors.

Explanation: For the purpose of this clause the expression 'independent directors' means directors who apart from receiving director's remuneration, do not have any other material pecuniary relationship or transactions with the company, its promoters, its management or its subsidiaries, which in judgement of the board may affect independence of judgement of the director. Except in the case of government companies, institutional directors on the boards of companies should be considered as independent directors whether the institution is an investing institution or a lending institution.

B. The company agrees that all pecuniary relationship or transactions of the non-executive directors vis-à-vis the company should be disclosed in the Annual Report.

ANNEXURE-II of O.M. dated 26.11.2001

Schedule of Implementation

The above amendments to the listing agreement have to be implemented as per schedule of implementation given below:

- By all entities seeking listing for the first time, at the time of listing.
- Within financial year 2000-2001, but not later than March 31, 2001 by all entities, which are included either in Group 'A' of the BSE or in S&P CNX Nifty index as on January 1, 2000. However to comply with the recommendations, these companies may have to begin the process of implementation as early as possible.
- Within financial year 2001-2002, but not later than March 31, 2002 by all the entities which are presently

listed, with paid up share capital of ₹ 10/- crore and above, or networth of ₹ 25 crore or more any time in the history of the company.

- Within financial year 2002-2003, but not later than March 31, 2003 by all other entities, which are presently listed, with paid up share capital of ₹ 3 crore and above.
- As regards the non-mandatory requirement given in Annexure-3, they shall be implemented as per the discretion of the company. However, the disclosures of the adoption/non-adoption of the non-mandatory requirements shall be made in the section on corporate governance of the Annual Report.

ANNEX-III

EXTRACTS FROM THE COMPANIES ACT, 1956

Section 2 (41) "relative" means, with reference to any person, any one who is related to such person in any of the ways specified in Section 6, and no others;

Section 6 – Meaning of "relative"

A person shall be deemed to be a relative of another, if, and only if,

(a) they are members of a Hindu undivided family; or

(b) they are husband and wife; or

(c) the one is related to the other in the manner indicated in Schedule IA.

SCHEDULE IA [See section 6(c)]

List of Relatives

1. Father
2. Mother (including step-mother)
3. Son (including step-son)
4. Son's wife
5. Daughter (including step-daughter)
6. Father's father
7. Father's mother

8. Mother's mother
9. Mother' father
10. Son's son
11. Son's son's wife
12. Son's daughter
13. Son's daughter's husband
14. Daughter's husband
15. Daughter's son
16. Daughter's son's wife
17. Daughter's daughter
18. Daughter's daughter's husband
19. Brother (inclucding step-brother)
20. Brother's wife
21. Sister (including step-sister)
22. Sister's husband

ANNEX-IV

INFORMATION TO BE PLACED BEFORE BOARD OF DIRECTORS

1. Annual operating plans and budgets and any updates.
2. Capital budgets and any updates.
3. Quarterly results for the company and its operating divisions or business segments.
4. Minutes of meetings of audit committee and other committees of the board.
5. The information on recruitment and remuneration of senior officers just below the board level, including appointment or removal of Chief Financial Officer and the Company Secretary.
6. Show cause, demand, prosecution notices and penalty notices which are materially important.
7. Fatal or serious accidents, dangerous occurrences, any material effluent or pollution problems.

8. Any material default in financial obligations to and by the company, or substantial nonpayment for goods sold by the company.
9. Any issue, which involves possible public or product liability claims of substantial nature, including any judgment or order which, may have passed strictures on the conduct of the company or taken an adverse view regarding another enterprise that can have negative implications on the company.
10. Details of any joint venture or collaboration agreement.
11. Transactions that involve substantial payment towards goodwill, brand equity, or intellectual property.
12. Significant labour problems and their proposed solutions. Any significant development in Human Resources/ Industrial Relations Front like signing of wage agreement, implementation of Voluntary Retirement Scheme, etc.
13. Sale of material nature, of investments, subsidiaries, assets, which is not in normal course of business.
14. Quarterly details of foreign exchange exposures and the steps taken by management to limit the risks of adverse exchange rate movement, if material.
15. Non-compliance of any regulatory, statutory or listing requirements and shareholders service such as nonpayment of dividend, delay in share transfer, etc.

ANNEX-V

SUGGESTED LIST OF ITEMS TO BE INCLUDED IN THE CODE OF CONDUCT

The Board of Directors of the company will formulate the code of conduct for the Directors and senior Management Personnel and while doing so the code of conduct would, *inter alia*, include the following:

1. Act in the best interests of, and fulfill their fiduciary obligations to the Company
2. Act honestly, fairly, ethically and with integrity;

3. Conduct themselves in a professional, courteous and respectful manner and not take improper advantage of the position of Director;
4. Act in a socially responsible manner, within the applicable laws, rules and regulations, customs and traditions of the countries in which the Company operates.
5. Comply with communication and other policies of the Company;
6. Act in good faith, responsibly, with due care, competence and diligence, without allowing their independent judgment to be subordinated;
7. Not to use the Company's property or position for personal gain;
8. Not to use any information or opportunity received by them in their capacity as Directors in a manner that would be detrimental to the Company's interests;
9. Act in a manner to enhance and maintain the reputation of the Company;
10. Disclose any personal interest that they may have regarding any matters that may come before the Board and abstain from discussion, voting or otherwise influencing a decision on any matter in which the concerned Director has or may have such an interest;
11. Abstain from discussion, voting or otherwise influencing a decision on any matters that may come before the board in which they may have a conflict or potential conflict of interest;
12. Respect the confidentiality of information relating to the affairs of the Company acquired in the course of their service as Directors, except when authorized or legally required to disclose such information;
13. Not to use confidential information acquired in the course of their service as Directors for their personal advantage or for the advantage of any other entity;
14. Help create and maintain a culture of high ethical standards and commitment to compliance;

15. Keep the Board informed in an appropriate and timely manner any information in the knowledge of the member which is related to the decision making or is otherwise critical for the company.
16. Treat the other members of the Board and other persons connected with the Company with respect, dignity, fairness and courtesy.

ANNEX-VI

MODEL CODE OF BUSINESS CONDUCT AND ETHICS FOR BOARD MEMBERS AND SENIOR MANAGEMENT

1.0 Introduction

1.1 This Code shall be called "The Code of Business Conduct & Ethics for Board Members and Senior Management" of_________(hereinafter referred to as "the Company").

1.2 The purpose of this Code is to enhance ethical and transparent process in managing the affairs of the Company.

1.3 This Code for Board Members and Senior Management has been framed specially in compliance of the provisions of Clause 49 of the Listing Agreement with Stock Exchanges and as per the Guidelines of DPE.

1.4 It shall come into force with effect from the_________(year and month).

2.0 Definitions and Interpretations

2.1 The term "Board Members" shall mean Directors on the Board of Directors of the Company.

2.2 The term "Whole-time Directors" or "Functional Directors" shall be the Directors on the Board of Directors of the Company who are in whole-time employment of the company.

2.3 The term "Part-time Directors" shall mean Directors on the Board of Directors of the Company who are not in whole time employment of the Company.

2.4 The term "Relative" shall have the same meaning as defined in Section 6 of the Companies Act, 1956.

2.5 The term "Senior Management" shall mean personnel of the Company who are members of its core management team excluding Board of Directors and would comprise all members of management one level below the Whole time Directors, including all functional heads.

2.6 The term "the Company" shall mean_________(name of the Company).

Note: In this Code, words importing the masculine gender shall include feminine gender and words importing singular shall include the plural or vice-versa.

3.0 Applicability

3.1 This code shall be applicable to the following personnel:

a. All Whole-time Directors including the Chairman & Managing Director of the Company.

b. All Part-time Directors including Independent Directors under the provisions of law.

c. Senior Management.

3.2 The Whole-time Directors and Senior Management should continue to comply with other applicable/to be applicable policies, rules and procedures of the Company.

4.0 Contents of Code

Part I General Moral Imperatives

Part II Specific Professional Responsibilities

Part III Specific Additional Provisions for Board Members and Senior Management

This code is intended to serve as a basis for ethical decision making in the conduct of professional work. It may also serve as a basis for judging the merit of a formal complaint pertaining to violation of professional ethical standards.

It is understood that some words and phrases in the code of ethics and conduct document are subject to varying interpretations. In case of any conflict, the decision of the Board shall be final.

PART-I

5.0 General Moral Imperatives

5.1 Contribute to Society and Human Well-being

5.1.1 This principle concerning the quality of life of all people, affirms an obligation to protect fundamental human rights and to respect the diversity of all cultures. We must attempt to ensure that the products of our efforts will be used in socially responsible ways, will meet social needs and will avoid harmful effects to health and welfare of others. In addition to a safe social environment, human well being includes a safe natural environment.

5.1.2 Therefore, all Board Members and Senior Management who are accountable for the design, development, manufacture and promotion of company's products, must be alert to, and make others aware of, both a legal and a moral responsibility for the safety and the protection of human life and environment.

5.2 Be Honest and Trustworthy and Practice Integrity

5.2.1 Integrity and honesty are essential components of trust. Without trust an organization cannot function effectively.

5.2.2 All Board Members and Senior Management are expected to act in accordance with highest standards of personal and professional integrity, honesty and ethical conduct, while conducting business of the Public Enterprise.

5.3 Be Fair and Take Action not to Discriminate

5.3.1 The values of equality, tolerance, respect for others, and the principles of equity and justice govern this imperative. Discrimination, on the basis of race, sex, religion, caste, age, disability, national origins or other such factors, is an explicit violation of this Code.

5.4 Honour Confidentiality

5.4.1 The principle of honesty extends to issues of confidentiality of information. The ethical concern is to respect all obligations of confidentiality to all stakeholders unless discharged from such obligations by requirements of the law or other principles of this Code.

5.4.2 All Board Members and Senior Management, therefore, shall maintain the confidentiality of all confidential unpublished information about business and affairs of the CPSE.

5.5 Pledge and Practice

5.5.1 To strive continuously to bring about integrity and transparency in all spheres of the activities.

5.5.2 Work unstintingly for eradication of corruption in all spheres of life.

5.5.3 Remain vigilant and work towards growth and reputation of the Company.

5.5.4 Bring pride to the organization and provide value-based services to Company's stakeholders.

5.5.5 Do duty conscientiously and without fear or favour.

PART-II

6.0 Specific Professional Responsibilities

6.1 Live the Vision, Mission and Values of CPSE–each day

Live the Vision, Mission and Values of___________(name of CPSE) each day. For quick reference they are as under:

Vision

[Incorporate here vision of the CPSE, for example, A World-class Engineering Enterprise committed to enhancing Stakeholder Value]

Mission

[Incorporate here the mission of the CPSE, for example, To be an Indian Multinational Engineering Enterprise providing total business solutions through quality products, systems and services in the fields of__________and other potential areas]

Values

- Zeal to excel and zest for change
- Integrity and fairness in all matters
- Respect for dignity and potential of individuals

- Strict adherence to commitments
- Ensure speed of response
- Foster learning, creativity and team-work
- Loyalty and pride in the CPSE

6.2 Strive to Achieve the Highest Quality, Effectiveness and Dignity in both the Processes and Products of Professional Work

Excellence is perhaps the most important obligation of a professional. Everyone, therefore, should strive to achieve the highest quality, effectiveness and dignity in their professional work.

6.3 Acquire and Maintain Professional Competence

Excellence depends on individuals who take responsibility for acquiring and maintaining professional competence. All are, therefore, expected to participate in setting standards for appropriate levels of competence, and strive to achieve those standards.

6.4 Compliance with Laws

The Board Members and Senior Management of the CPSE shall comply with all the applicable provisions of existing local, state, national, and international laws. They should also follow and obey the policies, procedures, rules and regulations relating to business of the CPSE.

6.5 Accept and Provide Appropriate Professional Review

Quality professional work depends on professional review and comments. Whenever appropriate, individual members should seek and utilize peer review as well as provide critical review of the work of theirs.

6.6 Manage Personnel and Resources to Enhance the Quality of Working Life

Organizational leaders are responsible for ensuring that a conducive working and business environment is created for fellow employees to enable them delivering their best. The Board Members and Senior Management would be responsible for ensuring human dignity of all employees, would encourage and support the professional development of the employees of the CPSE by providing them all necessary assistance and cooperation, thus enhancing the quality of working.

6.7 Be Upright and Avoid any Inducements

The Board Members and Senior Management shall not, directly or indirectly through their family and other connections, solicit any personal fee, commission or other form of remuneration arising out of transactions involving Company. This includes gifts or other benefits of significant value, which might be extended at times, to influence business for the organization or awarding a contract to an agency, etc.

6.8 Observe Corporate Discipline

The flow of communication within the CPSE is not rigid and people are free to express themselves at all levels. Though there is a free exchange of opinions in the process of arriving at a decision, but after the debate is over and a policy consensus has been established, all are expected to adhere and abide by it, even when in certain instances one may not agree with it individually. In some cases policies act as a guide to action, in others they are designed to put a constraint on action. All must learn to recognize the difference and appreciate why they need to observe them.

6.9 Conduct in a Manner that Reflects Credit to the Company

All are expected to conduct themselves, both on and off duty, in a manner that reflects credit to the Company. The sum total of their personal attitude and behaviour has a bearing on the standing of Company and the way in which it is perceived within the organization and by the public at large.

6.10 Be Accountable to Company's Stakeholders

All of those whom we serve, be it our Customers, without whom the Company will not be in business, the Shareholders, who have an important stake in its business, the Employees, who have a vested interest in making it all happen, the Vendors, who support the Company to deliver in time and Society to which Company is responsible for its actions—are stakeholders of the Company. All, therefore, must keep in mind at all times that they are accountable to Company's stakeholders.

6.11 Prevention of Insider Trading

The Board Members and Senior Management shall comply with the code of Internal Procedures and conduct for prevention of Insider Trading in dealing with Securities of the Company.

6.12 Identify, Mitigate and Manage Business Risks

It is everybody's responsibility to follow the Risk Management Framework of the Company to identify the business risks that surround function or area of operation of the Company and to assist in the company-wide process of managing such risks, so that Company may achieve its wider business objectives.

6.13 Protect Properties of the Company

The Board Members and Senior Management shall protect the assets including physical assets, information and intellectual rights of the Company and shall not use the same for personal gains.

PART-III

7.0 Specific Additional Provisions for Board Members and Senior Management

7.1 As Board Members and Senior Management

They shall undertake to actively participate in the meetings of the Board and Committees on which they serve.

7.2 As Board Members

7.2.1 Undertake to inform the Chairman and Managing Director/Company Secretary of the Company of any changes in their other Board positions, relationship with other business and other events/circumstances/conditions that may interfere with their ability to perform Board/ Board Committee duties or may impact the judgement of the Board as to whether they meet the independence requirements of Listing Agreement with Stock Exchanges and the Guidelines of DPE.

7.2.2 Undertake that without prior approval of the disinterested members of the Board, they will avoid apparent conflict of interest. Conflict of interest may exist when they have personal interest that may have a potential conflict with the interest of the Company. Illustrative cases can be:

Related Party Transactions: Entering into any transactions or relationship with Company or its subsidiaries in which they have a financial or other personal interest (either directly or indirectly such as through a family member or relation or other person or other organization with which they are associated).

Outside Directorship: Accepting Directorship on the Board of any other Company that competes with the business of the Company.

Consultancy/Business/Employment: Engaging in any activity (be it in the nature of providing consultancy service, carrying on business, accepting employment) which is likely to interfere or conflict with their duties/ responsibilities towards Company. They should not invest or associate themselves in any other manner with any supplier, service provider or customer of the company.

Use of Official position for personal gains: Should not use their official position for personal gains.

7.3 Compliance with the Code of Business Conduct and Ethics

7.3.1 **All Members of the Board and Senior Management of Company shall uphold and promote the principles of this code:** The future of the organization depends on both technical and ethical excellence. Not only it is important for Board Members and Senior Management to adhere to the principles expressed in this Code, each of them should also encourage and support adherence by others.

7.3.2 **Treat violations of this code as inconsistent association with the organization:** Adherence of professionals to a code of ethics is largely and generally a voluntary matter. However, if any of Board Members and Senior

Management does not follow this Code, the matter would be reviewed by the Board and its decision shall be final. The Company reserves the right to take appropriate action against the defaulter.

7.4 Miscellaneous Points

7.4.1 **Continual updation of Code:** This Code is subject to continuous review and updation in line with any changes in law, changes in Company's philosophy, vision, business plans or otherwise as may be deemed necessary by the Board and all such amendments/modifications shall take effect prospectively from the date stated therein.

7.4.2 **Where to seek clarifications:** Any member of Board or Senior Management requiring any clarification regarding this code of conduct may contact Director (HR)/Company Secretary/any officer specifically designated by the Board of Directors.

ACKNOWLEDGEMENT OF RECEIPT OF CODE OF BUSINESS CONDUCT AND ETHICS FOR BOARD MEMBERS AND SENIOR MANAGEMENT

I have received and read the code of Business Conduct and Ethics for Board Members and Senior Management of__________(name of the Company) I understand the standards and policies contained in the said Code of Business Conduct and Ethics and understand that there may be additional policies or laws specific to my job. I further agree to comply with the said Code of Business Conduct and Ethics.

If I have questions concerning the meaning or application of the said Code of Business Conduct and Ethics, any policies of the CPSE or the legal and regulatory requirements applicable to my job, I know I can consult Director or Company Secretary concerned the CPSE knowing that my questions or reports will be maintained in confidence.

Further, I undertake to provide following Affirmation on an Annual basis to the Company within 30 days from the end of 31st March every year.

AFFIRMATION

(By Board Members/Senior Management of the Company on Annual basis by 30th April of every year)

I,__________(name),__________(designation), having read and understood the Code of Business Conduct and Ethics for Board Members and Senior Management, hereby solemnly affirm that I have complied with and has not violated any of the provisions of the Code during the year ended 31st March__________

Signature

Name __________

Designation __________

Place: Employment Number __________

Telephone No. __________

Date: __________

ANNEX-VII

SUGGESTED LIST OF ITEMS TO BE INCLUDED IN THE REPORT ON CORPORATE GOVERNANCE IN THE ANNUAL REPORT OF COMPANIES

1. **A brief statement** on company's philosophy on Guidelines on Corporate Governance.
2. **Board of Directors**
   (i) Composition and category of directors, for example, promoter, executive, non-executive, independent nonexecutive, nominee director.
   (ii) Attendance of each director at the Board meetings and the last AGM.
   (iii) Number of other Boards or Board Committees in which he/she is a member or Chairperson
   (iv) Number of Board meetings held, dates on which held.
   (v) In case of appointment of new Director/re-appointment of a Director following information may be provided:

a. brief resume of Director
b. nature of his expertise in specific functional areas; and
c. names of companies in which the person holds the Directorship and the membership of committees of the Board.

3. **Audit Committee**
   (i) Brief description of terms of reference
   (ii) Composition, name of members and Chairperson
   (iii) Meetings and attendance during the year

4. **Remuneration Committee**
   (i) Brief description of terms of reference
   (ii) Composition, name of members and Chairperson
   (iii) Meetings and attendance during the year
   (iv) Remuneration policy/Details of remuneration to all the Directors

5. **General Body Meetings**
   (i) Date, Time and Venue of the last three AGMs
   (ii) Whether any special resolutions passed in the previous three AGMs
   (iii) AGM of the current year: Date, Time and Venue

6. **Disclosures**
   (i) Disclosures on materially significant related party transactions that may have potential conflict with the interests of company at large.
   (ii) Details of non-compliance by the company, penalties, strictures imposed on the company by any statutory authority, on any matter related to any guidelines issued by Government, during the last three years.
   (iii) Whistle Blower policy and affirmation that no personnel has been denied access to the Audit Committee.
   (iv) Details of compliance with the requirements of these guidelines.

(v) Details of Presidential Directives issued by the Central Government and their compliance during the year and also in the last three years.

(vi) Items of expenditure debited in books of accounts, which are not for the purposes of the business.

(vii) Expenses incurred which are personal in nature and incurred for the Board of Directors and Top Management.

(viii) Details of Administrative and office expenses as a percentage of total expenses vis-à-vis financial expenses and reasons for increase.

7. Means of Communication

i. Quarterly results

ii. Newspapers wherein results normally published

iii. Any website, where displayed

iv. Whether it also displays official news releases;

8. Audit Qualifications

Company may move towards a regime of unqualified financial statements.

9. Training of Board Members

A company may train its Board members (Functional, Government Nominee and Independent) in the business model of the company as well as the risk profile of the business parameters of the company, their responsibilities as directors, and the best ways to discharge them.

10. Whistle Blower Policy

The company may establish a mechanism for employees to report to the management concerns about unethical behaviour, actual or suspected fraud, or violation of the Company's General guidelines on conduct or ethics policy. This mechanism could also provide for adequate safeguards against victimization of employees who avail of the mechanism and also provide for direct access to the Chairman of the Audit Committee in exceptional cases. Once established, the existence of the mechanism may be appropriately communicated within the organization.

ANNEX-VIII

FORMAT OF QUARTERLY COMPLIANCE REPORT BY CPSEs TO NODAL ADMINISTRATIVE MINISTRIES/DEPARTMENTS UNDER PARA 8.3 OF DPE's GUIDELINES ON CORPORATE GOVERNANCE FOR CPSEs

Name of the CPSE:

Administrative Ministry/Department:

Whether listed or unlisted:

Quarter ending on:

S.No.	Activity	CG Guidelines Clause[1]	Status of compliance with the CG guidelines (Yes/No/NA)	Remarks
1	2	3	4	5
I Board of Directors				
1.	Composition of Board	3.1		
2.	Non-official Directors	3.1		
3.	Part-time directors compensation and disclosures	3.2		
4.	Number of Board meetings	3.3.1		
5.	Review of compliance of laws	3.3.3		
6.	Code of Conduct	3.4		
7.	Risk management	3.6		
8.	Training for new Board members	3.7		
II Audit Committee				
9.	Constitution of Audit Committee	4.1		
10.	Audit Committee assigned due role	4.2		
11.	Audit Committee vested adequate powers	4.3		
12.	Meetings of Audit Committee	4.4		
13.	Review of information by Audit Committee	4.5		
III Remuneration Committee				
14.	Constitution of remuneration Committee	5.1		
IV Subsidiary Companies				
15.	Board of subsidiary companies	6.1		
16.	Review of financial statements of subsidiary by Audit Committee	6.2		
17.	Review of performance of subsidiary by Board	6.3		

1. Refers to the relevant provision in the Guidelines on Corporate Governance issued by DPE

1	2	3	4	5
V Disclosures				
18.	Transactions	7.1		
19.	Accounting Standards	7.2.1		
20.	Consolidated financial statements	7.2.3		
21.	Segment-wise profit and loss statement	7.2.4		
22.	Board Disclosures—Risk management	7.3		
23.	Remuneration of Directors	7.4		
24.	Management Discussion and Analysis	7.5		
25.	Disclosures by Senior management.	7.5.2		
VI Report and Compliance				
26.	Report on Corporate Governance	8.1		
27.	Compliance Certificate	8.2.1		
28.	Chairman' speech in AGM and annual report	8.2.2		
29.	Holding of AGM, Adoption of audited accounts and filing of adopted accounts with the Registrar of Companies within the stipulated time@			
30.	Timely submission of Compliance report	8.3		

@ Information in respect of this item should be furnished at the end of the relevant quarter of the relevant year.

(Name and Signature of the Chief Executive)

Dated:

Annexure–III

White Paper on Disinvestment of Central Public Sector Enterprises 31 July 2007 (Deptt. of Disinvestment, Ministry of Finance, Govt. of India)

CHAPTER 1: BACKGROUND

1.1 Overview of the Public Sector

1.1.1 There were 5 CPSEs owned by the Central Government at the beginning of the First Five-Year Plan with a total investment of ₹ 29 crore. By the end of the Seventh Plan in 1990, the number of CPSEs had increased to 244 with a total investment of ₹ 99,329 crore. Thereafter, though the capital invested increased to ₹ 3,93,057 crore in 2005-06, the number of CPSEs declined to 239.

1.1.2 The public sector presence is predominant in public utilities and infrastructure. Railways, post and telegraph, ports, airports and power are dominated by CPSEs or department-owned enterprises. In the roads sector, while some roads are owned and maintained by the private sector, publicly owned and maintained roads dominate. Road freight capacity is almost entirely private, while road passenger traffic capacity is also significantly privately owned and managed. In telecom, the public sector continues to be dominant in the provision of fixed line telephone services, while private licencees are operating in some urban areas. Mobile services are predominantly private, particularly in urban areas, while inter-state and international linking services are significantly privately managed and owned.

1.1.3 In the tradable goods sector, the public sector is dominant in coal; oil and gas exploration, development, extraction and transportation, though nearly one-third of oil refining capacity is now owned by the private sector. The public sector is also a significant player in steel, fertilizer, aluminum and copper. In the engineering industry, the public sector has been losing market share except in electrical machinery, where BHEL is a significant player. In construction and project services, the public sector is a minor player. The bulk of the remaining tradable sector is privately owned and managed.

1.1.4 The highlights of the performance of CPSEs during 2005-06 are as under:

(a) The share of CPSEs in GDP at market price stood at 11.12 per cent in 2005-06, and 11.68 per cent in 2004-05.

(b) The cumulative investment in all CPSEs, as on 31st March, 2006 was ₹ 3,93,057 crore. The share of manufacturing CPSEs in total investment was the highest at 51 per cent, followed by service CPSEs at 40 per cent and mining CPSEs at 7 per cent during 2005-06.

(c) The overall growth in turnover of CPSEs, during 2005-06 over 2004-05, was 11.86 per cent. The growth in the turnover of 'heavy engineering' and 'construction services' groups was the highest at 39 per cent during the year.

(d) The aggregate reserves and surpluses of all CPSEs have gone up to ₹ 3,59,077 crore in 2005-06.

(e) The accumulated losses of all CPSEs declined by ₹ 10,578 crore from ₹ 83,725 crore in 2004-05 to ₹ 73,147 crore in 2005-06.

(f) The share of 'taxes and duties' in net value addition of CPSEs at market prices during 2005-06 was the highest at 46 per cent, amongst all constituents. This was followed by 'net profit' (26 per cent), 'salaries and wages' (19 per cent) and 'interest' (9 per cent).

1.2 Evolution of the Disinvestment Policy

1.2.1 The Statement of Industrial Policy of July 24, 1991 stated that in order to raise resources and encourage wider public participation, a part of the government's shareholding in the public sector would be offered to mutual funds, financial institutions, general public and workers. Thus, disinvestment of the government's equity in CPSEs started in 1991-92, when minority shareholding of the Central Government in 30 individual CPSEs was sold to selected financial institutions (LIC, GIC, UTI) in bundles. The shares were sold in bundles to ensure that along with the attractive shares, the not so attractive shares also got sold. Subsequently, shares of individual CPSEs were sold and the category of eligible buyers was gradually expanded to include individuals, NRIs and registered FIIs. After 1996, sale through the GDR route was also initiated and MTNL (1997-98), VSNL (1996-97 and 1998-99) and GAIL (1999-2000) all used the opportunity to access the GDR market. The number of listed CPSEs on domestic stock exchange stood at 44 as on 31 July 2007 and the list is given at Annexure-1.

1.2.2 The policy on disinvestment has evolved largely through statements of Finance Ministers in their budget speeches. In the interim budget 1991-92, it was announced that the Government would disinvest up to 20 per cent of its equity in selected public sector undertakings in favour of mutual funds and financial or investment institutions in the public sector to broad-base the shareholding, improve management, enhance availability of resources for these CPSEs and yield resources for the exchequer.

1.2.3 The Rangarajan Committee recommended in April 1993, that the percentage of equity to be disinvested should be generally under 49 per cent in industries reserved for the public sector and over 74 per cent in other industries. As per Statement of Industrial Policy of 24 July 1991 the following industries were proposed to be reserved for the public sector:

(a) Arms and ammunition and allied items of defence equipment, defence aircraft and warships.
(b) Atomic Energy.
(c) Coal and lignite.
(d) Mineral oils.
(e) Mining of iron ore, manganese ore, chrome ore, gypsum, sulphur, gold and diamond.
(f) Mining of copper, lead, zinc, tin, molybdenum and wolfram.
(g) Minerals specified in the Schedule to the Atomic Energy (Control of Production and Use) Order, 1953.
(h) Railway transport.

1.2.4 In the budget speech of 1996-97, the proposal to establish a Disinvestment Commission was announced. It was also stated that the revenues generated from such disinvestment will be utilised for allocations to education and health and for creating a fund to strengthen CPSEs.

Public Sector Disinvestment Commission

1.2.5 The Public Sector Disinvestment Commission was established on 23 August 1996, for a period of three years, as an independent, non-statutory, advisory body with Shri G.V. Ramakrishna as full time Chairman, four other Members (part time) and a full time Member Secretary. 72 CPSEs were referred to the Commission. Subsequently, 8 cases were withdrawn. The Commission did not take up examination of the cases of six CPSEs, which were registered with the Board for Industrial and Financial Reconstruction (BIFR). The Commission submitted 12 reports covering 58 CPSEs, recommending strategic sale in 25 cases and disinvestment through modes other than strategic sale in 33 cases. The tenure of the Chairman of the Commission was extended till 30 November 1999.

1.2.6 In the budget speech of 1998-99, it was announced that, in the generality of cases, the government's shareholding in CPSEs would be brought down to 26 per cent. In the case of CPSEs involving strategic considerations, the government would continue to retain majority shareholding. The interest of workers would be protected in all cases.

1.2.7 In the budget speech of 1999-2000, it was announced that government's strategy towards the CPSEs would continue to encompass a judicious mix of strengthening strategic units, privatising non-strategic ones through gradual disinvestment or strategic sale and devising viable rehabilitation strategies for weak units.

1.2.8 On 16 March 1999, the government classified the CPSEs into strategic and non-strategic areas for the purpose of disinvestment. It was decided that the strategic CPSEs would be those functioning in the areas of:

(a) Arms and ammunition and the allied items of defence equipment, defence aircrafts and warships;

(b) Atomic energy (except in the areas related to the generation of nuclear power and applications of radiation and radio-isotopes to agriculture, medicine and non-strategic industries);

(c) Railway transport.

All other CPSEs were to be considered as being non-strategic. For the non-strategic CPSEs, it was decided that reduction of the government's shareholding to 26 per cent would not be automatic and the manner and pace of doing so would be decided on a case-by-case basis on the following considerations:

(a) Whether the industrial sector required the presence of the public sector as a countervailing force to prevent concentration of power in private hands; and

(b) Whether the industrial sector required a proper regulatory mechanism to protect the consumer interests before Public Sector Enterprises were privatised.

1.2.9 It was also decided to establish a new Department for Disinvestment and the following business was allocated to it:

(a) All matters relating to disinvestment of Central Government equity from Central Public Sector Undertakings.

(b) Decisions on the recommendations of the Disinvestment Commission on the modalities of disinvestment, including restructuring.

(c) Implementation of disinvestment decisions, including appointment of advisers, pricing of shares, and other terms and conditions of disinvestment.

(d) Disinvestment Commission.

(e) Central Public Sector Undertakings for purposes of disinvestment of government equity only.

The Department came into being on 10 December 1999.

1.2.10 In the budget speech of 2000-2001, it was announced that the main elements of the Government's policy were to restructure and revive potentially viable CPSEs; close down CPSEs which cannot be revived; bring down government's shareholding in all non-strategic CPSEs to 26 per cent or lower, if necessary; and fully protect the interests of workers. The receipts from disinvestment and privatisation will be used for meeting expenditure on social sectors, restructuring of CPSEs and for retiring public debt.

Re-constituted Public Sector Disinvestment Commission

1.2.11 The Public Sector Disinvestment Commission was re-constituted on 24 July 2001 for a period of two years with Dr. R.H. Patil as Chairman (part time) along with four other Members (part time) and a full time Member Secretary. The then Ministry of Disinvestment had informed the Commission on 23 January 2002 that all non-strategic CPSEs, including subsidiaries, excluding IOC, ONGC and GAIL, stood referred to the Commission for it to prioritize, examine and make recommendations in the light of the Government policies articulated earlier on 16 March 1999 and the budget speeches of Finance Ministers from time to time. The re-constituted Disinvestment Commission in 13 reports examined 41 CPSEs (including 4 review cases), recommending strategic sale in 34 cases (including 4 review cases) and disinvestment through other modes in 7 cases. The term of the Commission was subsequently extended till 31 October 2004. The Commission ceased to exist from 1 November 2004.

1.2.12 In the budget speech of 2001-2002, it was announced that CPSEs must be strengthened to compete and prosper in the new environment.

1.2.13 The government decided in September 2002 that CPSEs and Central Government owned cooperative societies (where government's ownership is 51 per cent or more) should not be permitted to participate, as bidders, in the disinvestment of other CPSEs, unless specifically approved by the Core Group of Secretaries on Disinvestment (CGD). In December 2002, on the basis of a proposal of the Department of Fertilizers, it was decided that Multi-State Cooperative Societies under the Department of Fertilizers be allowed to participate in the disinvestment of fertilizer CPSEs including NFL.

1.2.14 In a *suo motu* statement made in both Houses of Parliament on 9 December 2002, by the then Minister of Disinvestment, the government reiterated the policy as:

"The main objective of disinvestment is to put national resources and assets to optimal use and in particular to unleash the productive potential inherent in our public sector enterprises. The policy of disinvestment specifically aims at:

- Modernization and upgradation of Public Sector Enterprises;

- Creation of new assets;
- Generation of employment; and
- Retiring of public debt.

Government would continue to ensure that disinvestment does not result in alienation of national assets, which, through the process of disinvestment, remain where they are. It will also ensure that disinvestment does not result in private monopolies. In order to provide complete visibility to the Government's continued commitment of utilisation of disinvestment proceeds for social and infrastructure sectors, the government would set up a Disinvestment Proceeds Fund. This Fund will be used for financing fresh employment opportunities and investment, and for retirement of public debt. For the disinvestment of natural asset companies, the Ministry of Finance and the Ministry of Disinvestment will work out guidelines. The Ministry of Finance will also prepare for consideration of the Cabinet Committee on Disinvestment a paper on the feasibility and modalities of setting up an Asset Management Company to hold, manage and dispose the residual holding of the government in the companies in which government's equity has been disinvested to a strategic partner."

1.2.15 The then Ministry of Disinvestment issued guidelines regarding Management-Employee Bids in Strategic Sale on 25 April 2003 to encourage and facilitate the participation of employees in strategic sales.

1.2.16 In the budget speech for 2003-04, the Government announced that details regarding the already announced Disinvestment Fund and Asset Management Company, to hold residual shares post disinvestment, would be finalized early in 2003-04.

1.2.17 The disinvestment policy was changed with the formation of the present Government in May 2004. The new policy is described in detail in Chapter 8.

CHAPTER 2: DISINVESTMENT TRANSACTIONS AND REALISATIONS

2.1 Disinvestment Transactions Undertaken can be Classified into Five Main Categories

(a) Transactions involving the sale of minority shareholding of the Government, subject to the residual equity of the Government remaining at least 51 per cent.

(b) Sale of majority shareholding in one CPSE to another CPSE.

(c) Sale of a large block of shares in a CPSE (including subsidiary of a CPSE) along with transfer of management control to a strategic partner identified through a process of competitive bidding. This was termed as strategic sale. After the strategic sale, the CPSE ceased to be a Government Company as defined in Section 617 of the Companies Act, 1956.

(d) Slump sale of 2 hotel units of HCI and other related transactions during 1999-00 to 2005-06.

(e) Sale of all or part of Government's residual shareholding in disinvested CPSEs/companies either through a public offering or private placement, viz. CMC, IBP, IPCL, MUL and ICI.

These five categories of transactions are narrated separately below.

2.2 Sale of Minority Shareholding in CPSEs

2.2.1 Disinvestment of government's shareholding in CPSEs started in 1991-92. In that year government disinvested an average of about 8 per cent of the shareholding in 30 CPSEs and realised ₹ 3037.74 crore over two auctions. The sale was made exclusively to financial institutions, mutual funds and banks in the public sector on competitive basis for the shares which were offered in mixed bundles of CPSEs classified as Very Good, Good and Average.

2.2.2 During 1992-93, government disinvested on an average less than 5 per cent of the aggregate equity over three auctions and realised a total amount of ₹ 1,912.51 crore.

Unlike the case in 1991-92, the shares were not bundled in 1992-93 and were offered for sale individually by auction. The auctions were open not only to public sector institutions, but also to private firms, brokers and any person, who was legally permitted to buy, hold and sell shares in India. Reserve price for each CPSE's share was fixed with the help of professional advice from merchant bankers and only bids in excess of the reserve price were accepted.

2.2.3 During 1993-94, government enlarged the range of bidders to include FIIs. This was based on the recommendations of the Rangarajan Committee on "Disinvestment of Shares in Public Sector Enterprises" which were given in April 1993. In March 1994, small portions of shareholding in six CPSEs were disinvested for an amount of ₹ 2282.16 crore which was received during 1994-95. Towards the end of 1993-94, government made an offer for sale to employees in 8 CPSEs where disinvestment had already occurred. The offer was for a maximum of 200 shares per employee, subject to a ceiling of 5 per cent of the paid-up capital of CPSE and at a 15 per cent discount to the average price realised by the government at the auctions held during 1992-93. A total of ₹ 333.57 crore was collected by such sale to employees during 1994-95.

2.2.4 In October 1994, the range of bidders was further enlarged so as to include NRIs and OCBs. Small portions of equity in 10 CPSEs was disinvested for a total realisation of ₹ 2,560.93 crore. In 1995-96 small portions of government's shareholding in 4 CPSEs was sold realising ₹ 168.48 crore. In 1996-97, 0.39 crore shares of VSNL were sold through a GDR issue realising ₹ 379.67 crore at a price of ₹ 973.51 per share. In 1997-98, 4.00 crore shares held by government along with 3.00 crore new shares of MTNL were sold through a GDR issue. The government thereby realised an amount of about ₹ 910 crore from this GDR issue.

2.2.5 During the year 1998-99, government sold a small portion of its shareholding in one CPSE to another CPSE. Through this mechanism, ONGC and IOC each purchased 4.85 per cent shares of GAIL's equity shareholding. IOC purchased 10 per cent of the shareholding of ONGC, whereas ONGC purchased 10 per cent of equity shareholding of IOC. In addition 0.90 crore shares of CONCOR and 3.06 crore shares of GAIL were sold to institutional investors in the domestic market while 1 crore shares of VSNL were sold in the GDR market. The net realisation for government from these disinvestment transactions in 1998-99 was ₹ 5,371.11 crore.

2.2.6 During the years 1999-2000 to 2002-03 the receipts from sale of minority shares were minimal, since the emphasis shifted to Strategic Sale. During 1999-2000 the proceeds were only from the sale of 0.10 crore shares of VSNL in the domestic market and 13.50 crore shares of GAIL in the GDR market. In addition, the remaining amount from the sale of shareholding in one CPSE to another CPSE carried out in the previous year and amounting to ₹ 459.27 crore was also received, giving a total receipt of ₹ 1,479.27 crore during that year. During the following years 2000-01 to 2002-03 there were no receipts from sale of minority shareholding.

2.2.7 In the year 2003-04, after the Supreme Court judgement in the case of HPCL/BPCL, the sale of government's minority shareholding through public offers was resumed. The Offer for Sale of 20 per cent of DCIL's paid up equity out of the government's shareholding was decided in July, 2003, while the decision to sell small portions of government's stake in GAIL and ONGC was taken in December, 2003. The decision for sale of government's residual shareholding of 26 per cent through an Offer for Sale in IBP was taken in July, 2003. In February and March 2004 these four issues raised ₹ 12,757.61 crore. ONGC was a single issue, which raised ₹ 10,558.40 crore and remains one of the largest offerings so far in the Indian market.

2.2.8 This trend was continued in 2004-05 in which the major receipt of ₹ 2,684.07 crore was from the sale of 43.29 crore equity shares of ₹ 10 each out of the government's equity in NTPC, along with a fresh issue of equity of a similar quantum by NTPC through an IPO in October, 2004. Annexure-2 tabulates details of these five Offers for Sale implemented during the years 2003-04 and 2004-05.

2.2.9 The total realisation from sale of minority shareholding of equity in CPSEs has been ₹ 33,543.56 crore, which is approximately two-third of the total receipts of ₹ 51,608.58 crore from disinvestment till July, 2007. The year-wise and company-wise receipts from disinvestment of minority shareholding in CPSEs are given in Annexure-3.

2.3 Sale of Majority Shareholding to CPSEs

There are only three instances where government divested itself of a majority shareholding in a CPSE by selling the shares to another CPSE without going through a process of competitive bidding. In 2000-01, 74.46 per cent of the equity of BRPL was disinvested to IOC for ₹ 148.80 crore, 51.81 per cent of equity in CPCL was sold to IOC for ₹ 509.33 crore and 55.04 per cent of the equity of KRL was off-loaded to BPCL for ₹ 659.10 crore. Subsequently, it was felt that disinvestment by sale of shares to CPSEs did not result in any of the advantages normally associated with the block transfer of majority shareholding, since the public sector character of the company did not change. Thereafter, government on 18 September 2002 issued guidelines that the CPSEs should be prohibited from participating in disinvestment transactions, unless an exemption was specifically given in a particular case. The total amount raised through the block sale of shares in one CPSE to another CPSE was ₹ 1317.23 crore which is less than 3 per cent of the total amount of ₹ 51,608.58 crore raised from disinvestment till July 2007.

2.4 Strategic Sale

MUL was the first government company to be privatized. It ceased to be a government company in 1992, when government entered into an agreement with SMC allowing it to raise its shareholding from 40 per cent to 50 per cent, by subscribing to

22,04,860 shares of face value of ₹ 100 each at a price of ₹ 269 per share. However, strategic sale as a policy measure commenced in 1999-2000 with the sale of 74 per cent of the government's equity in MFIL for ₹ 105.45 crore. Thereafter, twelve CPSEs (including four subsidiaries of CPSEs), and seventeen hotels of ITDC were sold to private investors along with transfer of management control by the government. In addition, the strategic sale of 33.58 per cent IBP's shareholding was effected to IOC. IBP remained a CPSE after strategic sale, since IOC held 53.58 per cent of its paid-up equity. The names of the CPSEs in which strategic sale were effected, the years of strategic sale, the percentage of equity sold, the residual equity of the government and the amounts realized from disinvestment are given in Annexure-4. The total realisation from these strategic sale transactions was ₹ 6,344.35 crore, which is around one-eighth of the total amount of ₹ 51,608.58 crore raised from disinvestment till 31st July, 2007.

2.5 Slump Sale of Two Hotels of HCI and Other Transactions

The receipts from slump sale of two hotels of HCI (Hotel Centaur Juhu Beach, Mumbai and Centaur Hotel Mumbai Airport, Mumbai), lease-cum-management contract of Hotel Ashok Bangalore and other disinvestment transactions during 1999-00 to 2005-06 were ₹ 4,005.17 crore. The details of these transactions are given in Annexure-5.

2.6 Sale of All or Part of the Residual Equity in Privatised CPSEs/Companies

2.6.1 MUL was the first privatized CPSE to come out with an IPO, which consisted of an Offer for Sale of 27.51 per cent of MUL's paid up equity capital, out of government's residual shareholding of 45.79 per cent. The IPO, which was completed in June, 2003 was oversubscribed by 8.92 times realizing ₹ 993.34 crore for the government. Thereafter, in January, 2006 government realised a sum of ₹ 1,567.60 crore from the sale of 8 per cent of equity out of its shareholding of 18.28 per cent in MUL, to public sector financial institutions and banks. Another, ₹ 2.08 crore was received by the government in March

2006 from the sale of 31,507 (0.01 per cent) equity shares in MUL to employees of MUL. In May 2007, the government realized ₹ 2,366.94 crore from the sale of its entire residual equity of 10.27 per cent in MUL to public sector financial institutions, public sector banks and Indian mutual funds.

2.6.2 In the year 2003-04 government's residual stake in two other privatized CPSEs, viz. CMC and IPCL was sold to the public. Government also divested its shareholding in ICI Limited, a private company.

2.6.3 Government thus, realized ₹ 6,398.27 crore from these transactions. Annexure-6 details the receipts from these transactions.

2.7 Disinvestment Receipts vis-à-vis Budget Estimates

Annexure-7 provides the year-wise budgeted receipt from disinvestment and the achievement in each year since 1991-92. The realisations exceeded the budgeted receipts in the years 1991-92, 1994-95, 1998-99, and 2003-04. The realization of 1994-95 includes ₹ 2,282.16 crore being the proceeds of sale of small portions of its shareholding in six CPSEs disinvested in March 1994.

CHAPTER 3: DISINVESTMENT PROCEDURES

3.1 From 1991-92, when it started and till 1996-97, disinvestment was handled by the Department of Public Enterprises (Ministry of Heavy Industries) and subsequently, from 1 April 1997 till 9 December 1999, by the Department of Economic Affairs (Ministry of Finance). The Department of Disinvestment (DoD) was set up as a separate department on 10 December 1999 and was subsequently renamed as Ministry of Disinvestment (MODI) from 6 September 2001. From 27 May 2004, the Department of Disinvestment is one of the Departments under the Ministry of Finance.

3.2 The procedures followed for disinvestment have evolved over a period of time. These were based on decision-making through inter-ministerial consultations and involvement of professionals and experts, in view of the technical and complex nature of transactions and the need for transparency and fair play. The decision making process, the bidding procedure and the methods used for valuation of equity of CPSE sold are described below for the different modes of sales.

3.3 Decision-Making Process

3.3.1 Strategic Sale

3.3.1.1 The decision-making process consisted of the following steps:

(a) Identification of the CPSE whose shares were to be sold, the percentage of shares to be sold and the mode of sale.

(b) Appointment of various advisers who would assist in the process of sale.

(c) Selection of the bidders.

(d) Determination of the reserve price; and

(e) Approval of the price and other terms at which the shares were to be sold.

These are dealt with sequentially in the succeeding paragraphs.

3.3.1.2 Generally, though not universally, the starting point till May 2004 was study of the target CPSE by the Disinvestment Commission. In June 1997, the Government decided that the recommendations of the Disinvestment Commission would be processed by the Department of Economic Affairs (Ministry of Finance) through a Core Group of Secretaries on Disinvestment (CGD), chaired by the Cabinet Secretary, for obtaining the decision of the Cabinet thereon. At that time, it was also decided that for disinvestment transactions exceeding ₹ 500 crore, CGD would directly supervise the implementation of the Cabinet decision through an inter-ministerial operational group. This group consisted of Joint Secretaries from Ministry of Finance, Department of Public Enterprises, the administrative ministry concerned and the CMD of the CPSE concerned. In all the cases, where CGD was to directly supervise the disinvestment, CGD would recommend the timing, pricing and extent of disinvestment, etc. based upon the advice of the inter-ministerial operational group, to the Finance Minister, Industry Minister and the Minister of the administrative ministry for approval. For disinvestment transactions below ₹ 500 crore, the administrative ministry concerned would be responsible for implementing Cabinet decisions, though they were to be monitored by CGD. The administrative ministries concerned would be provided appropriate technical assistance by the Department of Public Enterprises and Ministry of Finance.

3.3.1.3 This system was further modified in 1999 when the Department of Disinvestment (converted into Ministry of Disinvestment on 6 September 2001) was established and issues, such as, which company was to be sold, the percentage of shares and the mode of sale were decided, on a case-by-case basis, by the Cabinet or one of its committees duly authorized in this regard. Generally, DOD/MODI would initiate a proposal for consideration of CGD which would further recommend the case to the Cabinet Committee on Disinvestment. Thus, there was a three-tier structure for decision-making and implementation of decisions:

- Cabinet Committee on Disinvestment (CCD) at the apex level;
- Core Group of Secretaries on Disinvestment (CGD) as a recommendatory body; and
- Inter-Ministerial Group (IMG) as a consultative group.

3.3.1.4 CCD was chaired by the Prime Minister. The functions of CCD, constituted in January, 2000 were as follows:

(a) To consider the advice of the Core Group of Secretaries regarding policy issues relating to the disinvestment programme;

(b) To decide the price band for the sale of government's shares through international/domestic capital market route prior to the book building exercise, and to decide the final price of sale in all cases;

(c) To decide the final pricing of the transaction and the strategic partner in case of strategic sales;

(d) To decide on cases where there is disagreement between the recommendations of the Disinvestment Commission and the views of DOD/MODI; and

(e) To approve the three-year rolling plan and the annual programme of disinvestment every year.

3.3.1.5 CGD was headed by the Cabinet Secretary. CGD functioned as the Empowered Group for vetting the recommendations of the Disinvestment Commission, monitored the progress of implementation of CCD decisions, in disinvestment transactions exceeding ₹ 500 crore directly supervised the process of disinvestment and made recommendations to CCD on disinvestment policy matters.

3.3.1.6 A separate IMG was formed for each case of disinvestment. Generally, it was chaired by Secretary, DOD/MODI and comprised the officers of Ministry of Finance, Department of Public Enterprises, Department of Legal Affairs, Department of Company Affairs, the Administrative Ministry, the CMD and the Director (Finance) of the CPSE concerned. IMG was the forum where inter-ministerial consultation took place at the primary level. Recommendations of the IMG were considered by the CGD.

3.3.1.7 **Appointment of Advisers:** In September 1997, government decided that merchant bankers/global advisers would be appointed through a global process of competitive selection. The Expressions of Interest submitted by the advisers/merchant bankers were first considered by IMG comprising representatives from the Administrative Ministry concerned, the Department of Public Enterprises, the Department of Economic

Affairs and the Chief Executive of the CPSE concerned. The recommendations of IMG were considered by CGD and approved by the Minister in-charge of the Administrative Ministry concerned, the Minister of Industry and the Finance Minister. The criteria and marking system for selection of Adviser for strategic sale were laid down by the CGD in its meeting held on 1 April 1999. In July 1999, the government modified the procedure to the extent that intermediary advisers like Legal Advisers, Accounting Advisers, Asset Valuers, Environmental Advisers, etc. should in future be appointed by the CPSE concerned following its internal procedure which would also bear the related expenditure. On 23 June 2000, the government further modified the procedure and decided that Global Advisers would be termed as Advisers and be appointed with the approval of Minister of State of the Department of Disinvestment instead of the Group of Ministers. In February 2001 the Ministry of Law advised that all advisers including the intermediary advisers should be appointed by the government and not by the CPSE concerned. Subsequently, the government decided in July 2001 that, appointment of intermediary advisers would be made by Department of Disinvestment, after making selection from the list provided by the General Advisers. The actual appointment of intermediary advisers was typically made on the recommendations of an Inter-Ministerial Selection Committee and with the approval of the Minister in-charge of Department of Disinvestment. The criteria and the marking system were further revised with the approval of CGD in January 2002.

3.3.1.8 **Selection of Bidders:** The procedure generally followed for selection of bidders was that IMG constituted for the specific disinvestment transaction determined the qualification requirements based on the recommendations of the Adviser. Thereafter, Expressions of Interest (EoI) were invited through public advertisements in leading business newspapers and also simultaneously placing the advertisement as well as the Preliminary Information Memorandum containing the requisite details including qualification requirements, the format of submission of EoI, the last date of submission, etc. on the websites of DoD, the administrative ministry and CPSE concerned. The IMG concerned decided, on the basis of the recommendations of the Advisers, on the eligibility of the bidders to participate further in the process.

3.3.1.9 **Determination of Reserve Price:** Valuation was carried out to determine the Reserve Price. The Evaluation Committee (EC), generally consisting of the Financial Adviser of the Ministry/Department administratively concerned with the CPSE, a representative each from the Administrative Ministry/Department concerned, the Department of Economic Affairs, the Department of Disinvestment, the Department of Public Enterprises, the Chief Executive and Director (Finance), wherever available, of the CPSE concerned, made recommendations regarding fixation of the Reserve Price. The recommendations of EC were then considered by the IMG which also included the Chief Executive and Director (Finance) and a representative each of the Administrative Ministry and the Department of Public Enterprises. The Adviser concerned submitted the valuation report and the asset valuation report to the EC and made presentations on the values arrived at by different methodologies and merits and demerits of the various methods. The Valuation Report of the Advisers contained details of assumptions and basis of their recommendations. The CGD considered and forwarded the recommendations of IMG to CCD, which approved the valuation. However, MFIL was an exception, where the bid submitted by Hindustan Lever Limited was evaluated and recommended to CCD, for acceptance directly by EC without fixing the reserve price.

3.3.2 *Offer for Sale*

3.3.2.1 During February-March 2004, government sold its entire residual equity in IBP, CMC and the residual equity of 28.945 per cent in the case of IPCL. Government also sold small portions of equity in DCI, GAIL and ONGC. To assist the government in selling its equity, Book Running Lead Managers (BRLMs) were appointed, the BRLMs were selected through a competitive bidding procedure and appointed after obtaining the approval of the Minister-in-charge of the Department on the basis of the recommendations of CGD and IMG. The proposals for fixation of floor price/price band and the offer price were first considered by a High-level Committee comprising Secretary, Ministry of Disinvestment, Secretary of the Administrative Ministry concerned, Joint Secretary, Department of Economic Affairs and Joint Secretary, Department of Disinvestment. The recommendations of the High-level Committee were submitted for approval to the Group of Ministers constituted for this purpose.

3.3.2.2 Subsequently in June 2004, the following disinvestment related functions were allocated to the Cabinet Committee on Economic Affairs (CCEA).

(a) to consider issues relating to disinvestment;

(b) to decide price band for the sale of government shares through Global Depository Receipt/domestic capital market route prior to the book building exercise, and to decide the final price of sale in all cases;

(c) to decide the final pricing of the transaction and the strategic partner in case of the strategic sales;

(d) to decide on cases where there is disagreement between the recommendations of the Disinvestment Commission and the views of the Department of Disinvestment.

3.3.2.3 During July 2004, government decided to piggyback with an offer for sale on the fresh issue of equity that was being undertaken by NTPC. At the time of seeking government's approval, it was considered that the procedure to be followed by NTPC for determining and approving the floor price/price band and offer price and sale price would also be applicable to the government shares and this activity would be performed simultaneously taking the entire offer as one. DOD would participate in all monitoring level meetings in the Ministry of Power. A separate IMG was not to be formed.

3.3.2.4 In September 2004, government constituted an Empowered Group of Ministers (EGoM) to decide all issues related to the price band for the sale of Government's shares through GDR/domestic capital market route prior to the book building exercise and to decide the final price of sale in all such cases. EGoM comprises the Minister of Finance, the Minister of the Administrative Ministry concerned and Deputy Chairman, Planning Commission. EGoM would be serviced by Department of Disinvestment.

3.4 Sale of Residual Equity by the Auction Method

3.4.1 The government's residual equity of 18.28 per cent in MUL was sold in two tranches of 8 per cent and 10.27 per cent in January 2006 and May 2007 respectively. Another 0.01 per cent was sold to employees in March 2006.

3.4.2 In the case of sale of 8 per cent government equity in MUL to public sector financial institutions and public sector banks, an IMG finalized its recommendation on appointment of Advisers after going through the presentations made by merchant bankers/investment bankers. The recommendations of IMG were later considered by CGD and approved by the Finance Minister. The same advisers were retained for the sale of government's remaining stake of 10.27 per cent to public sector financial institutions, public sector banks and Indian mutual funds.

3.4.3 An Evaluation Committee under the Chairmanship of JS&FA, DoD with JS, DHI; JS, DoD; and JS (PSE), Department of Economic Affairs, as members, was constituted for recommending the floor price, final sale price and allocation of shares. The Committee's recommendations were submitted to EGoM for approval.

3.5 Bidding Procedure

3.5.1 *Strategic Sale*

The bidding procedure for strategic sale was evolved keeping in view the principles of transparency, administrative simplicity and fair play. Bidding was done in a two-stage process. In the first stage, all those bidders meeting the eligibility criteria were shortlisted by an IMG and were invited to do the due diligence of the company. Simultaneously, the transaction documents were firmed up by the Advisers in consultation with the CPSE concerned, the shortlisted interested parties and IMG. Once the government approved the draft transaction documents, which defined the future rights and obligations of the government and the strategic partner, the conditions for sale of shares, etc. financial bids were invited from the shortlisted bidders who had completed due diligence. After determination of the Reserve Price, the financial bids were opened and the highest eligible bidder was recommended by EC/IMG to CGD. The recommendations of IMG together with the recommendations of CGD in regard to sale price and the buyer were placed before CCD for approval.

3.5.2 *Offers for Sale*

Since 2003, eight Offers for Sale have been concluded. All of them utilized the Book Building route. Under this methodology, bids were invited within a pre-determined floor price/price band from the investors during a specific period. Each investor submitted bid specifying the number of shares bid for and the price. After the end of the bidding period, the bids were consolidated and a cut off price was recommended by the Inter-Ministerial

Committee, constituted separately for each transaction, for approval to the EGoM, which took the final decision regarding allocation of shares to investors and the cut-off price.

3.5.3 *Auction Method*

3.5.3.1 In the initial phase (December 1991 to 1995-96), disinvestment of shares of select CPSEs was through the auction method. The reserve price was first determined by the Core Group of Secretaries and then the bids were invited from pre-determined target group of investors. Shares were allotted to the bidders in order of the bid prices, first to the highest bidder and then to next and so on until the shares were exhausted or the reserve price reached, whichever was earlier.

3.5.3.2 For the sale of residual shareholding of government in MUL undertaken in January 2006 and May 2007, the government first fixed the reserve price and then the bids were invited from the target group of investors. The shares were sold through the auction method described above.

3.6 Valuation

3.6.1 As mentioned earlier, valuation was carried out to determine the Reserve Price. The objective of valuation is to determine the fair value of an asset, which in turn is based on the assessment of its intrinsic value accruing from the fundamentals of the asset on a stand-alone basis. A purchase and sale is concluded only when two parties, with varying views on the value of an asset, reach an agreement on the same price. Thus the sale price is different from the Reserve Price, the latter being a benchmark for evaluation of bids received through the bidding process.

3.6.2 **Disinvestment Commission's Recommendations on Valuation**

3.6.2.1 The Disinvestment Commission, in its Report on Disinvestment: Strategy and Issues, submitted in

December 1996, while underlining the importance of the subject of valuation, discussed three basic approaches to valuation:

(a) Discounted Cash flow (DCF).

(b) Relative valuation.

(c) Net asset value.

3.6.2.2 The Commission was of the further view that the use of a particular method of valuation would depend upon the health of the company being evaluated, the nature of the industry in which it operated and the company's intrinsic strengths. The depth of the capital markets would also have an impact on the valuation.

3.6.2.3 The Commission also discussed several factors, which impact valuation. Although valuation methods itself generate a range of valuations in each case, some discounts may need to be applied due to the following reasons:

- The lack of marketability.
- Minority Discount.
- Multi-Business Discount.

3.6.2.4 The Commission also sought to correct some erroneous perceptions about valuation. There is a general perception that since valuation models are quantitative, valuation is objective. The Commission felt that though valuation does make use of quantitative models, the assumptions made as inputs to the model leave plenty of room for subjective judgments. At the same time, there is no such thing as a precise estimate of a value. Even at the end of the most careful and detailed valuation of a company, there could be uncertainty about the final numbers, as they are shaped by assumptions about the future of the company's operations.

3.6.2.5 Another perception sought to be corrected by the Commission was the relationship attributed between valuation and market price. The benchmark for most valuations remains the market price (either the company's own price, if it is listed, or that of a comparable company). The Commission felt that the valuation done before listing takes into account anticipated factors, whereas market price reflects realised events that are influenced by unanticipated factors. Moreover, a specific valuation itself may not be valid over a period of time as it is a function of the competitive position of the company, the nature of market in which it operates and Government policies. Therefore, it may be appropriate to update or revise valuations.

3.6.3 *Valuation Methodologies Followed in the Case of Strategic Sale*

3.6.3.1 The following four methodologies were used for valuation of CPSEs:

(a) Discounted Cash Flow (DCF) Method.

(b) Balance Sheet Method.

(c) Transaction Multiple/Comparable Companies/ Relative Valuation Method.

(d) Asset Valuation Method.

3.6.3.2 The Reserve Price was fixed on the DCF method in the case of BALCO, CMC, HTL, VSNL, IBP, IPCL, HZL, ITDC and HCI Hotel units. In the case of MFIL, the reserve price was not fixed, whereas in the case of PPL, the reserve price was determined by giving weightages of two to DCF value and one to the Replacement Value based Asset Value.

3.6.3.3 A statement indicating the valuation of the CPSEs, which were sold through strategic sale, under different methods of valuation, the Reserve Price and Sale Price in each case is given at Annexure-8. The statement indicates that the bid price realized by the Government was always more than the Reserve Price, except in the case of PPL. The statement on Reserve Price and the amount realised in respect of disinvestment of hotel properties is at Annexure-9.

3.6.4 *Valuation Methodologies Followed in the Case of Sale of Small Portions of Equity*

3.6.4.1 **Auction Method:** During 1991-96 shares were sold by the auction method. The basis of fixation of the Reserve Price is given hereinunder:

(a) In the first year of disinvestment, i.e. 1991-92, government sold shares in bundles belonging to Very Good, Good and Average CPSEs. The auctions were open only to financial institutions, mutual funds and public sector banks which were finally subjected to a reserve price computed on the basis of the then prevailing formula of the Controller of Capital Issues. The second tranche of disinvestment was based on reserve prices recommended by the Industrial Credit and Investment Corporation of India.

(b) In the subsequent year (1992-93), the shares were sold individually in auctions which elicited more competition with the presence of firms, corporate bodies as well as individuals who had permission to buy, hold and sale shares in India. Reserve prices at the auctions were fixed with the help of professional advice from merchant bankers and only bids in excess of the reserve prices were accepted. Shares were allotted in the order of bid prices, first to the highest bidder, then to the next and so on until the shares were exhausted or the reserve price reached, whichever was earlier.

(c) In 1993-94, the reserve price was the higher of the highest price realized for each CPSE's share at the last year's auction or average of the prices indicated by the merchant bankers (IDBI and ICICI) for that CPSE. Towards the end of 1993, the government offered shares to employees in eight CPSEs where disinvestment had already occurred, at a 15 per cent discount to the average price realized by the government at the auctions held during 1992-93.

(d) The formula for fixation of reserve price was revised in 1994-95 as the higher of (i) average price indicated by the merchant bankers engaged for that purpose; or (ii) average price realized at any preceding auction. Where there was more than one previous auction in which the share had been sold individually, the highest of the average price realized at any of the preceding auctions was considered.

(e) During 1995-96, the reserve price was taken as the average of the price indications given by a panel of three institutions namely, IDBI, ICICI Securities and SBI Capital Markets.

(f) In the year 2005-06, the government sold 8 per cent of the paid equity capital of MUL through the auction method to public sector financial institutions and public sector banks. A floor price of ₹ 620 per share was fixed for the share of the face value of ₹ 5. The shares were allotted to the bidders in the order of the bid prices, first to the highest bidder and then to the next and so on until the shares were exhausted at a cut off price of ₹ 660 per share. The weighted average price worked out to ₹ 678.24 per share in a bid range of ₹ 660-725. Another 0.01 per cent was sold to employees at the cut-off price of ₹ 660 per share. Each employee was offered 20 shares.

g. In May 2007 the government sold its residual 10.27 per cent paid up equity capital in MUL through the auction method to the public sector financial institutions, public sector banks and Indian mutual funds. A floor price of ₹ 760 per share was fixed for the share of face value of

₹ 5. The weighted average price of the shares sold worked out to ₹ 797.49 per share in a bid range of ₹ 775-850.

3.6.4.2 **Public Offerings**

(a) The government through the 'Offer for Sale' route, divested all or a portion of its equity in six listed companies, viz. DCI, CMC, ONGC, GAIL, IBP and IPCL. While disinvesting in these six listed companies, the government was required to fix a Floor Price/Price Band. The Floor Price/Price Band was fixed by the Group of Ministers on the recommendations of a High-level Inter-Ministerial Committee. While making its recommendations, the High-level Committee was, by and large, guided by the market price and its trends. In some cases, multiples provided by BRLMs were also considered for assessing the reasonableness of the recommended Floor Price/Price Band. The Floor Price per share recommended in the cases of CMC, GAIL, IBP and IPCL was ₹ 475, ₹ 185, ₹ 620 and ₹ 170 respectively. In the cases of DCI and ONGC, the price bands of ₹ 385-400 and ₹ 680-750 per share respectively were fixed.

(b) The IPO of MUL in 2003 consisted only of an Offer for Sale for 27.51 per cent of MUL's paid-up equity, out of government's shareholding. Based on the recommendation of the BRLMs, the floor price of the issue for the face value of ₹ 5 per share was fixed at ₹ 115 per share.

(c) The IPO of NTPC in 2004-05 consisted of an Offer for Sale for 5.25 per cent and Fresh Issue of 5.25 per cent of the post-issue paid up equity of NTPC. A price band of ₹ 52 to ₹ 62 per equity share was fixed after studying the ratios pertaining to P/E, P/BV, EV/Adjusted EBITDA, Dividend Yield, DCF, etc.

CHAPTER 4: POST STRATEGIC SALE TRANSACTIONS FOR RESIDUAL HOLDING AND POST CLOSING ADJUSTMENTS

4.1 In all cases of strategic sale, (except hotel properties of ITDC and HCI), government/BBUNL (in the case of LJMC and JCL being the holding company) retained a part of the equity with it, though management control was transferred to the strategic partner. The percentage of shares sold in the first instance to the SP varied from case to case. Except for the SHAs of HTL and LJMC, other SHAs, provided for the manner of sale for the residual equity. In some cases a 'Put' option was made available to the government under which it was compulsory for the SP to buy the shares being offered by the government. In some cases a 'Call' option was made available to the SP. In some other cases, both 'Put' and 'Call' options were made available. In all the cases of both 'Put' and 'Call' options, the period in which or the date from which the option could be exercised was pre-defined. The principles for determining the price at which the options were to be exercised was also predefined in the SHA. The procedure of exercising the option was also provided in the SHA.

4.2 The government retained at least 26 per cent shareholding of the divested CPSE with it for a certain length of time. Annexure-10 provides details of the 'Put' and 'Call' options available in different CPSEs sold through strategic sale, specifying the percentage of shares associated with the option, the time period as well as the basis of pricing.

4.3 A CPSE-wise Summary of How 'Put'/'Call' Options were Exercised in the Past

4.3.1 MFIL, an unlisted CPSE was privatised in January, 2000 through a sale of 74 per cent of the paid up equity. 26 per cent of the equity was left with the government. The SHA provided for a 'Put' option to the government to sell the residual shares to the SP from January 2001 at higher of the Fair Market Value or the price at which shares were sold in the strategic sale. The 'Put' option was followed by a 'Call' option to SP. The 'Put' option was exercised by the government on 28 November 2002. The government's residual equity was sold at the strategic sale price, i.e. ₹ 11,489.56 per share, whose Face Value was ₹ 1,000, realising an amount of ₹ 44.07 crore.

4.3.2 BALCO is an unlisted CPSE in which 51 per cent of the equity was sold by the government in March 2001. A 'Call' option for the residual 49 per cent shares exercisable from 3 March 2004 at the higher of the Fair Value or the strategic sale price plus 14 per cent annual interest compounded half yearly after giving credit for dividend received by the government, was available to SP. In the context of the 'Call' option exercised by SP on 22 March 2004, the Attorney General for India (AG), in his opinion dated 27 April 2006, advised that the 'Call' option provisions in the SHA place restriction on the right of the GOI to transfer its shares freely and such a restriction would be void and unenforceable. A final decision on sale of the 'Called Shares' is yet to be taken as AG has opined against the validity of the Call Option provisions and the matter is under dispute.

4.3.3 CMC was a listed CPSE, when government disinvested 51 per cent of the paid up equity through strategic sale in October 2001, leaving a residual equity of 32.31 per cent with the government, which got reduced to 26.25 per cent after sale of shares to employees. The SHA provided for a 'Put' option for the government effective from 16 October 2002 to 15 October 2003 not exceeding 10 per cent of the paid up equity out of the residual shares and from 16 October 2003 to 15 October 2004 for some or all of the remaining shares at Fair Value as defined in the SHA. The 'Call' option was provided to the SP from 16 October 2004 to 15 October 2006 at higher of the Fair Value or the Market Value of the called shares. In February 2004 the entire residual shareholding of 26.25 per cent was sold through an Offer for Sale to the public after getting the concurrence of the SP under the 'Right of First Refusal' clause of the SHA. The government realised an amount of ₹ 190.44 crore from this transaction.

4.3.4 **VSNL** was a listed CPSE when the government disinvested 25 per cent of the paid up equity capital through strategic sale in February 2002, leaving a residual shareholding of 27.97 per cent. Out of the residual shareholding, 1.85 per cent shareholding was sold to the employees. As per the SHA, the SP could exercise a 'Call' option for the entire residual shareholding of the government, except one share, during the period from 13 February 2006 to 12 February 2007 at Fair Value of the called shares, to be determined as per SHA. However, the SP did not exercise the 'Call' option and the period of one year, during which the SP could have exercised the call option, expired on 12 February 2007.

4.3.5 **IBP:** The government disinvested 33.58 per cent of the paid up equity in February 2002 in this listed CPSE leaving a residual shareholding of 26 per cent. The SHA provided for a 'Put' option to the Government from 8 February 2003 to 7 February 2005 at Fair Value and a 'Call' option to the SP from 8 February 2005 to 7 February 2007 at Fair Value. However, government sold its entire residual shareholding through an Offer for Sale to the public in February 2004.

4.3.6 **PPL:** The government sold 74 per cent of the paid up equity capital in February 2002 through strategic sale in this unlisted CPSE leaving a residual shareholding of 26 per cent. The shareholding of the government in PPL came down to 19.55 per cent, consequent to a Rights Issue by the company, which was not subscribed to by the government. The SHA provides for a 'Put' option right to the government for some or all of the residual shares held by the government at the time it exercises the put option at the fair value of the put shares. It further provides for a Call Option right to the SP from 1 March 2005, requiring government to sell to the SP all but not less than all of the equity shares held by the government on date of issue of the Call Option Notice at a price which is higher of the fair value of the called shares or, if the company is listed, the highest price of the equity shares (during the period 15-days prior to the date of the call option notice) as quoted in the Stock Exchange or the price at which the shares were sold to SP at the time of strategic sale. In view of the opinion of AG referred to in Para 4.3.2 the government has decided to repudiate the Call Option if and when exercised.

4.3.7 **HZL:** The government sold 26 per cent of the paid up equity capital of the company through a strategic sale in April 2002, retaining a shareholding of 49.92 per cent in this listed CPSE. Out of the residual shareholding, 1.465 per cent shareholding was sold to the employees. The SHA provided for the first 'Call' option to the SP from 11 October 2002 to 10 October 2003 for 18.92 per cent of the equity at higher of the Market Value of the shares or strategic sale price. This option was exercised by the SP in August 2003 against which government realised ₹ 323.88 crore at the strategic sale price. A 'Put' option was available to the Government from 11 October 2004 to 10 April 2005 at higher of the Market Value of the shares or the strategic sale price for the shareholding in excess of 26 per cent. The government decided not to exercise the 'Put' option. The residual shareholding of the government is now 29.535 per cent for which a 'Call' option is available to the SP from 11 April 2007 at the Fair Market Value. In view of the opinion of AG referred to in Para 4.3.2 the government has decided to repudiate the Call Option if and when exercised.

4.3.8 **IPCL:** The government sold 26 per cent of the equity in this listed CPSE through strategic sale in June 2002 leaving a residual shareholding of 33.95 per cent for which the SHA provided a 'Put' option to the government from 4 June 2004 to 3 June 2005 and a 'Call' option to the SP from 4 June 2005 to 3 June 2006 both at Fair Value. However, in February 2004 the government, after obtaining concurrence of the SP under the 'Right of First Refusal' clause of the SHA, sold 28.95 per cent through an Offer for Sale to the public realising ₹ 1203 crore and the residual holding of 5 per cent was offered to the employees of IPCL at discounted price, out of which 4.58 per cent shares were actually allotted. The existing shareholding of the government in IPCL is 0.42 per cent.

4.3.9 **JCL:** At the time of strategic sale, BBUNL, a CPSE held 99 per cent of the paid up equity capital of JCL, a listed company. BBUNL sold 72 per cent of the paid up equity through the strategic sale to Indo-Wagon Engineering Limited (IWEL), leaving a residual shareholding of 27 per cent. The SHA provided for a 'Put' option to BBUNL from 29 August 2004 to 28 August 2006 and a 'Call' option to the SP from 29 August 2006 to 28 August 2008 both at Fair Value, to be determined as per the SHA. The shareholding in JCL got further reduced from 27 per cent to 4.16 per cent, consequent to a Rights Issue made by JCL in 2005 which was not subscribed by BBUNL. IWEL exercised the 'Call' option on 4 September 2006. In view of the opinion of AG referred to in Para 4.3.2, the government has decided to repudiate the Call Option already exercised by SP.

4.3.10 MUL was an unlisted company when the government renounced a Rights Issue of 4.21 per cent of the paid up equity in June, 2002, in favour of SMC, thereby reducing its shareholding to 45.79 per cent. SMC paid ₹ 1000 crore as control premium to the government for renouncing the Rights Offer. The RJVA provided for a 'Put' option from 8 November 2003 to 8 July 2005 at a price to be determined through a pre-defined formula. The government, however, sold 27.51 per cent out of its shareholding through an IPO in July 2003 realising ₹ 993.30 crore. Out of the residual shareholding of 18.28 per cent, the government sold 8 per cent equity of MUL to public sector financial institutions and public sector banks in January 2006 for ₹ 1,567.60 crore and 0.01 per cent equity to the employees of MUL for ₹ 2.08 crore in March 2006. In May 2007, the government sold its residual 10.27 per cent shareholding in MUL for the consideration of ₹ 2,366.94 crore to public sector financial institutions, public sector banks and Indian mutual funds.

Sale of Shares to Employees

4.4 Five SHAs relating to strategic sale provided for offer of shares to employees. These are detailed below:

4.4.1 **BALCO:** The SHA provided for an offer of up to 5 per cent equity of the company out of the residual shareholding of government to the employees. A final decision in the matter is yet to be taken.

4.4.2 **CMC:** The SHA provided for an offer of not more than 6.31 per cent of the equity of the company out of the residual shareholding of government to the employees. The strategic sale was completed in October 2001 and the offer of shares to the employees was completed in June/July 2002 at a price of ₹ 66 per share, i.e. at one-third of the strategic sale price of ₹ 197 approximately. All regular employees of the company including full time functional Directors of the company, on the specified date, were eligible to acquire shares under this scheme. 3,208 employees availed of this offer, realising ₹ 6.07 crore for the Government by subscribing to 6.06 per cent of the equity. The offer involved a sacrifice of around ₹ 12.04 crore for the government vis-a-vis the strategic sale price and an average benefit of ₹ 0.38 lakh per employee. The shares were non-transferable/non-tradeable for one year from the date of issue.

4.4.3 **VSNL:** The SHA provided for an offer up to 2 per cent shares of the company out of the government's residual shareholding to the employees. The company ceased to be a government company in February 2002 and the offer to the employees was made in the same month at one-third of the price offered by the strategic partner or one-third of listed market value calculated as the average of the closing price on BSE for 30 days, whichever was less, subject to a minimum of par value of ₹ 10 per equity share. 52,64,555 shares representing

1.85 per cent equity of the company were subscribed by the employees. The shares were offered at ₹ 47.85 per share against the strategic sale price of ₹ 202 per share, involving a sacrifice of ₹ 81.15 crore by the government and an average benefit of ₹ 2,71,304 per employee. The shares were made non-transferable/ tradable for one year.

4.4.4 **HZL:** The SHA provided for an offer of up to 5 per cent equity of the company to the employees out of the residual shareholding of the government. It was decided to offer the shares at one-third of the Listed Market Value or one-third of strategic sale price whichever was lower subject to a minimum of the face value. Accordingly, in November 2002 the shares were offered at the face value of ₹ 10 per share against a prevailing Listed Market Value of ₹ 22.52 per share and strategic sale price of ₹ 40.50 per share. 61.90 lakh shares or 1.465 per cent of the equity was subscribed by the employees. This transaction involved a sacrifice of ₹ 18.88 crore by the government and an average benefit of ₹ 0.66 lakh per employee vis-à-vis the strategic sale price. The shares were non-transferable/ non-tradable for one year.

4.4.5 **IPCL:** The SHA provided for an offer up to 5 per cent equity of the company out of government residual shareholding to the employees. The strategic sale was completed in June 2002. Thereafter, the offer of shares to the employees was made in April 2004 at one-third of the price at which the shares were sold in February 2004 through an Offer for Sale, i.e. ₹ 170. Accordingly, 5 per cent shares were offered to employees, out of which 4.58 per cent shares were actually allotted at ₹ 57 per share. This involved a sacrifice of ₹ 197.85 crore for the government vis-à-vis the strategic sale price of ₹ 231. An average benefit of ₹ 1.61 lakh accrued to each employee. The shares were non-transferable/non-tradable for three years.

4.4.6 A tabular presentation of these transactions is available in Annexure-11. While the terms and conditions of sale of shares to employees varied, there are some common features. A matrix of distribution of shares among employees was adopted. Secondly, the ratio of distribution from the lowest to the highest level ranged between 1:2.75 and 1:5. Thirdly, the regular employees including the functional Directors of the Board at the time of disinvestment were eligible for subscribing to the shares. Fourthly, in all the schemes, the shares were offered at a discount to the prevailing price.

4.5 Post Closing Adjustments

In the case of 4 unlisted companies and the hotel properties of HCI and ITDC, the Share Purchase Agreement/ Agreement to Sell provided for a Post Closing Adjustment to cover the change in the financial status of the company between the date upto which the audited accounts were provided to the parties at the time of due diligence and the date of actual disinvestment. The difference in the Net Assets on the date of the last audited balance sheet and the closing date was called post closing adjustment and depending on whether there was an accretion or depletion of the Net Assets, this amount become payable to the government or SP.

4.5.1 The details of cases where Post Closing Adjustments were provided for in the Share Purchase Agreement/ relevant transaction agreement and the status of each case as given below:

4.5.2 **MFIL:** MFIL was disinvested through sale of 74 per cent Government's equity to HLL for an amount of ₹ 105.45 crore. Financial bids were invited/received on the basis of audited accounts of MFIL as on 31 March 1999. The transaction agreements were executed on 31 January 2000. The appointed accounting firm had submitted a statement on 26 April 2000 which required the government to pay ₹ 17.48 crore to the SP but the government accepted a claim amounting to ₹ 12.64 crore and released payment of

₹ 10.94 crore in October 2000 and ₹ 1.70 crore in November 2001. HLL, the purchaser still claims ₹ 4.43 crore under post closing adjustment on account of gratuity and recovery from U.P. Government. The matter is under consideration of the Ministry of Food Processing Industries.

4.5.3 **BALCO:** 51 per cent equity of BALCO was disinvested in favour of SIIL on 2 March 2001 for an amount of ₹ 551. 50 crore. The SHA and SPA were signed on 2 March 2001 and the SP took over the management control. The SPA provided that within 90 days following the Closing Date, the government and the Purchaser shall jointly select an accounting firm to prepare a statement showing the Closing Date Net Assets Amount. If the Closing Date Net Assets Amount were higher than the Adjusted Net Assets Amount on 31 March 2000 (₹ 590.95 crore), the Purchaser shall pay 51 per cent of the difference to the government and if the Closing Date Net Assets Amount was lower than the Adjusted Net Assets Amount, the government shall pay 51 per cent of the difference to the Purchaser. In terms of the SPA, the government and the SP jointly appointed Price Waterhouse to compute the Closing Date Net Assets Amount. Price Waterhouse initially computed the Net Assets of BALCO as on 2 March 2001 at ₹ 478.08 crore which was subsequently increased to ₹ 558.17 crore as against the Adjusted Net Assets of ₹ 590.95 crore as on 31 March 2000. The matter is under examination in the Ministry of Mines.

4.5.4 **PPL:** Financial bids for the disinvestment of 74 per cent of the equity in PPL were invited on the basis of audited accounts of the company as on 31 March 2001. Only one financial bid of Zuari Maroc Phosphate Pvt. Limited (ZMPPL) was received. The transaction agreements for strategic sale were executed on 28 February 2002. As per the joint audit, on the post closing claim, initially conducted by Price Waterhouse,

Kolkota, the total deterioration in the net assets of PPL between 31 March 2001 and 28 February 2002 was at ₹ 204.80 crore (approx.) out of which ₹ 151.55 crore was due to ZMPPL. No agreement could be reached between ZMPPL and the government on the amount of the post-closing claim. Thereafter, the government appointed Patro & Co. who arrived at a post-closing claim of ₹ 108.8 crore. In view of the discrepancies in the reports of the two auditors mentioned above, KPMG Private Limited was jointly engaged for conducting a full audit. In the report of KPMG, the amount payable to ZMPPL was computed to be ₹ 141.32 crore. While this case was under examination of the Department of Fertilizer, ZMPPL initiated arbitration proceedings under the SPA. The matter is pending before an Arbitral Tribunal.

4.5.5 **HTL:** 74 per cent equity of HTL was disinvested through Strategic Sale to HFCL on 16 October 2001. The Post Closing adjustment claim filed by the strategic partner in terms of the provisions of SPA was not acceptable to the Department of Telecommunications and the matter is under arbitration.

4.5.6 **HCI:** HCI is a subsidiary of Air India Limited. Transactions relating to two hotel businesses of HCI, viz., Hotel Centaur Juhu Beach Mumbai and Centaur Hotel Mumbai Airport, Mumbai and a subsidiary hotel of HCI, viz. Indo Hokke Hotels Limited, Rajgir were based upon the audited accounts of 31 March 2001. The transfer dates of these 3 hotels were: Indo Hokke Hotels Limited, Rajgir-26 March 2002, Hotel Centaur Juhu Beach, Mumbai-31 May 2002 and Centaur Hotel Mumbai Airport, Mumbai-5 June 2002.

4.5.6.1 Post closing adjustment in terms of the provisions of SPA was completed in respect of Indo Hokke Hotels Limited, Rajgir. HCI paid an amount of ₹ 4.33 lakh to the purchaser in settlement of the claim. Post closing adjustments in respect of the other two hotels in terms of the Agreement to Sell have not yet been completed.

4.5.6.2 In the case of Centaur Hotel Mumbai Airport, Mumbai, the purchaser raised a claim of ₹ 235.67 lakh, whereas HCI raised a claim of ₹ 497.71 lakh to be recovered from the purchaser. Since both the parties have disputed the claims of each other, the matter has been referred to arbitration.

4.5.6.3 In the case of Hotel Centaur Juhu Beach, Mumbai, the post closing adjustments in respect of (i) additional provision towards doubtful debts, (ii) additional provision towards leave encashment and gratuity and (iii) insurance claim and advances paid to suppliers have not been concluded. The parties have mutually agreed to refer the matter to Ministry of Civil Aviation (MoCA) for the award. MoCA informed that Additional Secretary and Financial Adviser, MoCA was appointed as the Arbitrator. The purchaser did not agree to this. HCI after taking legal opinion from their solicitors issued legal notice to the purchaser in October 2005. The Board of HCI decided in March 2006 to go ahead with arbitration proceedings. In June 2006, HCI requested Arbitrator to proceed further in the matter. The matter is still pending.

4.5.7 **ITDC:** The position regarding post closing adjustments in respect of the disinvested ITDC properties is at Annexure-12.

CHAPTER 5: POST DISINVESTMENT EMPLOYEES ISSUES IN PRIVATIZED CPSES

5.1 There are two primary employees issues, which are voiced with respect to privatization. First there is a concern about change in the terms of services of employees and secondly there is a concern that the reservation policy of the government for the Scheduled Castes/Scheduled Tribes and other categories would be diluted.

5.2 Terms and Conditions of Services

The concern of the employees regarding alteration in the terms and conditions of the services were sought to be addressed through provisions in the Shareholders Agreement/Share Purchase Agreement entered into with the Strategic Partner at the time of strategic sale. The typical provisions are given below:

Recitals:

Subject to the substantive clauses in this regard, the Parties envision that all Employees of the Company on the date hereof will continue in the employment of the Company.

Substantive Clauses

The SP covenants with the government that:

(a) notwithstanding anything to the contrary in this Agreement, it shall not retrench any of the Employees of the Company for a period of 1 (one) year from the Closing Date other than any dismissal or termination of Employees of the Company from their employment in accordance with the applicable staff regulations and standing orders of the Company or applicable Laws.

(b) notwithstanding anything to the contrary in this Agreement, but subject to Sub-Clause (a) above, any restructuring of the labour force of the Company shall be implemented in the manner recommended by the Board and in accordance with all applicable Laws;

(c) notwithstanding anything to the contrary in this Agreement, but subject to Sub-Clause (a) above, in the event of any reduction of the strength of the Company's Employees, the SP shall ensure that the Company offers its Employees an option to voluntarily retire on terms that are not, in any manner, less favourable than the VRS applicable before disinvestment.

5.3 Reservation Policy

In the strategic sale transactions, the interest of SC/ST employees were also sought to be protected through the provisions in the Shareholders' Agreement. A typical Recital clause provided in the SHA is reproduced below:

The SP recognizes that the government in relation to its employment policies follows certain principles for the benefit of the members of the Scheduled Castes/Scheduled Tribes, physically handicapped persons and other socially disadvantaged categories of the society. The SP shall use its best efforts to cause the Company to provide adequate job opportunities for such persons. Further, in the event of any reduction in the strength of the employees of the Company, the SP shall use its best efforts to ensure that the physically handicapped persons are retrenched at the end.

CHAPTER 6: DISINVESTMENT RELATED LEGAL CASES

6.1 Review of Legal Cases

6.1.1 Ninety-six disinvestment related lawsuits, including transfer petitions, have been filed between December 1999 (when the Department of Disinvestment was established) and 30 June 2007. Out of these, sixteen writ petitions were transferred to the Supreme Court from different High Courts. At the end of July 2007, twenty four matters were pending before different High Courts and two matters before the Supreme Court, details of which are given below:

Summary of Legal cases

Sl. No.	Court	Total number filed (including transfer cases)	Disposed/ Dismissed	Transferred to Supreme Court	Number pending
1.	Supreme Court	15	13	Not applicable	2*
2.	Karnataka High Court	5	4	1	Nil
3.	Delhi High Court	19	13	4	2
4.	Chhattisgarh High Court	1	Nil	1	Nil
5.	Madras High Court	7	2	2	3
6.	Allahabad High Court	3	Nil	2	1
7.	Patna High Court	2	2	Nil	Nil
8.	J&K High Court	1	Nil	1	Nil

(Contd.)

9.	Calcutta High Court	10	4	1	5
10.	Rajasthan High Court	6	3	1	2
11.	Kerala High Court	1	1	Nil	Nil
12.	Orissa High Court	5	2	Nil	3
13.	Bombay High Court	10	4	2	4
14.	Bombay High Court (Nagpur Bench)	1	Nil	Nil	1
15.	Bombay High Court (Aurangabad Bench)	1	Nil	Nil	1
16.	High Court of MP (Gwalior Bench)	1	1	Nil	Nil
17.	High Court of MP (Jabalpur Bench)	3	2	Nil	1
18.	Gujarat High Court	1	Nil	Nil	1
19.	Andhra Pradesh High Court	2	2	Nil	Nil
20.	Punjab & Haryana High Court	1	1	Nil	Nil
21.	Jharkhand High Court	1	Nil	1	Nil
	Total	**96**	**54**	**16**	**26**

*2 matters consisting of Transferred Cases (i) 5 Writ Petitions involving issues arising out of the Supreme Court judgment in HPCL/BPCL case and clubbed together and (ii) 1 Writ Petition relating to HZL transferred from Rajasthan High Court.

6.1.2 Out of the cases which were either disposed or dismissed by various courts, there are three important judgements of the Supreme Court. These are the judgement dated 10 December 2001 in the BALCO matter, the judgement dated 16 September 2003 in the Centre for Public Interest Litigation and Others vs. Union of India and Others in HPCL/BPCL matter and the judgement dated 31 October 2006 in the matter of All India ITDC Workers Union & Others viz. ITDC and Others.

6.1.3 The Supreme Court in its judgement dated 10 December 2001 in the BALCO case (AIR 2002 SC 350) has observed as follows:

> In a democracy, it is the prerogative of each elected Government to follow its own policy. Often a change in Government may result in the shift in focus or change in economic policies. Any such

change may result in adversely affecting some vested interests. Unless any illegality is committed in the execution of the policy or the same is contrary to law or *mala fide*, a decision bringing about change cannot *per se* be interfered with the Court.

Wisdom and advisability of economic policies are ordinarily not amenable to judicial review unless it can be demonstrated that the policy is contrary to any statutory provision or the Constitution. In other words, it is not for the Courts to consider relative merits of different economic policies and consider whether a wiser or better one can be evolved. For testing the correctness of a policy, the appropriate forum is the Parliament and not the Courts. Here the policy was tested and the Motion defeated in the Lok Sabha on 1st March, 2001.

Thus, apart from the fact that the policy of disinvestment cannot be questioned as such, the facts herein show that fair, just and equitable procedure has been followed in carrying out this disinvestment. The allegations of lack of transparency or that the decision was taken in a hurry or there has been an arbitrary exercise of power are without any basis.

The offer of the highest bidder has been accepted. This was more than the reserve price which was arrived at by a method which is well recognized and, therefore, we have not examined the details in the matter or arriving at the valuation figure. Moreover, valuation is question of fact and the Court will not interfere in matters of valuation unless the methodology adopted is arbitrary.

In the case of a policy decision on economic matters, the courts should be very circumspect in conducting any enquiry or investigation and must be most reluctant to impugn the judgement of the experts who may have arrived at a conclusion unless the

Court is satisfied that there is illegality in the decision itself.

6.1.4 In the matter of Centre for Public Interest Litigation *versus* Union of India and Another, challenging the disinvestment in regard to HPCL/BPCL, the Supreme Court, through the judgement delivered on 16 September 2003 (AIR 2003 SC 3277) upheld the challenge to the proposed Strategic Sale of HPCL and the proposed dilution in equity in the case of BPCL to below 51 per cent through an Offer for Sale of the government's equity. The Supreme Court took the view that, since both these companies were established through Acts of Parliament under which the undertakings and assets of private companies were acquired and transferred to these government Companies, it was not open for the government to proceed with disinvestment that would result in HPCL and BPCL ceasing to be government Companies without appropriately amending the statutes concerned. The Court also held that setting up of government Companies is by way of Parliamentary approval for expenditure from the Consolidated Fund of India and hence privatisation of government Companies can therefore be only with approval of Parliament. This Judgement laid down principles, which would apply to all cases of privatization of government companies. Subsequently, several ongoing disinvestment proposals were challenged in various High Courts. On petitions filed by the government under Article 139A of the Constitution, 6 writ petitions (in the cases of Burn Standard Company Limited, Shipping Corporation of India Limited, Hindustan Copper Limited, Hindustan Zinc Limited) pending in various High Courts were transferred to the Supreme Court. Further, four Writ Petitions were directly filed before the Supreme Court. All the transferred cases and the Writ Petitions directly filed before the Supreme Court were tagged with the Civil Appeal SLP (C) No. 12203/2003 (Civil Appeal No. 6780/2004) filed by Jessop & Co. Limited Staff Association, in which the government, through its Counter Affidavit dated 11 November 2003, sought reconsideration of the ratios of the judgment dated 16 September 2003 in the Centre for Public Interest Litigation case (HPCL/BPCL). The Supreme Court on 11 October 2004 passed orders (a) granting the Special Leave to Jessop & Co. Limited Staff Association; (b) allowing the transfer petitions filed by the Union of India; and (c) admitting the Writ Petitions filed by EIL Officers' Association, NFL Officers' Association and Khetri Tamba Shramik Sangh. The Court also observed that, in view of the importance of the issues involved, a larger bench should hear these matters. Subsequently, the writ petitions filed by EIL Officers' Association, NFL Officers' Association were dismissed as withdrawn and the writ petition filed by Khetri Tamba Shramik Sangh was dismissed as premature. Jessop & Co. Staff Association filed an application in June 2007 seeking permission for withdrawing the Civil Appeal No. 6780 of 2004. The Supreme Court has through orders dated 24 July 2007 allowed the application and dismissed the appeal as withdrawn. Rest of the matters and the transferred cases are before the Supreme Court.

6.1.5 In the matter of All India ITDC Workers' Association *versus* ITDC & Others [Transfer Case (Civil) No. 73 of 2002 alongwith Transfer Case (Civil) No. 76 of 2002], the Supreme Court, through the judgement delivered on 31 October 2006, upheld the disinvestment in Hotel Agra Ashok. The Supreme Court has, referring to and relying on the judgement dated 10 December 2001 in BALCO matter, observed *inter alia* that disinvestment was a policy decision of the Government of India and the said policy decision should be least interfered in judicial review.

CHAPTER 7: AUDIT AND INTERNAL EXAMINATION OF DISINVESTMENT TRANSACTIONS

7.1 In accordance with the established procedure, subsequent to the completion of disinvestment transactions, the cases are made available to the Comptroller and Auditor General (CAG) for audit. The details of the audit of the transactions and the reports received from CAG, after formation of this Department are given below.

7.2 Audit of the Strategic Sale of the Hotel Properties of HCI

7.2.1 The sale of Centaur Hotel Mumbai Airport, Mumbai was completed on 18 April 2002 in favour of Batra Hospitality Private Limited. CAG took up the audit of this transaction in the month of February 2004. The Preliminary Inspection Report from CAG was received in January 2005. Reply of the government was sent by April 2005. The Final Report was received in May 2005. The Action Taken Note duly vetted by the audit, was sent to the Monitoring Cell (Ministry of Finance) on 1 September 2005.

7.2.2 The sale of Hotel Centaur Juhu Beach, Mumbai was completed on 11 March 2002 in favour of Tulip Hospitality Services Limited. CAG took up audit of this transaction in the month of February 2004. The Preliminary Inspection Report from CAG was received in January 2005. The reply of the government was sent by April 2005. The Final Report was received in May 2005. The Action Taken Note, duly vetted by the audit, was sent to Monitoring Cell (Ministry of Finance) on 1 September 2005.

7.2.3 The sale of Indo Hokke Hotels Limited, Rajgir was completed on 26 March 2002 in favour of Inpac Travels (India) Private Limited. CAG took up the audit of this transaction in August 2004. Preliminary Inspection Report from CAG was received in October 2005. Reply of the government was sent to Audit by 22 September 2006.

7.2.4 In the light of CAG report in the matter, the government of India has referred the strategic sale of Centaur Hotel Mumbai Airport, Mumbai and Hotel Centaur Juhu Beach, Mumbai for enquiry to Central Bureau of Investigation in July 2005.

7.3 Audit of the Strategic Sale of Hotel Properties of ITDC

CAG had commenced audit of strategic sale transactions in the case of six hotel properties of ITDC (Hotel Ashok Bangalore; Hotel Agra Ashok; Hotel Bodhgaya Ashok; Temple Bay Ashok Beach Resort, Mamallapuram; Hotel Madurai Ashok and Hotel Hassan Ashok) in April 2003. For the remaining 13 ITDC hotels (Laxmi Vilas Palace Hotel, Udaipur; Hotel Aurangabad Ashok; Hotel Airport Ashok, Kolkata; Lodhi Hotel, New Delhi; Qutab Hotel, New Delhi; Hotel Ranjit, New Delhi; Hotel Indraprastha, New Delhi; Hotel Kanishka, New Delhi; Hotel Varanasi Ashok; Hotel Manali Ashok; Kovalam Ashok Beach Resort; Hotel Khajuraho Ashok and Chandigarh Project of Punjab Hotels Limited), CAG commenced audit of the transaction in April 2006 and competed it in January 2007. The draft Preliminary Inspection Report for all nineteen hotel transactions was received in February 2007. The reply to the Preliminary Inspection Report was sent in May 2007.

7.4 Audit of Single Bid Strategic Sale Transaction

In November 2004, government decided to examine nine cases of Single Bid transactions, namely (i) MFIL, (ii) CMC, (iii) PPL, (iv) Hotel Ashok Agra, (v) Hotel Ashok Bodhgaya (vi) Hotel Ashok Mamallapuram (vii) Hotel Ashok Bangalore, (viii) LVPH, Udaipur, (ix) Indo Hokke Hotels Limited (Rajgir). Shri S. Lakshminarayanan ex-Deputy CAG was appointed for the purpose in November 2004 and submitted his reports in February/March 2005, which were processed and referred to the office of CAG for appropriate action.

7.5 Audit of the 2002 MUL Rights Issue Transaction

The renunciation of rights shares of Maruti Udyog Limited (MUL) by government in favour of Suzuki Motor Corporation was completed on 15 May 2002. CAG took up the audit of this transaction in July 2005. Preliminary Inspection Report from CAG was received in December 2005. The reply to the Preliminary Inspection Report is being prepared.

7.6 Audit of Sale of Government's Residual Shareholding in MFIL

The residual shareholding of 26 per cent held by government in Modern Food Industries (India) Limited (MFIL) was sold to the Strategic Partner, i.e. Hindustan Lever Limited in November 2002 by exercising 'Put Option' in terms of the provisions of SHA. A Preliminary Inspection Report on this transaction was received from CAG in August 2006. Reply was sent by 1 November 2006. The draft audit para on this transaction has been received from audit. The reply to the draft audit para is under preparation.

7.7 Audit of Strategic Sale of Jessop & Company Limited

In August 2005, government disinvested 72 per cent equity capital of Jessop & Company Limited (JCL) through strategic sale in favour of Indo-Wagon Engineers Limited for an amount of ₹ 18.18 crore. CAG conducted the audit for this transaction and the Preliminary Inspection Report was received on 23 August 2006. The reply to the Preliminary Inspection Report is being prepared.

7.8 Audit of Strategic Sale of Government's Stake in Nine CPSEs, Namely MFIL, BALCO, HTL, CMC, HZL, VSNL, IBP, IPCL and PPL

CAG conducted audit of the transactions relating to disinvestment of government equity through the strategic sale mode in nine CPSEs, viz. MFIL, BALCO, HTL, CMC, HZL, VSNL, IBP, IPCL and PPL. The final Report (Report No. 17/2006) of CAG was tabled in the Parliament on 25 August 2006. This Report has been selected by the Public Accounts Committee for detailed examination during 2006-07. A background note detailing the functions of the Department, evolution of the disinvestment policy and information of general nature was forwarded to Lok Sabha Secretariat on 29 September 2006. The Action Taken Notes were also sent on 11 December 2006. Replies to the questions received from Lok Sabha Secretariat were sent on 20 March 2007. The vetting comments of CAG on the ATN and the Questionnaire have been received.

CHAPTER 8: THE NEW DISINVESTMENT POLICY AND PROGRAMME

8.1 Current Policy on Disinvestment

8.1.1 In May 2004, government adopted the National Common Minimum Programme (NCMP), which outlines the policy of the government with respect to the public sector. The relevant extracts of NCMP are given hereinunder:

> The UPA Government is committed to a strong and effective public sector whose social objectives are met by its commercial functioning. But for this, there is need for selectivity and a strategic focus. The UPA is pledged to devolve full managerial and commercial autonomy to successful, profit-making companies operating in a competitive environment. Generally profit-making companies will not be privatized.
>
> All privatizations will be considered on a transparent and consultative case-by-case basis. The UPA will retain existing "navratna" companies in the public sector while these companies raise resources from the capital market. While every effort will be made to modernize and restructure sick public sector companies and revive sick industry, chronically loss-making companies will either be sold-off, or closed, after all workers have got their legitimate dues and compensation. The UPA will induct private industry to turn around companies that have potential for revival.
>
> The UPA Government believes that privatization should increase competition, not decrease it. It will not support the emergence of any monopoly that only restricts competition. It also believes that there must be a direct link between privatization and social needs—like, for example, the use of privatization revenues for designated social sector schemes. Public sector companies and nationalized banks will be encouraged to enter the capital market to raise resources and offer new investment avenues to retail investors.

8.2 Calling Off of the Ongoing Cases of Strategic Sale

In conformity with the policy enunciated in NCMP, it was decided in February 2005 to formally call off the process of disinvestment through Strategic Sale of profit making CPSEs, as enumerated below:

S. No.	Name of the PSE	Percentage of equity which was earlier proposed to be sold through Strategic Sale
1.	Manganese Ore India Limited	51 per cent
2.	Sponge Iron India Limited	100 per cent
3.	Shipping Corporation of India Limited	54.12 per cent (51 per cent through Strategic Sale and 3.12 per cent to Employees)
4.	National Aluminium Company Limited	61.15 per cent (10 per cent Domestic Issue, 20 per cent ADR Issue, 29.15 per cent Strategic Sale, 2 per cent to Employees)
5.	National Building Construction Corporation Limited	74 per cent
6.	National Fertilizers Limited	53 per cent (51 per cent through Strategic Sale and 2 per cent to Employees)
7.	Rashtriya Chemicals and Fertilizers Limited	53 per cent (51 per cent through Strategic Sale and 2 per cent to Employees)
8.	Hindustan Petroleum Corporation Limited	39.01 per cent (34.01 per cent through Strategic Sale and 5 per cent to Employees)
9.	Engineers India Limited	61 per cent (51 per cent through Strategic Sale and 10 per cent to Employees)
10.	Balmer Lawrie and Company Limited	61.8 per cent
11.	Engineering Projects India Limited	74 per cent
12.	Hindustan Paper Corporation Limited	74 per cent
13.	State Trading Corporation of India Limited	75 per cent (65 per cent through Strategic Sale and 10 per cent to Employees)

8.3 Sale of Small Portions of Government Equity through an IPO or FPO without Changing the Public Sector Character of CPSE

8.3.1 The government has also approved, in principle, the following:

(a) Listing of currently unlisted profitable CPSEs (other than Navratnas) each with a Net Worth in excess of

₹ 200 crore, through an Initial Public Offering (IPO), either in conjunction with a fresh equity issue by the CPSE concerned or independently by the government, on a case by case basis, subject to the residual equity of the government remaining at least 51 per cent and the government retaining management control of the CPSE;

(b) The sale of minority shareholding of the government in listed, profitable CPSEs either in conjunction with a Public Issue of fresh equity by the CPSE concerned or independently by the government subject to the residual equity of the government remaining at least 51 per cent and the government retaining management control of the CPSE; and

(c) Constitution of a "National Investment Fund" (NIF).

8.3.2 On 6 July 2006, government decided to keep all disinvestment decisions and proposals on hold, pending further review. The disinvestment decisions covered under this decision were: disinvestment of 5 per cent of government's holding in Power Finance Corporation Limited (PFC) riding piggy-back on fresh issue of PFC; offer for sale, through book building process, of 15 per cent equity in National Mineral Development Corporation (NMDC) and 10 per cent equity each in Neyveli Lignite Corporation Limited (NLC) and National Aluminium Company Ltd. (NALCO). Later, on 23 November 2006, government approved an IPO by PFC consisting of a fresh issue of equity only. The IPO of PFC was completed in February 2007.

8.4 National Investment Fund

8.4.1 In pursuance of the policy laid down in NCMP and the decision of the government to constitute NIF, the proposal for its operationalisation was approved on 3 November 2005. Accordingly, DoD has issued a Resolution on 23 November 2005 (Annexure-13) constituting 'NIF' with the following objectives, structure and administrative arrangements, investment strategy and accounting procedure:

(a) Objectives

(i) The proceeds from disinvestment of CPSEs will be channelised into NIF, which is to be maintained outside the Consolidated Fund of India (CFI).

(ii) The corpus of NIF will be of a permanent nature.

(iii) NIF will be professionally managed to provide sustainable returns to the government, without depleting the corpus. Selected Public Sector Mutual Funds will be entrusted with the management of the corpus of NIF.

(iv) 75 per cent of the annual income of NIF will be used to finance selected social sector schemes, which promote education, health and employment. The residual 25 per cent of the annual income of the Fund will be used to meet the capital investment requirements of profitable and revivable CPSEs that yield adequate returns, in order to enlarge their capital base to finance expansion/diversification.

(b) Structure and Administrative Arrangements

NIF will be operated by the selected Fund Managers under the 'discretionary mode' of the Portfolio Management Scheme, which is governed by SEBI guidelines. The entire work of NIF will be supervised by the Chief Executive Officer (CEO) of NIF, a senior officer of the government. A part time Advisory Board consisting of three eminent persons, with the requisite expertise to be appointed by the government, would advise CEO on various aspects of the functioning of NIF.

(c) Investment Strategy

(i) The broad investment strategy is to provide sustainable returns without depleting the corpus.

(ii) The investment strategy for NIF will be formulated by CEO based on the advice of the Advisory Board so as to ensure that government has a hands-off relationship in terms of the actual investment to be done by the Fund Managers.

(iii) Only broad guidelines are to be provided under the "discretionary mode" to the Fund Managers, within which individual investments would be made independently by the Fund Managers. More detailed guidelines specifying investment instruments and limits for investment in such instruments will be separately specified in the agreements to be entered into between the Fund Managers and CEO of NIF on behalf of the government.

(iv) Other operational details such as allocation of funds to the selected Fund Managers, negotiations of management fee and charges to be paid to the Fund Managers, etc. will be also decided by CEO based on the advice of the Advisory Board. Appropriate mechanisms for regular review and monitoring of the functioning of NIF, emerging market trends and future prospects will be instituted.

(d) Accounting Procedure

(i) The receipts from disinvestment of CPSEs will be deposited in CFI under the designated Head. Thereafter, these amounts would be appropriated from the CFI, with due approval, by the Department of Disinvestment and transferred to the selected Fund Managers through CEO of NIF.

(ii) Income from NIF will similarly be deposited in CFI and would be appropriated from it for specific purposes as per the scheme of appropriation approved from time to time by the Department of Expenditure.

8.4.2 Fund Managers of NIF

The following Public Sector Mutual Funds have been appointed initially as Fund Managers to manage the funds of NIF under the 'discretionary mode' of the Portfolio Management Scheme which is governed by SEBI guidelines.

(a) UTI Asset Management Company Limited

(b) SBI Funds Management (Private) Limited

(c) Jeevan Bima Sahayog, Asset Management Company Limited.

8.5 Disinvestment Programme for 2007-08

8.5.1 MUL—In December 2006 the government decided to sell its residual 10.27 per cent equity in MUL through the differential pricing method to Indian public sector financial institutions, public sector banks and Indian mutual funds. The sale was completed in May 2007 realising ₹ 2366.94 crore for the exchequer.

8.5.2 Power Companies (REC, PGCIL and NHPC)

8.5.2.1 On 23 November 2006, the government had approved the proposals for fresh issue of 20 per cent of the pre-issue paid-up equity capital in Rural Electrification Corporation and fresh issue not exceeding 24 per cent of the Power Grid Corporation of India Limited's paid-up equity capital in tranches, first tranche being limited to 10 per cent only. Subsequently, on 7 December 2006, government approved the proposal for fresh issue not exceeding 24 per cent of the paid-up equity capital of National Hydro-electric Power Corporation Limited in one or more tranches.

8.5.2.2 Thereafter, on 8 February 2007 government decided to piggy-back with an Offer for Sale of 10 per cent, 5 per cent and 5 per cent of the pre-issue paid-up equity of REC, PGCIL and NHPC respectively. The details of expected realization from these disinvestments are given below:

Sl. No	PSE	Equity as on 31.3.06 (in ₹ Crore)	GOI holding Pre-issue (%)	Book value as on 31.3.06 (in ₹) (Face value of ₹ 10)	Proposed fresh issue of equity by CPSE	Proposed disinvest-ment out of Govt's shareholding	Realisation based on book value as on 31.3.06 in (₹ crore)		GOI holding after the IPO %
					% of Equity Capital (Per Issue)	% of Equity Capital (Per Issue)	CPSE	GOI	
1	REC	780.60	100	53.78	10	10	420	420	81.22
2	PGCIL	3,623.44	100	26.80	10	5	971	486	86.36
3	NHPC	10,349.00	100	14.40	10	5	1,490	745	86.36
Total							**2,881**	**1651**	

Note: The actual realization is expected to be higher and would depend on the prevailing market conditions.

ANNEXURE-I

REF (Para 1.2.1)

MARKET CAPITALISATION OF CPSEs as ON 31.07.2007

Sl.	Code	Name	Rate (₹ per share)	Market Capitalisation (₹ in Crore)
1	526173	Andrew Yule & Company Ltd.	26.75	155.86
2	523319	Balmer Lawrie & Co. Ltd.	432.30	725.83
3	532485	Balmer Lawrie Investment Ltd.	91.60	203.33
4	500048	Bharat Earth Movers Ltd.	1247.90	5228.70
5	500049	Bharat Electronics Ltd.	1770.10	14160.80
6	500103	Bharat Heavy Electricals Ltd.	1731.70	84770.18
7	524663	Bharat Immunological & Biologicals Ltd.	13.51	34.30
8	500547	Bharat Petroleum Corporation Ltd.	321.00	11605.50
9	500072	Bongai Refinery and Petrochemicals Ltd.	52.60	1051.04
10	500110	Chennai Petroleum Corporation Ltd.	288.50	4392.80
11	531344	Container Corporation of India	2200.30	14300.06
12	523618	Dredging Corporation of India	546.90	1531.32
13	532178	Engineers India Ltd.	479.70	2694.00
14	*590024	Fertilizers and Chemicals (Travancore) Ltd.	22.45	796.46
15	532155	Gail (India) Ltd.	337.60	28549.20
16	513599	Hindustan Copper Ltd.	101.85	7416.90
17	500191	Hindustan Machine Tools Ltd.	65.95	3087.59
18	500449	Hindustan Organic Chemical Ltd.	47.35	318.98
19	500104	Hindustan Petroleum Corporation Ltd.	257.40	8734.35
20	524316	Hindustan Photo Films Manufacturing Ltd.	30.00	575.71
21	532189	India Tourism Development Corporation	78.10	52.87
22	530965	Indian Oil Corporation Ltd.	402.90	48039.55
23	523596	IRCON International Ltd.	152.50	150.94
24	523610	ITI Ltd.	43.00	378.40
25	513377	MMTC Ltd.	3190.60	15953.00
26	500108	Mahanagar Telephone Nigam Ltd.	150.45	9478.35
27	504824	Maharashtra Elecktrosmelt Ltd.	158.70	380.88
28	500109	Mangalore Refinery & Petrochemicals Ltd.	44.30	7766.44
29	532234	National Aluminium Co. Ltd.	263.00	16945.34
30	523630	National Fertilisers Ltd.	32.05	1572.30
31	526371	National Mineral Development Corporation Ltd.	3537.00	46744.00
32	532555	National Thermal Power Corporation Ltd.	165.65	136586.12
33	513683	Neyveli Lignite Corporation Ltd.	81.65	13698.50
34	500312	Oil and Natural Gas Corporation Ltd.	914.00	195492.95
35	532810	Power Finance Corporation Ltd.	185.75	21319.77
36	524230	Rashtriya Chemicals and Fertilizers Ltd.	46.85	2584.66
37	505141	Scooters India Ltd.	24.45	97.78
38	523598	Shipping Corporation of India Ltd.	208.85	5895.89
39	512531	State Trading Corporation of India Ltd.	166.05	498.15

(Contd.)

40	500113	Steel Authority of India Ltd.	150.05	61976.66
41	532168	Madras Fertilisers Ltd.	Delisted from BSE effective 13/04/2005. Market Capitalisation Data on other exchanges not available.	
42	NA	Kudremukh Iron Ore Ltd.	Quoted on Bangalore & Madras Stock Exchange, quotes are not available.	
43	524013	Hindustan Fluorocorbons Ltd.	Trading suspended since 1988 on BSE. Quoted on Hyderabad Stock Exchange, quotes are not available.	
44	NA	Hindustan Cables Ltd.	Quoted on Calcutta Stock Exchange, quotes are not available.	
		Total		**775945.46**

Source - **BSE:** * Trading in Fertilisers and Chemical Travancore Limited was shifted to Permitted Category w.e.f. 04/10/2004.

Kochi Refinieries Ltd. since merged with BPCL w.e.f. 22 September 2006.

IBP Co. Ltd. since merged with IOC w.e.f. 4 June 2007.

ANNEXURE-II

REF (Para 2.2.8)

REALISATION FROM OFFER FOR SALE OF SHARES IN CPSEs DURING 2003-04 AND 2004-05

	DCI	*GAIL*	*IBP*	*ONGC*	*NTPC*
Bid opening date	26.2.2004	27.2.2004	23.2.2004	5.3.2004	7.10.2004
Bid closing date	4.3.2004	5.3.2004	1.3.2004	13.3.2004	14.10.2004
Floor price per share/Price Band (₹)	385-400	185	620	680-750	52-62
% of Government equity prior to the Offer	98.56	67.35	26	84.11	100
% of CPSE's equity offered for sale	20	10	26	10	5.25
Shares offered for sale (crore Nos)	0.56	8.457	0.576	14.26	43.2915
Ratio of bids received to shares offered (No. of times)	17.78	6.71	2.66	5.88	13.14
No of bidders allocated shares (lakhs)	2.19	3.41	0.86	7.43	12.46
Final price per share (in ₹)	400	195	620	750	62
Discount for Retail Bidders	5%	5%	5%	5%	-
Effectiive price for Retail Bidders	380	185.25	589	712.5	62
Total amount realised (₹ crore)	**221.2**	**1627.36**	**350.66**	**10558.4**	**2684.07**
Cumulative total (₹ crore)					**15441.7**

ANNEXURE-III

REF (Para 2.2.9)

DISINVESTMENT PROCEEDS FROM SALE OF MINORITY SHAREHOLDING IN CPSEs

(₹ crore)

		1991-92	1992-93	1994-95	1995-96	1996-97	1997-98	1998-99	1999-00	2003-04	2004-05
S. No.	Name of CPSEs	Amount	Amount	Amount	Amount	Amount	Amount	Amount	Amount	Amount	Amount
1	AYL	*									
2	BEL	*		47.17							
3	BEML	*		48.27							
4	BHEL	*	8.21	301.34							
5	BPCL	*	331.18								
6	BRPL	*	45.40								
7	CMC	*									
8	CONCOR			99.71	14.12			221.65			
9	CPCL	*									
10	DCIL	*								221.20	
11	EIL			67.53							
12	FACT	*	1.30								
13	GAIL			194.12				671.86	945.00	1627.36	
14	HCL	*	8.07								
15	Hind. Cables	*									
16	HMT	*	23.38								
17	HOCL	*									
18	HPCL	*	331.85	563.11							
19	HPF	*									
20	HZL	*	81.55								
21	IBP									350.66	
22	IOC			1033.65				1208.96	162.79		

(Contd.)

23	IPCL	*									
24	IRCON	*									
25	ITDC			51.99							
26	ITI	*	15.63								
27	KIOCL			11.40							
28	KRL	*									
29	MMTC	*									
30	MTNL	*		1322.17	135.90		910.00				
31	NALCO	*	244.20	0.10							
32	NFL	*	0.72	0.28							
33	NLC	*	70.43								
34	NMDC		17.88								
35	NTPC										2684.07
36	PGCIL										
37	RCF	*	30.36								
38	SAIL	*	700.1	22.66	13.30						
39	SCI	*		28.08							
40	STC	*	2.25								
41	VSNL	*				379.67		783.68	75.00		
Total		**3037.74**	**1912.51**	**3791.58**	**163.32**	**379.67**	**910.00**	**2886.15**	**1182.79**	**2199.22**	**2684.07**
Grand Total											**33543.56**

Note: In 1991-92 shares of the CPSEs (marked*above) were sold in bundles, amount realised CPSE-wise is not available. There was no receipt from sale of minority shares in 1993-94, 2000-01, 2005-06, 2006-07.

ANNEXURE-IV

REF (Para 2.4)

RECEIPTS FROM STRATEGIC SALE DURING 1999-2000 TO 2003-04

S.No.	Name of CPSE disinvested	Type of disinvestment	Name of buyer	Percentage of equity sold	Percentage of residual equity of Govt.	Amount realised (₹ crore)
1999-00						
1.	Modern Food Industries (India) Ltd.	Strategic sale	Hindustan Lever Ltd.	74	26	105.45
					Sub Total	**105.45**
2000-01						
1.	Bharat Aluminium Company Ltd.	Strategic sale	Sterlite Industries (India) Ltd.	51	49	551.50
2.	Lagan Jute Machinery Company Ltd.^^	Strategic sale	Murlidhar Ratanlal Exports Ltd.	74	26	2.53
					Sub Total	**554.03**
2001-02						
1.	HTL Ltd.	Strategic sale	Himachal Futuristic Communications Ltd.	74	26	55.00
2.	CMC Ltd.	Strategic sale	Tata Sons Ltd.	51	32.31	152.00
3.	India Tourism Development Corporation (ITDC)					
	(i) Hotel Hassan Ashok	Strategic sale	Malnad Hotels& Resorts(P) Ltd.	89.97		*2.27
	(ii) Hotel Bodhgaya Ashok	Strategic sale	Lotus Nikko Hotels	89.97	-	1.81
	(iii) Hotel Madurai Ashok	Strategic sale	Sangu Chakra Hotels Pvt. Ltd.	89.97	-	*4.98

(Contd.)

S.No.	Name of CPSE disinvested	Type of disinvestment	Name of buyer	Percentage of equity sold	Percentage of residual equity of Govt.	Amount realised (₹ crore)
	(iv) Temple Bay Ashok Beach Resort, Mamallapuram	Strategic sale	G.R. Thanga Maligai (P) Ltd.	89.97		6.13
	(v) Hotel Agra Ashok	Strategic sale	Mohan Singh	89.97	-	*3.61
	(vi) Laxmi Vilas Palace Hotel, Udaipur	Strategic sale	Bharat Hotels Ltd.	89.97	-	6.77
	(vii) Qutab Hotel, New Delhi	Strategic sale	Consortium of Sushil Gupta and Others	89.97	-	*34.45
	(viii) Lodhi Hotel, New Delhi	Strategic sale	Silverlink Holdings Ltd. & Consortium	89.97	-	*71.93
4.	IBP Ltd.	Strategic sale	Indian Oil Corpn.	33.58	26	1,153.68
5.	Videsh Sanchar Nigam Ltd.	Strategic sale	Panatone Finvest Ltd. (a Tata Group Co.)	25	27.97	1439.25
6.	Paradeep Phosphates Ltd.	Strategic sale	Zuari Maroc Phosphates Pvt. Ltd.	74	26	151.70
7.	HCI# -Indo Hokke Hotels Ltd., Rajgir	Strategic sale	Inpac Travels (India) Pvt. Ltd.	100	-	# 6.51
					Sub Total	**3,090.09**
2002-03						
1.	Hindustan Zinc Ltd.	Strategic sale	Sterlite Opportunities & Ventures Ltd.	26	49.92	445.00
2.	Indian Petrochemicals Corporation Ltd.	Strategic sale	Reliance Petro Investments Ltd.	26	33.95	1,490.84
3.	ITDC					
	(i) Hotel Airport Ashok, Kolkata	Strategic sale	Bright Enterprises (P) Ltd. & Consortium	89.97	-	*19.39

(Contd.)

	(ii) Kovalam Ashok Beach Resort	Strategic sale	M Far Hotels Limited	89.97	-	*40.38
	(iii) Hotel Aurangabad Ashok	Strategic sale	Loksangam Hotels & Resorts Pvt. Ltd. & Consortium	89.97	-	*16.50
	(iv) Hotel Manali Ashok	Strategic sale	Auto Impex Limited	89.97	-	*3.66
	(v) Hotel Khajuraho Ashok	Strategic sale	Bharat Hotels Ltd.	89.97	-	*2.19
	(vi) Hotel Varanasi Ashok	Strategic sale	Consortium of Ramnath Hotels(P) Ltd.	89.97	-	*8.38
	(vii) Hotel Ranjit, New Delhi	Strategic sale	Consortium of Unison Hotels Ltd. & Formax	89.97	-	*29.28
	(viii) Hotel Kanishka, New Delhi	Strategic sale	Nehru Place Hotels Ltd.	89.97	-	*92.38
	(ix) Hotel Indraprastha, New Delhi	Strategic sale	Moral Trading & Investment Ltd.	89.97	-	*43.38
	(x) Chandigarh Project of Punjab Hotels Limited	Strategic sale	TAJGVK Hotels & Resorts Ltd.	100	-	**17.27
4.	Modern Foods Industries (India) Ltd.	Sale of residual shares to SP (Put Option by GoI)	Hindustan Lever Ltd.	25.995	-	44.07
					Sub Total	**2,252.72**
2003-04						
1.	Hindustan Zinc Ltd.	Call Option by SP	Sterlite Opportunities & Ventures Ltd.	18.92	29.53	323.88
2.	Jessop & Co. Ltd.^^	Strategic sale	Indo Wagon Engineering Ltd.	72	27	^^18.18
					Sub Total	**342.06**
					Grand Total	**6,344.35**

#Proceeds went to Air India, the holding company. ^^ Amount received by BBUNL, the holding company. *Inclusive of payments to GoI and statutory authorities and other payments. **Proceeds went to Chandigarh Administration and ITDC, the holding company.

ANNEXURE-V

REF (Para 2.5)

RECEIPTS FROM OTHER RELATED TRANSACTIONS UNDERTAKEN DURING 1999-00 TO 2005-06

S.No.	Name of CPSE	Type of transaction	Name of buyer, if any	Percentage of equity sold	Percentage of residual equity of Govt.	Amount realised (Rs crore)
Receipts from Capital Receipts, Special Dividends and Dividend Tax in CPSEs.						
1999-00						
1.	Bharat Aluminium Co. Ltd.	Capital reduction and special dividend	-	-	-	244.42 31.00
					Sub Total	**275.42**
2001-02						
1.	Videsh Sanchar Nigam Ltd.	(i) Dividend (ii) Dividend Tax	-	-	-	1887.00 363.00
2.	State Trading Corporation of India Ltd.	Special dividend	-	-	-	40.00
3.	Minerals and Metals Trading Corporation of India Ltd.	Special dividend	-	-	-	60.00
					Sub Total	**2350.00**
Receipts from Slump Sale						
2001-02						
1.	**HCI***-Hotel Centaur Juhu Beach, Mumbai	Slump Sale	Tulip Hospitality Services Ltd.	-	-	*153.00
					Sub Total	**153.00**
2002-03						
1.	**HCI**-Centaur Hotel Mumbai Airport, Mumbai*	Slump Sale	Batra Hospitality Pvt. Ltd.	-	-	*83.00
					Sub Total	**83.00**

(Contd.)

Receipts from Sale of Shares to Employees in Privatised CPSEs						
2001-02						
1.	Videsh Sanchar Nigam Ltd.	Sale of shares to Employees	Employees	1.85	26.12	25.19
					Sub Total	**25.19**
2002-03						
1.	Hindustan Zinc Ltd.	-do-	Employees	1.46	48.45	6.19
2.	CMC Ltd.	-do-	Employees	6.06	26.25	6.07
					Sub Total	**12.26**
2004-05						
1.	Indian Petrochemicals Corporation Ltd.	-do-	Employees	4.58	0.42	64.81
					Sub Total	**64.81**
2005-06						
1.	Maruti Udyog Limited	-do-	Employees	0.01	10.27	2.08
					Sub Total	**2.08**
Receipts from Control Premium Given by Suzuki Motors Co. (SMC) to GOI For Renunciation of Rights Shares in Favour of SMC						
2002-03						
1.	Maruti Udyog Ltd.^	Control premium for Rights Shares	SMC		45.79	^1,000.00
					Sub Total	**1,000.00**
Receipts from Leasing of Hotel of ITDC						
2001-02						
1.	ITDC - Ashok Bangalore	30 years lease-cum-management contract	Bharat Hotels Ltd.	-	-	@39.41
					Sub Total	**39.41**
					Grand Total	**4,005.17**

*Proceeds went to Air India. ^ ₹ 1,000 crore as control premium for the rights issue of 6,06,585 shares. @ Inclusive of 50% of discounted Minimum Guaranteed Annual Payment (MGAP) for thirty years, Security Deposit and Business Transfer Consideration. The proceeds went to Kumarakruppa Frontier Hotels Ltd. (a CPSE under the Ministry of Tourism) and Airports Authority of India.

ANNEXURE-VI

REF (Para 2.6.3)

REALISATION FROM SALE OF ALL OR PART OF THE RESIDUAL EQUITY IN DISINVESTED CPSEs/COMPANIES DURING 2003-04 TO JULY 2007

	MUL IPO	*IPCL Offer for Sale*	*CMC Offer for Sale*	*ICI*	*MUL Private Placement*	
					Tranche I	*Tranche II*
			2003-04		*2005-06*	*2007-08*
Bid opening date	12.6.2003	20.2.2004	23.2.2004	-	05.01.2006	27.04.2007
Bid closing date	19.6.2003	27.2.2004	28.2.2004	27.10.2003	11.01.2006	08.05.2007
Floor price per share (in ₹)	*115	170	475	-	620	760
% of company's equity with the Government prior to the Offer	45.79	33.95	26.25	9.20	18.28	10.27
% of company's equity offered for sale	27.51	28.95	26.25	9.20	8.00	10.27
Shares offered for sale (crore Nos)	7.947	7.185	0.397	0.3761	2.31	2.97
Ratio of bids received to shares offered (No. of times)	8.92	4.9	9.60	-	1.78	1.12
No of bidders allocated shares	2.48 lakh	1.95 lakh	1.28 lakh	^1	8	32
Final price per share (in ₹)	125	170	485	205	**678.24	**797.49
Discount for Retail Bidders	-	5%	5%	-	-	-
Effective price for Retail Bidders	125	161.5	460.75	-	-	-
Total amount realised (₹ crore)	**993.34**	**1202.85**	**190.44**	**77.1**	**1567.6**	**2366.94**
Cumulative amount realised (₹ crore)						**6398.27**

* Face value was ₹ 5 per share. Face value of shares of other companies was ₹ 10 each.

** The average price per share

^ Sold to Asian Paints (India) Ltd.

ANNEXURE-VII

REF (Para 2.7)

SUMMARY OF RECEIPTS FROM DISINVESTMENT: 1991-92 TO JULY 2007

Year	*Budgeted receipt (₹ crore)*	*Receipts through sale of minority shareholding in CPSEs (₹ crore)*	*Receipts through sale of majority shareholding of one CPSE to another CPSE (₹ crore)*	*Receipts through Strategic sale (₹ crore)*	*Receipts from other related transactions (₹ crore)*	*Receipts from sale of residual shareholding in disinvested CPSEs/companies (₹ crore)*	*Total receipts (₹ crore)*	*Transactions*
		Ann. II	*Para 2.3*	*Ann. IV*	*Ann. V*	*Ann. VI*		
1991-92	2,500	3,037.74	-	-	-	-	**3,037.74**	Minority shares sold in Dec, 1991 and Feb, 1992 by auction method in bundles of "very good", "good" and "average" companies
1992-93	2,500	1,912.51	-	-	-	-	**1,912.51**	Shares sold separately for each company by auction method.
1993-94	3,500	-	-	-	-	-	**-**	Equity of 6 companies sold by auction method but proceeds received in 94-95.
1994-95	4,000	4,843.10	-	-	-	-	**4,843.10**	Shares sold by auction method.
1995-96	7,000	168.48	-	-	-	-	**168.48**	Shares sold by auction method.
1996-97	5,000	379.67	-	-	-	-	**379.67**	GDR-VSNL
1997-98	4,800	910.00	-	-	-	-	**910.00**	GDR-MTNL
1998-99	5,000	*5371.11	-	-	-	-	**5,371.11**	GDR-VSNL; Domestic offerings of CONCOR and GAIL; Cross purchase by 3 Oil sector companies i.e. GAIL, ONGC and IOC.
1999-00	10,000	**1479.27	-	105.45	275.42	-	**1,860.14**	GDR-GAIL; Domestic offering of VSNL; capital reduction and dividend from BALCO; Strategic sale of MFIL.

(Contd.)

2000-01	10,000	-	1,317.23	554.03	-	-	**1,871.26**	Sale of KRL, CPCL and BRPL to CPSEs; Strategic sale of BALCO and LJMC.
2001-02	12,000	-	-	3,090.09	2,567.60	-	**5,657.69**	Strategic sale of CMC, HTL, VSNL, IBP, PPL, hotel properties of ITDC and HCI, slump sale of Hotel Centaur Juhu Beach, Mumbai and leasing of Ashok Bangalore; Special dividend from VSNL, STC and MMTC; sale of shares to VSNL employees.
2002-03	12,000	-	-	2,252.72	1,095.26	-	**3,347.98**	Strategic sale of HZL, IPCL, hotel properties of ITDC, slump sale of Centaur Hotel Mumbai Airport, Mumbai; Premium for renunciation of rights issue in favour of SMC; Put Option of MFIL; Sale of shares to employees of HZL and CMC.
2003-04	14,500	12,741.62	-	342.06	-	2,463.73	**15,547.41**	Strategic sale of JCL; Call Option of HZL; Offer for Sale of MUL, IBP, IPCL, CMC, DCI, GAIL and ONGC; Sale of shares of ICI Ltd.
2004-05	4,000	2,700.06	-	-	64.81	-	**2,764.87**	Offer for Sale of NTPC and spill over of ONGC; sale of shares to IPCL employees
2005-06	No target fixed	-	-	-	2.08	1,567.60	**1,569.68**	Sale of MUL shares to Indian public sector financial institutions & banks and employees
2006-07	No target fixed	-	-	-	-	-	-	
2007-08	No target fixed	-	-	-	-	2,366.94	**2,366.94**	Sale of MUL shares to public sector financial institutions, public sector banks and Indian mutual funds.
Total		**33,543.56**	**1,317.23**	**6,344.35**	**4,005.17**	**6,398.27**	**51,608.58**	

* Out of ₹ 5371.11, ₹ 4184 crore constitute receipts from cross purchase of shares of ONGC, GAIL and IOC.

** Out of ₹ 1479.27, ₹ 459.27 crore constitute receipts from cross purchase of shares of ONGC, GAIL and IOC.

ANNEXURE-VIII

REF (Para 3.6.3.3)

VALUATION UNDER DIFFERENT METHODS, RESERVE PRICE AND SALE PRICE OF STRATEGIC SALE

Sr. No.	*CP SEs*	*Date of EoI*	*No. of EoIs/ QIPs/ Valid Bids*	*Date of CCD decision*	*% of GoI equity at the time of disinvestment*	*% of equity sold*	*No. of shares sold (in Lakh)*	*Advisors valuation for 100% equity (₹ in crore)*				*Reserve price for equity sold (₹ in crore)*	*Sale price (₹ in crore)*	*Name of successful Bidder*
1	2	3	4	5	6	7	8	9	10	11	12	13	14	15
								BV	AVM	CC	DCF			
1	MFIL*	21.05 1999	10\10\1	25.01 2000	100	74	*0.92	28.51	68.18	78.55	Negligible	-	* 105.45	Hindustan Lever Ltd.
2	BALCO	30.06 2000	8\3\2	21.02 2001	100	51	1125.2	597.2-681.9	1072.3	587.0 909.0	651.2-994.7	514.4	551.5	Sterlite Industries (India) Ltd.
3	CMC	30.03 2001	14\14\1	05.10 2001	83.31	51	77.27	72.74	37.58	102.53	213.49	108.88	152	Tata Sons Ltd.
4	HTL*	01.08 2000	6\4\2	05.10 2001	100	74	11.10	57.473	52.792	40.317	52.436	38.8	55	Himachal Futuristic Communication Ltd.
5	VSNL	10.04 2001	6\6\2	05.02 2002	52.97	25	712.5	4018.5	5301	5871	4873.5	1218.38	1439.25	Panatone Finvest Ltd. (a Tata Group Co.)
6	IBP	28.02 2001	15\15\7	05\02 2002	59.8	33.8	74.38	608	445	972-1382	1124	377	1153.68	Indian Oil Company Ltd.
7	PPL*	15.05 2001	4\4\1	14.02 2002	100	74	32.02	48.9	206.25-495.0	NA	111.8	176.09	151.7	Zuari Maroc Phosphates Pvt. Ltd.
8	HZL	15.01 2001	9\7\2	27.03 2002	75.92	26	1098.6	1186.9	1619	1023-1442	1073-1356	353.17	445	Sterlite Opportunities & Ventures Ltd.
9	JCL	23.03 2001	5\5\2	27.02 2002	99	72	681.34	-17.82	30.60\60.28	NA	13.5	12	18.18	Indo-Wagon Engineering Ltd.
10	IPCL	18.12 2001	4\3\3	18.05 2002	59.95	26	645.39	2554.4	3673.7	3648.9	3251.8	845	1490.84	Reliance Petro Investments Ltd.

BV–Book Value; AVM–Asset Valuation Method; CC–Comparable Companies/transaction multiple; DCF–Discounted Cash Flow; NA–Not Applicable. * Face Value–₹ 1000

ANNEXURE-IX

REF (Para 3.6.3.3)

STRATEGIC SALE/SLUMP SALE/LEASE OF ITDC AND HCI HOTEL PROPERTIES: VALUATION UNDER DIFFERENT METHODS, RESERVE PRICE AND REALISATION

S.No.	*Name of Hotel*	*Date of EOI*	*No. of EOIs/ QIPs/ Bids*	*Date of CCD decision*	*% of GOI equity*	*% of equity sold*	*Advisor's Valuation for 100% Equity (₹ In Crore)*					*Reserve price (100% equity)*	*Amont realized for Govt.'s equity + statutory & other payments, if any) (₹ In crore)*	*Name of Purchaser*
							DCF	BV	CC		AVM			
	ITDC - 19 Hotels								EBITDA	Net profit				
1	Hotel Hassan Ashok	25.01.2001	13/11/2	13.11.2001	89.97	89.97	2.19	0.17	1.55	2.12	4.96	2.19	*2.27	Malnad Hotels & Resorts(P) Ltd.
2	Hotel Bodhgaya Ashok	25.01.2001	14/13/1	13.11.2001	89.97	89.97	1.76	1.26	1.32	1.40	2.35	1.67	1.81	Lotus Nikko Hotels
3	Hotel Madurai Ashok	25.01.2001	24/22/2	13.11.2001	89.97	89.97	3.64	–0.33	2.57	2.02	3.91	3.64	*4.98	Sangu Chakra Hotels Pvt. Ltd.
4	Temple Bay Ashok Beach Resort, Mamallapuram	25.01.2001	29/26/1	13.11.2001	89.97	89.97	5.45	2.72	4.37	3.41	3.96	5.18	6.13	G.R. Thanga Maligai (P) Ltd.
5	Hotel Agra Ashok	25.01.2001	21/19/1	13.11.2001	89.97	89.97	3.43	1.16	2.65	2.29	3.84	3.26	*3.61	Mohan Singh
6	Laxmi Vilas Palace Hotel, Udaipur	25.03.2001	15/12/1	05.02.2002	89.97	89.97	6.12	1.74	5.90	4.26	5.93	6.12	6.77	Bharat Hotels Ltd.
7	Qutub Hotel, New Delhi	25.03.2001	22/19/2	05.02.2002	89.97	89.97	31.00	0.10	27.02	17.85	27.23	31.00	*34.45	Consortium of Sushil Gupta & Others
8	Lodhi Hotel, New Delhi	25.03.2001	27/25/3	05.02.2002	89.97	89.97	40.36	–5.87	14.91	11.08	35.82	40.36	*71.93	Consortium of Silverlink Holdings Ltd. and others.
9	Hotel Airport Ashok, Kolkata	15.02.2002	21/21/2	31.05.2002	89.97	89.97	14.83	–15.60	1.56	–4.10	–19.31	14.83	*19.39	Consortium of Bright Enterprises (P) Ltd. and Modern Publishers
10	Kovalam Ashok Beach Resort	15.02.2002	31/31/4	31.05.2002	89.97	89.97	41.75	–1.50	39.02	24.54	22.51	41.75	*40.38	M Far Hotels Limited
11	Hotel Aurangabad Ashok	15.02.2002	23/23/5	31.05.2002	89.97	89.97	15.05	0.82	-	-	13.28	15.05	*16.50	Consortium of Loksangam Hotels & Resorts Pvt. Ltd. and others.
12	Hotel Manali Ashok	15.02.2002	27/27/6	31.05.2002	89.97	89.97	1.91	1.25	1.66	0.53	1.63	1.91	*3.66	Auto Impex Limited.
13	Hotel Khajuraho Ashok	25.04.2002	12/12/2	05.07.2002	89.97	89.97	2.01	0.41	1.62	0.63	0.32	2.01	*2.19	Bharat Hotels Ltd.

(Contd.)

14	Hotel Varanasi Ashok	25.04.2002	14/14/3	05.07.2002	89.97	89.97	5.55	1.27	-	-	0.75	5.55	*8.38	Consortium of Ramnath Hotels Pvt. Ltd. and others.
15	Hotel Ranjit, New Delhi	25.04.2002	8/8/2	07.09.2002	89.97	89.97	25.18	–0.49	-	-	14.17	23.78	*29.28	Consortium of Unison Hotels Ltd. and Formax Commercial Pvt. Ltd.
16	Hotel Kanishka, New Delhi	25.04.2002	22/22/8	05.07.2002	89.97	89.97	70.90	3.95	39.80	32.86	45.81	70.90	*92.38	Nehru Place Hotels Ltd.
17	Hotel Indraprastha, New Delhi	25.04.2002	30/30/6	05.07.2002	89.97	89.97	18.34	1.70	-	-	19.58	18.34	*43.38	Moral Trading & Investment Ltd.
18	Chandigarh Project of Punjab Hotels Ltd.	25.04.2002	17/16/2	05.07.2002	100	100	14.01	8.18	-	-	9.50	14.01	$17.27	TAJGVK Hotels & Resorts Ltd.
19	Hotel Ashok Bangalore	25.01.2001	30/24/1	13.11.2001	This hote property of ITDC has been given on Lease-cum-Management Contract basis to Bharat Hotels Ltd. for a period of 30 years at Minimum Guaranteed Annual Payment of ₹ 4.11 Crore. The Lessee had made an upfront payment of ₹ 39.41 crore. It included payment of 50% of discounted Minimum Guaranteed Annual Payments for 30 years; security deposit and business transfer consideration. Proceeds went to Kumarakruppa Frontier Hotels Ltd. (A CPSU Under Ministry of Tourism) & Airport Authority of India.									
	HCI - 3 Hotels													
20	Hotel Centaur Juhu Beach, Mumbai	31.10.2000	20/17/1	10.11.2001/ 27.03.2002	100	Slump-sale	81.70-121.60	13.60	32.90-63.30	-	134.10	101.60	#153.00	Tulip Hospitality Services Ltd.
21	Indo Hokke Hotels Ltd., Rajgir	31.10.2000	8/8/1	10.11.2001/ 27.03.2002	100	100	2.90-5.10	4.60	3.60-5.80	-	6.10	3.86	#6.51	Inpac Travels (India) Private Ltd.
22	Hotel Centaur Mumbai Airport, Mumbai	31.10.2000	21/17/1	05.02.2002	100	Slump-sale	78.30-105.70	1.70	27.60-53.00	-	43.50	78.30	#83.00	Batra Hospitality Private Ltd.

* Inc usive of payments to GOI, statutory authorities and other payments.
$ Proceeds went to Chandigarh Administration & ITDC. # Proceeds went to Air India.

BV–BooK Value; AVM–Asset Valuation Method; CC–Comparable Companies/transaction multiple; DCF–Discounted Cash Flow; EBITDA–Earning Before Interest, Taxes, Depreciation & Amortisation.

ANNEXURE-X

REF (Para 4.2)

PUT/CALL OPTIONS FOR RESIDUAL SHARES IN DISINVESTED CPSEs

S.No.	*CPSEs*	*Date of CCD decision*	*% of equity disinvested*	*% of equity retained on the date of SS/JVA (in MUL)*	*Option*	*Period*	*Basis of valuation*	*Remarks*
1	MFIL	25.01.2000	74	26	Put Option	From 31st January 2001 till survival of the agreement	FV	Government exercised Put Option for remaining shares on 28.11.2002 at SS price.
2	LJMC	10.05.2000	74	26	No Call/Put Option	-	-	Government shareholding stands reduced to 18.3% consequent to a Rights Issue made by LJMC which was not subscribed by BBUNL
3	BALCO	21.02.2001	51	49	No Put Option	-	-	-
					Call Option for 49%	From 3rd March 2004 till survival of the agreement	FV or SS price+14% per annum interest half yearly	Strategic partner exercised Call Option on 22.03.2004. A final decision on the sale of Called Shares is yet to be taken.
4	CMC	05.10.2001	51	32.31	1st Put Option exceeding 10%.	16th Oct. 2002 to 15th Oct. 2003	FV	Put Option not exercised. 26.25% equity sold through
					2nd Put Option for some or all remaining share.	16th Oct. 2003 to 15th Oct. 2004	FV	OFS in Feb. 2004. 6.06% of the equity sold to employees.

(Contd.)

					Call Option for all but not less than all of the shares held by the Govt.	16th Oct. 2004 to 15th Oct. 2006	Higher of MP or FV	
5	VSNL	05.02.2002	25	27.97	No Put Option	-	-	1.85% equity sold to employees. Call Option not exercised.
					Call Option for all but one voting equity share in the company held by the Government.	13th Feb. 2006 to 12th Feb. 2007	FV	
6	IBP	05.02.2002	33.58	26	Put Option for some or all share	8th Feb. 2003 to 7th Feb. 2005	FV	Put Option not excercised. 26% equity sold through OFS in Feb. 2004.
					Call Option for all shares	8th Feb. 2005 to 7th Feb. 2007 to	FV	
7	PPL	14.02.2002	74	26	Put Option for some or all shares	1st March 2003 till survival of the agreement	FV	Neither put nor call option has been exercised till date. The call option if and when exercised would be repudiated.
					Call Option for all shares	1st March 2005 till survival of the agreement	Higher of FV MP or SS price	
8	HZL	27.03.2002	26	49.92	Call Option upto 18.92%	11th Oct. 2002 to 10th Oct. 2003	Higher of MV or SS price	1st Call Option exercised in August 2003 by SP at SS price. 1.465% equity sold to employees.
					GOI has a Put Option for its shareholding in excess of 26% of HZL's equity.	11th Oct. 2004 to 10th April 2005	Higher of MV or SS price	Government decided not to exercise Put Option.

(Contd.)

					2nd Call Option for all shares	11th Apr. 2007 onward till survival of agreement	FMV	Strategic Partner not yet exercised the call option. The call option if and when exercised would be repudiated.
9	IPCL	18.05.2002	26	33.95	Put Option	4th June 2004 to 3rd June 2005	FV	Put Option not exercised. 28.95% equity sold through
					Call Option for all but not less than all	4th June 2005 to 3rd June 2006	FV	OFS in Feb. 2004 and 5% offered to employees in April 2004, out of which 4.58% was allotted to the employees.
10	HTL	05.10.2001	74	26	No Call/Put Option	-	-	
11	JCL	27.02.2002	72	27	Put Option	29th August 2004 to 28th August 2006	FV	Put option not exercised.
					Call Option	29th August 2006 to 28th August 2008	FV	Government shareholding stands reduced to 4.16% consequent to a Rights Issue made by JCL in 2005 which was not subscribed by BBUNL. Call option exercised on 4.9.2006. The call option would be repudiated.
12	MUL	14.05.2002	-	45.79*	Put Option	8th Nov. 2003 to 8th July 2005	Price per share would be equal to the average of the daily closing prices of the shares of Maruti as quoted on NSE in the 90-day period preceding the date of the put option notice. If on	27.51% equity sold through IPO in July 2003. Put option not exercised. 8% equity sold to public sector financial institutions and public sector banks in January 2006. 0.01% equity sold to employees of MUL in March 2006. Balance GoI equity of

(Contd.)

the date of put option notice Govt. holds more than 1484006 shares, there shall be a discount of 15% on the shares above 1484006 and a discount of 10% on the remaining shares. If on the date of put option Government holds less than or equal to 1484006 shares, there will be a discount of 10% on the shares put by the Government.	10.27% was sold to public sector financial institutions, public sector banks and Indian mutual funds in May 2007.

ANNEXURE-XI

REF (Para 4.4.6)

STATUS OF ALLOTMENT OF SHARES TO THE EMPLOYEES OF CMC/VSNL/HZL/IPCL/BALCO

	CMC	VSNL	HZL	IPCL	BALCO
Number of shares	1,51,50,000	28,48,44,517	42,25,31,900	24,82,25,000	22,06,24,500
Number of employees	3,208	2,991	2,848	12,272	6,436
Percentage allotted to employees	6.065	1.85	1.4649	4.58	up to 5% (Yet to be decided)
Number of shares 1,10,31,225 allotted to employees	9,19,326	52,64,555	61,89,830	1,13,70,678	up to (Yet to be decided)
Average shares allotted per employee	287	1,760	2,173	927	Yet to be decided
Sacrifice by the Government	₹12.04 crore (Sale price of ₹66 per share against strategic sale price of ₹197 per share)	₹81.15 crore (Sale price of ₹47.85 per share against strategic sale price of ₹202 per share)	₹18.88 crore (Sale price of ₹10 per share against strategic sale price of ₹40.50 per share)	₹197.85 crore (Sale price of ₹57 per share against strategic sale price of ₹231 per share)	Yet to be decided
Average benefit to employees (approx.)	₹37,541	₹2,71,304	₹66,277	₹1,61,221	Yet to be decided
Ratio of distribution among employees Lowest: Highest	1:05	1:03	1:05	01:02.8	Yet to be decided
Offer to employees	June/July, 2002	February, 2002	November, 2002	April, 2004	Yet to be decided
Lock in period	1 Year	1 Year	1 Year	3 Year	Yet to be made

(Contd.)

Basis of pricing	1/3rd of the listed market value or 1/3rd or the strategic sale price per share, whichever is lower but not less than ₹10 (face value)	1/3rd of the price offered by the strategic partner or one-third of the listed marked value calculated on the average of the closing price on BSE for 30 days, whichever is less, subject to minimum of par value of ₹10 per equity share.	1/3rd of the Listed Market Value or Strategic sale price whichever is lower subject to minimum of face value	1/3rd of the offer price or the price quoted by the strategic partner at the time of disinvestment whichever is lower	Yet to be decided
Eligibility of employees	All existing regular employees including the NRIs/Foreign National on rolls of the company as on 1.9.2001 including Directors/CMD	All regular employees including full-time Directors as on 1.9.2001	All regular employees including full time functional Directors as as on 11.4.2002.	Regular employees on rolls as on 4.6.2002 who are alive including Directors	Yet to be decided

ANNEXURE-XII

REF (Para 4.5.7)

STATUS OF POST CLOSING ADJUSTMENT IN DISINVESTED ITDC HOTEL PROPERTIES

S.No.	Name of Hotel	Purchaser/Lessee	Closing Date	Amount of claim paid (₹)
1.	Hotel Ashok Bangalore	Bharat Hotels Ltd.	29.11.2001	4,98,11,483
2.	Hotel Hassan Ashok	Malnad Hotels & Resorts (P) Ltd.	29.11.2001	24,59,944
3.	Hotel Bodhgaya Ashok	Lotus Nikko Hotels	29.11.2001	46,19,593
4.	Hotel Madurai Ashok	Sangu Chakra Hotels Pvt. Ltd.	31.01.2002	39,78,892
5.	Temple Bay Ashok Beach Resort, Mamallapuram	G.R. Thanga Maligai (P) Ltd.	01.02.2002	49,86,640
6.	Hotel Agra Ashok	Mohan Singh	07.02.2002	87,47,725
7.	Laxmi Vilas Palace Hotel, Udaipur	Bharat Hotels Ltd.	26.02.2002	1,08,07,868
8.	Qutab Hotel, New Delhi	Consortium of Sushil Gupta and Others	20.03.2002	3,09,54,080
9.	Lodhi Hotel, New Delhi	Consortium of Silverlink Holdings Ltd. and others	22.03.2002	2,87,94,622
10.	Hotel Airport Ashok, Kolkata	Consortium of Bright Enterprises(P) Ltd. and Modern Publishers	08.07.2002	4,89,24,848
11.	Kovalam Ashok Beach Resort	M Far Hotels Limited	11.07.2002	2,36,39,576
12.	Hotel Aurangabad Ashok	Consortium of Loksangam Hotels & Resorts Pvt. Ltd and others	04.09.2002	76,49,690
13.	Hotel Manali Ashok	Auto Impex Limited	15.07.2002	3,94,874
14.	Hotel Khajuraho Ashok	Bharat Hotels Ltd.	07.08.2002	4,95,448
15.	Hotel Varanasi Ashok	Consortium of Ramnath Hotels (P) Ltd. and others	07.08.2002	1,52,43,715
16.	Hotel Ranjit, New Delhi	Consortium of Unison Hotels Ltd. and Formax Commercial Pvt. Ltd.	07.10.2002	1,19,45,307
17.	Hotel Kanishka, New Delhi	Nehru Place Hotels Ltd.	08.10.2002	4,51,11,608
18.	Hotel Indraprastha, New Delhi	Moral Trading & Investment Ltd.	08.10.2002	61,57,966
19.	Chandigarh project of Punjab Hotels Limited	TAJGVK Hotels & Resorts Ltd.	16.10.2002	Nil*
	Total			**30,47,23,879**

* ₹ 31,86,323 paid by Purchaser to ITDC

ANNEXURE-XIII

REF (Para 8.4.1)

(TO BE PUBLISHED IN THE GAZETTE OF INDIA, PART-I, SECTION 1)

F. NO. 2/3/2005-DD-II GOVERNMENT OF INDIA MINISTRY OF FINANCE DEPARTMENT OF DISINVESTMENT

BLOCKS NO. 11 & 14, CGO COMPLEX,
LODI ROAD, NEW DELHI

THE 23RD NOVEMBER 2005

RESOLUTION

In pursuance of the policy laid down in the National Common Minimum Programme, the Government of India has decided to constitute a separate fund, with the name and style of the 'National Investment Fund', with the following objectives, structure, investment strategy and administrative arrangements.

A. Objectives

(i) The proceeds from disinvestment of Central Public Sector Enterprises will be channelised into the National Investment Fund which is to be maintained outside the Consolidated Fund of India.

(ii) The corpus of the National Investment Fund will be of a permanent nature.

(iii) The Fund will be professionally managed to provide sustainable returns to the government, without depleting the corpus. Selected Public Sector Mutual Funds will be entrusted with the management of the corpus of the Fund.

(iv) 75% of the annual income of the Fund will be used to finance selected social sector schemes, which promote education, health and employment. The residual 25% of the annual income of the Fund will be used to meet the capital investment requirements of profitable and revivable CPSEs that yield adequate returns, in order to enlarge their capital base to finance expansion/diversification.

B. Structure and Administrative Arrangements

The National Investment Fund will be operated by the selected Fund Managers under the 'discretionary mode' of the

Portfolio Management scheme, which is governed by the SEBI guidelines. The entire work of the National Investment Fund will be supervised by Chief Executive Officer (CEO) of the Fund, an officer of the rank of Joint Secretary/Additional Secretary to the Government of India. A part time Advisory Board consisting of three eminent persons, with the requisite expertise to be appointed by the government, would advise the CEO on various aspects of the functioning of the Fund.

C. Investment Strategy

(i) The broad investment strategy is to provide sustainable returns without depleting the corpus.

(ii) The investment strategy for the Fund will be formulated by the Chief Executive Officer (CEO) based on the advice of the Advisory Board so as to ensure that government has a hands-off relationship in terms of the actual investment to be done by the Fund Managers.

(iii) Only broad guidelines are to be provided under the "discretionary mode" to the Fund Managers, within which individual investments would be made independently by the Fund Managers. More detailed guidelines specifying investment instruments and limits for investment in such instruments will be separately specified in the agreements to be entered into between the Fund Managers and the Chief Executive Officer of the Fund on behalf of the government.

(iv) Other operational details such as allocation of funds to the selected Fund Managers, negotiations of management fee and charges to be paid to the Fund Managers, etc. will be also decided by the CEO based on the advice of the Advisory Board.

(v) Appropriate mechanisms for regular review and monitoring of the functioning of the Fund, emerging market trends and future prospects will be instituted.

D. Accounting Procedure

(i) The receipts from disinvestment of CPSEs will be deposited in the Consolidated Fund of India (CFI) under the designated Head. Thereafter, these amounts would be appropriated from the CFI, with due approval, by the Department of Disinvestment and transferred to the selected Fund Managers through CEO of the Fund.

(ii) Income from the Fund will similarly be deposited in the CFI and would be appropriated from it for specific purposes as per the scheme of appropriation approved from time to time by the Department of Expenditure.

(Saurabh Chandra)

Joint Secretary to the Government of India

ORDER

ORDERED that a copy of the resolution be communicated to all Ministries/Departments of the Government of India. ORDERED also that the resolution be published in the Gazette of India for general information.

(Saurabh Chandra)

Joint Secretary to the Government of India

To

The Manager,
Government of India Press,
(Bharat Sarkar Press),
FARIDABAD

Bibliography

Abernethy, W. L., *Internal Audit in the Public Boards* (London, 1957).

Abrera, B.P., *Management of Public Enterprise in the Philippines* (New Delhi, 1959).

Agarwal, R.C., *State Enterprise in India* (Allahabad, 1961).

Aggarwal, Suresh C., *Human Resource in Public Enterprises*, Anmol Publications, New Delhi, 2003.

Alehin, D.J., *Planned State Industry in the U.S.S.R.* (New Delhi, 1959).

Allen, L.A., *Management and Organisation* (New York, 1958).

Annual Report 2009-10, Department of Heavy Industries and Public Enterprises, Govt. of India.

Appleby, Dean Paul H., *Re-examination of India's Administrative System with Special Reference to Administration of Government's Industrial and Commercial Enterprises* (New Delhi, 1956).

Balog, Nikota, *Some Experience in the Management of Yugoslav Industrial Enterprise* (New Delhi, 1959).

Batra, G.S., *Leading Issues in Public Enterprises: Control and Accountability*, Anmol Publications, New Delhi, 1993.

Bhambari, Chander Prakash, *Parliamentary Control over State Enterprise in India* (*A Study in Public Administration*) (Delhi, 1960).

Bhandari, K.C., *Nationalisation of Industries in India (doctrinaire adherence redundant)* (Calcutta, 1962).

Bienstock, Gregory et al., *Management in Russian Industry and Agriculture* (New York, 1950).

Chanda, A.K., "New Deal for Public Enterprises", *Hindustan Times*, 28 April 1966.

——, "Public Enterprises in India", *Industrial India* (Annual), 1960.

——, *Indian Administration* (London, 1958).

Chandra, J.P., *India's Socialistic Pattern of Society* (Delhi, 1956).

Clegg, H.A. and Chester, T.E., *The Future of Nationalisation* (Oxford, 1955).

Cole, G.D.H., "The Statutory Corporation in New South Wales", *Public Administration*, September 1952.

Das, Nabagopal, *The Public Sector* (Eastern Economist Pamphlet No. 32) (New Delhi, 1955).

——, *The Public Sector in India* (2nd Edition) (Bombay, 1961).

——, "Efficiency of State-run Enterprises in India", *Economic Times*, 30 November 1962.

——, "Factors Responsible for State Enterprises Inefficiency", *Economic Times*, 1 December 1962.

Dasappa, H.C., "Parliamentary Control and Accountability of Public Undertakings", *Indian Journal of Public Administration*, April-June 1961.

Dass, Radhika, and Manohar Pandit (Ed.), *Public Sector in India*, Atlantic Publishers and Distributors, New Delhi, 1989.

Davies, Ernest, *Problems of Public Ownership*, Labour Party (London, 1957).

Dewan, S.M. (Ed.), *Corporate Governance in Public Sector Enterprises*, Dorling Kindersley, New Delhi, 2006.

Dimock, M.E. and Dimock, G.O., *Public Administration* (New York, 1953).

Federation of Indian Chambers of Commerce and Industry, *Report on Seminar on Problems of Private and Public Industrial Undertakings*, August 6-8, 1963 (New Delhi, 1963).

Florence, P. Sargent, *Industry and State* (London, 1957).

Forum of Free Enterprise, *State Monopolies and the Citizen in Democracy* by V.K. Narasimhan (Bombay, 1959).

Gaitskell, Hugh, *Socialism and Nationalisation* (London, 1956).

Galbraith, J.K., *Some Notes on the Rationale of Indian Economic Organisation: A Report Submitted to the Government of India* (New Delhi, 1959).

Ganguly, D.S., *Public Corporations in National Economy—with Special Reference to India* (Calcutta, 1963).

Ghosh, S., *On the Public Sector* (Delhi, 1957).

Ginwala, F.R., *Company Law and Problems of Corporate Enterprise* (Bombay, 1958).

Goodman, Edward, *Forms of Public Control and Ownership* (London, 1951).

Gorwala, A.D., *Report on the Efficient Conduct of State Enterprises* (New Delhi, 1951).

——, *The Role of the Administrator* (Poona, 1952).

——, *Report on the Public Administration* (New Delhi, 1953).

Government of India, *A Brochure on Principal Public Sector Undertakings in India* (New Delhi, 1960).

Granick, David, *Management of the Industrial Firm in the U.S.S.R.—A Study in Soviet Economic Planning* (New York, 1954).

Grove, J.W., *Government and Industry in Britain* (Glasgow, 1962).

Hanson, A.H., *Parliament and the Nationalized Industries*, 1954.

——, *Public Enterprise and Economic Development* (London, 1959).

——, *Managerial Problems in Public Enterprise* (Bombay, 1962).

Hemming, Richard, and Ali M. Mansoor, "Privatization and Public Enterprises", International Monetary Fund, Washington D.C., 1988.

Indian Chamber of Commerce, *The Working of State Enterprises in India* (Calcutta, 1951).

Indian Institute of Public Administration, *Administrative Problems of State Enterprises in India: Report of Seminar,* December 1957 (New Delhi, 1958).

——, *Industrial Enterprises in the Public Sector in India* (New Delhi, 1959).

——, *Seminar Report on Management of Public Industrial Enterprises, Some Experience in the Management of Yugoslav Industrial Enterprises* (New Delhi, 1959).

——, *Seminar Report on Management of Public Industrial Enterprises, Industrial Enterprises in the Public Sector in India* (New Delhi, 1959).

——, *Seminar Report on Management of Public Industrial Enterprises: Measurement of Management* (New Delhi, 1959).

Indian Institute of Public Administration, *Seminar Report on Morale and Public Services* (New Delhi, 1959).

——, *The Questions of a Parliamentary Committee for Public Enterprises* (New Delhi, 1960).

——, *State Undertakings—Report of a Conference*, December 19-20, 1959 (New Delhi, 1960).

Institute of Management, *Report of Conference of Industrialists and Symposium on Nationalised Industries* (Bangalore, 1954).

Kaushal, O.P., *Management Organisation and Control in Public Enterprises* (Bombay, 1964).

Khera, S.S., *Government in Business* (Bombay, 1968).

——, *Management and Control in Public Enterprise* (Bombay, 1964).

Koontz, H. and Grable, R.W., *Public Control of Economic Enterprise* (New York, 1956).

Krishnamurti, B.V., *Pricing in Planned Economy* (Bombay, 1949).

Lewis, W.A., *British Planning and Nationalization* (London, 1952).

"Management of State Owned Commercial Undertakings", *Commerce*, 9 August 1958.

"Management of State Undertakings", *Commerce*, 20 June 1959.

Mehta, Ashok, *Democratic Socialism* (Bombay, 1958).

Ministry of Commerce and Industry, *Public Sector Industries* (*Supplement to the Journal of Industry and Trade,* December 1959) (New Delhi, 1959).

Mishra, R.K. and B. Navin, *Restructuring Public Enterprises in India*, Mittal Publications (New Delhi 2002).

Mishra, R.K., Lakshmi Kumari, and J. Kiranmai, *Reforming Public Enterprises*, Kalpaz Publications (Delhi, 2009).

Muhairwe, William T., *Making Public Enterprises Work: From Despair to Promise—A Turn Around Account*, IWA Publishing (London, 2009).

Murdeshwar, Anand K., *Administrative Problems Relating to Nationalization with Special Reference to Indian State Enterprises* (Bombay, 1957).

Musolf, Lloyd D., *Public Ownership and Accountability—The Canadian Experience* (Cambridge, 1959).

Neuman, *The Economic Aspects of Nationalization in Great Britain* (Cambridge, 1952).

Paranjape, H.K., *Public Enterprise in India* (New Delhi, 1953).

——, *Flight of Technical Personnel in Public Undertaking* (New Delhi, 1964).

Parkash, Om, *The Theory and Working of State Corporations with Special Reference to India* (London, 1962).

Prasad, B., *Some Economic Problems of Public Enterprises in India* (London, 1957).

Prasad, Parmanand, *Some Economic Problems of Public Enterprises in India* (London, 1957).

"Public versus Private Sector", *Commerce*, 2 May 1959.

"Public sector in free world", *Commerce*, 28 May 1960.

"Prof. Galbraith on public enterprises", *Commerce*, 3 December 1960.

——, *The Damodar Valley Corporation* (New Delhi, 1963).

Public Enterprises Survey, 2008-09, Vols. I, II and III, Department of Public Enterprises, Ministry of Heavy Industries and Public Enterprises, Govt. of India.

——, *Structure of Public Enterprise in India* (Bombay, 1961).

——, *Pricing, Labour and Efficiency in the Public Sector* (Hyderabad, 1962).

——, *The Finances of Public Enterprises* (Bombay, 1963).

——, *The Efficacy of Public Enterprise* (Bombay, 1963).

——, *The Control of Public Enterprises in India* (Bombay, 1964).

——, *Working of Public Sector* (Bombay, 1965).

Rogow, A.A. and Shore, P., *The Labour Government and British Industry, 1945-51* (Oxford, 1955).

Sachs, Igracy, *Patterns of Public Sector in Underdeveloped Economies* (Bombay, 1962).

Sadli, M., *Public Enterprises in Indonesia* (New Delhi, 1959).

Sarma, R.P., *Investment Pattern of Public Undertakings in India*, Mittal Publications, Delhi, 1987.

Sharma, Tirth Raj, *The Working of State Enterprises in India* (Bombay, 1961).

Shukla, M.C., *Administrative Problems of Public Enterprises in India* (Delhi, 1959).

Singh, A.B. and Anurag Singh, *Public Sector Reforms in India*, APH Publishing (New Delhi, 2004).

Singh, Ashok K., *Personnel Management in Public Enterprises*, Mittal Publications (Delhi, 1985).

Sleeman, J.F., *British Public Utilities* (London, 1953).

Spencer, D.L., *India, Mixed Enterprise and Western Business, Experiments in Controlled Change for Growth and Profit* (The Hague, 1959).

Spriegel and Lansburgh, *Industrial Management* (Bombay, 1962).

United Nations, *Public Industrial Management in Asia and Far East* (New Delhi, 1959).

——, *Papers of the ECAFE Seminar on Management of Public Industrial Enterprises* (New Delhi, 1959).

Wilcox, C., *Public Policies Towards Business* (Chicago, 1955).

"Working of public sector enterprises, accounts of running concerns analysed", *Commerce*, 31 August 1963.

Deshpande, R.A., "Pricing Policy of Public Enterprises", *Indian Journal of Public Administration*, January-March 1962.

Sharma, J.P., "Estimates Committee Reports on Public Enterprises", *Indian Journal of Public Administration*, January-March 1965.

——, "Estimates Committee reports on public enterprises", *Indian Journal of Public Administration*, April-June 1965.